This detailed work focuses on the formation of and challenges to early Christian community and identity in Roman Philippi in the first century. It brings forward a wealth of inscriptional and literary evidence useful for understanding the cultural setting in which Christians of first century Philippi lived out their daily lives. Against this backdrop, Sergienko probes the thesis that the Philippian Christians were compromising their commitment to Jesus Christ as Lord and Savior by participation in local voluntary organizations that included the practice of emperor worship. Paul challenges their allegiance to an earthly politeuma – a voluntary association – with his declaration that Christians in fact have their politeuma – source of authority – in heaven. Offering a fresh look at ancient evidence and the text of Philippians, Sergienko crafts a suggestive argument for reading this epistle and Paul's call for exclusive allegiance to Jesus Christ as Lord in light of various religious, social, and cultural obstacles faced by the church.

Marianne Meye Thompson
George Eldon Ladd Professor of New Testament
Fuller Theological Seminary, California, USA

"Our *Politeuma* is in Heaven!":
Paul's Polemical Engagement with the "Enemies of the Cross of Christ" in Philippians 3:18-20

Gennadi A. Sergienko

MONOGRAPHS

© 2013 by Gennadi Sergienko

Published 2013 by Langham Monographs
an imprint of Langham Creative Projects

Langham Partnership
PO Box 296, Carlisle, Cumbria CA3 9WZ, UK
www.langham.org

ISBNs:
978-1-907713-74-3 Print
978-1-907713-73-6 Mobi
978-1-907713-72-9 ePub

Gennadi Sergienko has asserted his right under the Copyright, Designs and Patents Act, 1988 to be identified as the Author of this work.

All rights reserved. No part of this publication may be reproduced, stored in a retrieval system or transmitted, in any form or by any means, electronic, mechanical, photocopying, recording or otherwise, without the prior written permission of the publisher or the Copyright Licensing Agency.

Unless otherwise stated, Scripture quotations are from the New Revised Standard Version Bible, copyright © 1989 National Council of the Churches of Christ in the United States of America. Used by permission. All rights reserved.

British Library Cataloguing in Publication Data
Sergienko, Gennadi Andreyevich, author.
　Our politeuma is in heaven!.
　1. Bible. Philippians, III, 18-20--Language, style.
　2. Paul, the Apostle, Saint--Language. 3. Hapax legomena.
　4. Paul, the Apostle, Saint--Political and social views.
　I. Title
　227.6'066-dc23

ISBN-13: 9781907713743

Cover & Book Design: projectluz.com

Langham Partnership actively supports theological dialogue and a scholars right to publish but does not necessarily endorse the views and opinions set forth, and works referenced within this publication, or guarantee its technical and grammatical correctness. Langham Partnership does not accept any responsibility or liability to persons or property as a consequence of the reading, use or interpretation of its published content.

Моей любимой жене Вере, благодаря терпению и поддержке которой, стало возможным написание этой работы

To my beloved wife, Vera. Thank you for the patience and support that made writing this work possible.

Contents

List of Abbreviations xi
    Modern Translations of the Bible xi
    Books of the Bible xi
    Old Testament Apocrypha and Psedepigrapha xii
    Dead Sea Scrolls xii
    Rabbinic Literature xiii
    Classical and Hellenictic Literature xiii
    Ancient Inscriptions xvi
    Modern Works xvii

Chapter 1 1
Introduction
    1.1 Topic and Goal of the Dissertation 1
    1.2 State of Scholarship 2
        1.2.1 Scholarly Contributions 2
        1.2.2 Scholarly Tendecies in Reading Philippians 10
        1.2.3 Pertinent Bibliography 12
    1.3 Voluntary Associations and the "Enemies of the Cross": The Thesis of the Dissertation 13
    1.4 Outline of the Dissertation 15

Chapter 2 19
Voluntary Associations within a Graeco-Roman City
    2.1 Religious and Professional Associations 22
    2.2 Membership 24
    2.3 Organizational Structure 30
    2.4 Social Function of Voluntary Associations 35
    2.5 Relating to Imperial Rome 41
    2.6 The Religious Function of Voluntary Associations 43
    Conclusion 50

Chapter 3 51
The Roman Colony of Philippi
    3.1 Historical Overview 52
    3.2 Demographic Situation 54
    3.3 Socio-Economic Features 58
    3.4 Political Profile 62

  3.5 Religious Profile 64
  Conclusion 66

Chapter 4 69
 Voluntary Associations at Philippi
  4.1 Silvanus Association 70
  4.2 Diana Association 75
  4.3 Dionysiac Association 78
  4.4 Associations of Isis and/or Serapis 80
  4.5 Associations of the Thracian deities Sourgethes and Hero 84
  4.6 Association of Dendrophorus Augustalis 85
  4.7 Association of the Purple-Dyers 86
  4.8 Association of Grave-Diggers 87
  4.9 Association of Gladiators 88
  Conclusion 89

Chapter 5 91
 Christian Ekklēsia *at Philippi and Voluntary Associations: Discovering the Points of Correlation*
  5.1 The social context of Paul's ministry..................................92
  5.2 Philippian Christian Community 98
   5.2.1 The Social and Ethnic Prosopography 99
   5.2.2 Elevated Status of Women 103
   5.2.3 Organizational Structure 107
   5.2.4 Community of Friends 112
   5.2.5 Seeking Honor and Creating Rivalry 118
  Conclusion 124

Chapter 6 127
 The Earthly Politeuma *of the Enemies of the Cross and Paul's Vision of the* Politeuma *in Heaven (Phil 3:18-20)*
  6.1 The Earthly Πολίτευμα of the Enemies of the Cross
  (Phil 3:18-20) 127
   6.1.1 What is the Πολίτευμα of Phil 3:20? 128
   6.1.2 The Alluring Walk of the "Enemies" (Phil 3:18) 141
   6.1.3 Paul's Polemical Characterization of the Opponents
   (Phil 3:19) 148
  6.2 Paul's Counter-Argument Against the "Enemies of the Cross" 153
   6.2.1 Paul's Vision of the Heavenly Πολίτευμα 153
   6.2.2 Paul's Anti-Imperial Polemics................................162

  6.2.3 Paul's Way of Discipleship: Κοινωνία in
    Christ's Sufferings 177
  Conclusion 181

Summary.. 183

Appendix 1... 187
  Cults Attested at and Near Philippi

Appendix 2... 191
  Membership List of the Silvanus Association at Philippi

Appendix 3... 193
  Graeco-Roman and Jewish Literary Sources on Πολιτευμα
    Aeschines (4th century BCE):..193
    Appian, *Civil Wars* (1st century CE): 193
    Aristotle, *Politics* (384-322 BCE): 194
    Epictetus (mid. 1st to 2nd century CE): 194
    Demosthenes (384-322 BCE):...195
    Diodorus Siculus, *Library* (1st century BCE):.........................195
    Isocrates (436-338 BCE): 196
    Josephus (1st century CE):..196
    Philo (1st century CE):..196
    Plato, *Laws* (429-347 BCE):...196
    Plutarch, *Lives* (1st century CE):..197
    Polybius (203-120 BCE):...197
    Strabo, *Geography* (64 BCE-21CE): 200

Bibliography.. 201
  1. Primary Sources 201
    1.1 Ancient Texts and Translations...201
    1.2 Inscriptions...203
    2.3 Sourcebooks 206
  3. Reference Works 207
  4. Secondary Literature 208

List of Abbreviations

Modern Translations of the Bible

NAB	New American Bible
NASB	New American Standard Bible
NIV	New International Version
NRSV	New Revised Standard Version
NJB	New Jerusalem Bible
RST	Русский Синодальный перевод (Russian Synodal Translation)

Books of the Bible

Exod	Exodus
Deut	Deuteronomy
Judg	Judges
2 Kgs	2 Kings
Neh	Nehemia
Ps	Psalms
Prov	Proverbs
Isa	Isaiah
Jer	Jeremiah
Ezek	Ezekiel
Dan	Daniel
Hos	Hosea
Mic	Micah
Hab	Habakkuk
Zeph	Zephaniah

Zech	Zechariah
Mal	Malachi
Matt	Matthew
Rom	Romans
1-2 Cor	1-2 Corinthians
Gal	Galatians
Eph	Ephesians
Phil	Philippians
1-2 Thess	1-2 Thessalonians
Phlm	Philemon
1 Tim	1 Timothy
Tit	Titus
1 Pet	1 Peter
Heb	Hebrews
Rev	Revelation

Old Testament Apocrypha and Psedepigrapha

2 Esd	2 Esrda
1-2 Macc	1-2 Maccabees
3-4 Macc	3-4 Maccabees
Sir	Sirach
Tob	Tobit
Wis	Wisdom of Solomon
Apoc. Abr.	*The Apocalypse of Abraham*
2 Bar.	*2 Baruch (Syriac Apocalypse)*
1 En.	*1 Enoch (Ethiopic Apocalypse)*
3 En.	*3 Enoch*
Jub.	*Jubilees*
T. Dan.	*Testament of Dan*
Sib. Or.	*Sibylline Oracles*

Dead Sea Scrolls

11QPs[a]	Psalms Scrolls

Rabbinic Literature

b. Ta'an.	Babylonian Talmud, tractate *Ta'anit*
b. Hag.	Babylonian Talmud, tractate *Hagigah*
Gen. Rab.	*Genesis Rabbah*
Num. Rab	*Numbers Rabbah*
Cant. Rab.	*Song of Songs Rabbah*
Midr. Teh.	*Midrash Tehillin* (midrash on Psalms)
Pesiq. R.	*Pesiqta Rabbati*
Tg. Ket.	*Targum on Writings*

Classical and Hellenictic Literature

Appian
B Civ.   *Civil Wars*

Aristotle
Eth. Nic.   *Nicomachean ethics*
Eud. Eth.   *Eudemean Ethics*
Pol.   *Politics*
Rhet.   *Rhetoric*

Aristides
Or.   *Orationes*

Asconius
Pis.   *Commentary on Against Piso*

Athenaeus
Deipn.   *Deipnosophistae*

Augustine
Civ. Dei.   *The City of God*

Cicero
Amic.   *De Amicia*
Rep.   *On the Republic*
Ver.   *Against Verres*

Dio Chrysostom
Or.   *Oration*

Euripides
Bacch.   *Bacchantes*
Cycl.   *Cyclops*

Hesiod
Op. — *Works and Days*
Isocrates
Areop. — *Areopagiticus*
Josephus
C. Ap. — *Against Apion*
Ant. — *Jewish Antiquities*
Bell — *Wars of the Jews*
Philo
Agr. — *On the Agriculture*
Conf. — *On the Confusion of Tongues*
Decal. — *On the Decalogue*
Ebr. — *On Drunkenness*
Flacc. — *Against Flaccus*
Ios. — *On the life of Josephus*
Leg. — *Allegorical Interpretation*
Legat. — *On the Embassy to Gaius*
Mos. — *Moses*
Opif. — *On the Creation of the World*
Praem. — *On Rewards and Punishments*
Quaest. in Gn. — *Questions and Answers of Genesis*
Spec. Leg. — *On the Special Laws*
Vit. Cont. — *On the Contemplative Life*
Plato
Grg. — *Gorgias*
Cleit. — *Cleitophon*
Menex. — *Menexenus*
Pliny the Elder
HN — *Natural History*
Pliny the Younger
Ep. — *Letters*

Plutarch
Alc. *Alcibiades*
Brut. *Brutus*
De com. *Against the Stoics on Common Conceptions*
De def. or. *On the Failure of Oracles*
Mor. *Moralia*
Per. *Pericles*
Sol. *Solon*
Sull. *Sulla*
Them. *Themistocles*
Thes. *Theseus*
Vit. *Lives*

Polybius
Hist. *Histories*

Seneca
Ben. *De Beneficiis*
Ep. *Epistles*

Strabo
Geog. *Geography*

Suetonius
Aug. *Augustus*
Calig. *Gaius Caligula*
Claud. *Divine Claudius*
Ner. *Nero*
Tib. *Tiberius*

Tacitus
Ann. *Annals*
Hist. *Histories*

Tertullian
Apol. *Apology*

Varro
Rust. *On Rustic Affairs*

Vegetius
Mil. *On Military Affairs*

Xenophon

Cyr. The Education of Cyrus

Ancient Inscriptions

CCET	Corpus cultus equities Thracii
CIG	Corpus Inscriptionum Graecarum
CIL	Corpus Inscriptionum Latinarum
CPJ	Corpus Papyrorum Judaicarum
EAM	Epigraphes Ano Makedonias
GIBM	Collection of Greek Inscriptions in the British Museum
IDelos	Inscriptions de Delos
IEph	Die Inschriften von Ephesos
IG	Inscriptiones Graecae
IGBulg	Inscriptiones graecae in Bulgaria repertae
IGCB	Corpus der griechisch christlichen inschriften von Hellas
IGL	Inscriptions grecques et latines de la Syrie
IGLAM	Inscriptions grecques et latines reueillies en Asie Mineure
IGRR	Inscriptiones Graecae ad Res Romanas Pertinentes
IGUR	Inscriptiones graecae urbis romae
ILS	Inscriptiones Latinae Selectae
IMAe	Incriptiones Graecae Insularum Maris Aegaei
ISmyrna	Die Inschriften von Smyrna
Mouseion	Mouseion kai Bibliotheke tes Euangelikes Sholes (Smyrna)
OGIS	Orientis Graeci Inscriptiones Selectae
POxy	The Oxyrhynchus Papyri
PRyl	Catalogue of the Greek Papyri in the John Rylands Library

Sardis	Sardis. Greek and Latin Inscriptions
SEG	Supplementum Epigraphicum Graecum
SIG	Sylloge Inscriptionum Graecarum
TAM	Tituli Asiae Minoris

Modern Works

ABD	The Anchor Bible Dictionary
ABSA	Annual of the British School at Athens
ANRW	Austieg und Niedergang der römischen Welt
ANTC	Abingdon New Testament Commentaries
AB	Anchor Yale Bible Commentary
BA	Biblical Archeologist
BBS	Bulletin of Biblical Studies
BDAG	Bauer's Greek-English Lexicon of the NT
BDB	Brown-Driver-Briggs Hebrew and English Lexicon
BDF	Blass and Debrunner's Greek Grammar of the New Testament
BECNT	Baker Exegetical Commentary on the New Testament
BHS	Biblia Hebraica Stuttgartensia
Bib	Biblica
BNTC	Black's New Testament Commentaries
BRev	Bible Review
BSac	Bibliotheca Sacra
BTB	Biblical Theology Bulletin
BW	Biblical World
CBQ	Catholic Biblical Quarterly
CJ	Classical Journal
ConBNT	Coniectanea Biblica: New Testament Series

CHECLT	Contributions to the History of Early Christian Literature and Theology
CQ	Classical Quarterly
ConBNT	Coniectanea Biblica: New Testament Series
DDD	Dictionary of Deities and Demons in the Bible
Digesta	The Digest of Justinian
DS	Dissertation Series
DNTB	Dictionary of New Testament Background
DPL	Dictionary of Paul and His Letters
DSS	García Martínez's The Dead Sea Scrolls Study Edition
EGT	Expositor's Greek Testament
EP	Epworth Commentaries
EPaROdLR	Etudes Préliminaires Aux Religions Orientales Dans L'empire Romain
GNT	Greek New Testament
EQ	Evangelical Quarterly
Exp	Expositor
FilNeot	Filologia Neotestamentica
HB	Hebrew Bible
HTR	Harvard Theological Review
HvTSt	Hervormde teologiese studies
IAOP	Institute of Archeology Occasional Publication
ICC	International Critical Commentary
Int	Interpretation
JAC	Jahrbuch für Antike und Christentum
JBL	Journal of Biblical Literature
JECS	Journal of Early Christian Studies
JFSR	Journal of Feminist Studies in Religion

JPFC	The Jewish People in the First Century.
JSNT	Journal for the Study of the New Testament
JTC	Journal for Theology and the Church
JTS	Journal of Theological Studies
LXX	Septuagint
LPS	Library of Pauline Studies
LSJ	Liddell-Scott-Jones' Greek-English Lexicon
LTQ	Lexington Theological Quarterly
MM	Moulton-Milligan's Vocabulary of the Greek Testament
NAC	New American Commentary
NewDocs	New Documents Illustrating Early Christianity
NICNT	The New International Commentary of the New Testament
NIGTC	The New International Greek Testament Commentary
NovTSup	Supplements to Novum Testamentum
NT	New Testament
NTinC	New Testament in Context
NTS	New Testament Studies
NTSR	New Testament for Spiritual Reading
OBT	Overtures to Biblical Theology
OCD	The Oxford Classical Dictionary
OT	Old Testament
PECS	The Princeton Encyclopedia of Classical Sites
PRSt	Perspectives in Religious Studies
RCSS	Records of Civilization, Sources and Studies
RevExp	Review and Expositor
SBL	Society of Biblical Literature

SecCent	Second Century
SJLA	Studies in Judaism in Late Antiquity
SJRS	Scottish Journal of Religious Studies
SJT	Scottish Journal of Theology
SNTSMS	Society for New Testament Studies Monograph Series
TAPA	Transactions of the American Philological Association
TDNT	Kittel's Theological Dictionary of the New Testament
THNTC	Two Horizons New Testament Commentary
TrinSR	Trinity Seminary Review
VT	Vetus Testamentum
WBC	Word Biblical Commentary
WUZNT	Wissenschaftliche Untersuchungen zum Neuen Testament
WW	Word & World
ZNW	Zeitschrift für die Neutestamentliche Wissenschaft
ZSNT	Zacchaeus Studies New Testament

CHAPTER 1

Introduction

1.1 Topic and Goal of the Dissertation

Our investigation will be centered around one particular text from Paul's letter to Philippians, namely, 3:18-20:

> For many of whom I often told you, and even now am writing with tears, walk as the enemies of the cross of Christ: they walk to their final destruction, their god is the belly and their glory is in shameful things, their minds are earthly bound. But our πολίτευμα is in heaven from where we expect the Lord Jesus Christ, who is our Savior.[1]

In this text we encounter one of Paul's *hapax legomena* (πολίτευμα) which is intentionally left untranslated. One of the objectives of our study will be to locate the meaning of this word in the Philippian context which in turn will help us understand the reasons why Paul felt comfortable using this Hellenistic term in the letter to the Philippians. We also are going to probe whether Paul's usage of πολίτευμα was inadvertently "sponsored" by the "enemies of the cross."

Those who study Paul's letters know that this rather outspoken man had plenty of opportunities to aggravate some of his contemporaries. So the presence of the opponents who disagreed with Paul or who were with

---

1. Translations from Greek, Latin, German, and Russian are mine unless otherwise noted.

him in a competitive relationship comes to us as no surprise. Yet whenever somebody labels someone as an "enemy" one thing is certain: it gets our attention. Who were these enemies? What did they do wrong? Why did they deserve destruction? In our search for the "enemies'" identity we will try to specify what in particular made them so dangerous.

An obvious predicament in answering these questions lies in the scarcity of the information at our disposal. As we shall see shortly, this textual brevity has opened the door for a variety of different, at times quite fanciful, reconstructions of their identity.

The issue of these "enemies" undoubtedly is related to a broader issue of the early Christian communities' formation within the socio-political realities of the urban centers of the Roman Empire. Being a new phenomenon, Christianity had to assess its chances of survival within the well-established and structured world of the *Pax Romana*. Many of those who became followers of Jesus had to reassess their former social and cultural affinities, as well as their political and religious allegiances. Whereas for some this reassessment meant radical re-socialization and thus a willingness to "share in Christ's suffering" (Phil 3:10), for others it meant something quite different. The very fact that in writing a letter to the Philippians Paul warns them against certain "enemies" eloquently speaks of the quite uneven and complex dynamics of the early Christian community's formation at Philippi.

1.2 State of Scholarship

We are going to limit our survey of NT scholarship to the more general issue of the social location of the early Christian community and to the more particular issue of the identity of the opponents mentioned in Philippians 3:18-20.

1.2.1 Scholarly Contributions

The pioneering attempts to locate the early Christian community within the social structures of Graeco-Roman society belong to the late-nineteenth century scholars Georg Heinrici[2] and Edwin Hatch.[3] Both of them advocated a thoroughly historical approach to the study of Christian origins. In his study of Christian origins at Corinth, G. Heinrici came to the conclusion that the closest analogue to the Christian *ekklēsia* was the Graeco-Roman cultic association. Similarly, E. Hatch insisted that religious associations were the closest category available for Christian groups to identify with: "To the eye of the outside observer they [Christian groups] were in the same category as the associations which already existed. They had the same names for their meetings, and some of the same names for their officers."[4]

Unfortunately the findings of both scholars became an object of severe criticism and remained unheeded until the work of Australian scholar, Edwin Judge, brought the issue again to the foreground.[5] As did his predecessors, he argued that the development of Christianity should be considered not in isolation from, but rather in interaction, with the wider civic society. Christianity, while it had "originated in Galilee, . . . [had been] nourished in the great cosmopolitan cities of the eastern Mediterranean."[6] E. Judge argued in favor of a "balanced appraisal" between what he called "Hebraic origins and Hellenic application" of the NT message.[7] The best way to ascertain the message is to "begin with the readers, and explain their social situation as it is shown in the Acts and Epistles."[8] "Once the sect is established beyond the homeland of its parent religion, at least within the Roman area, which is as far as our records go, it belongs inevitably, as a social phenomenon, to the Hellenistic republics."[9] E. Judge considered the

---

2. Georg Heinrici, "Die Christengemeinden Korinths und die religiösen Genossenschaften der Griechen," ZWT 19 (1876): 465-526.
3. Edwin Hatch, The Organization of the Early Christian Churches (London, New York and Bombay: Longmans, 1901).
4. Hatch, Organization, 30.
5. Edwin Judge, The Social Pattern of the Christian Groups in the First Century (London: Tyndale Press, 1960).
6. Judge, Social Pattern, 9.
7. Judge, Social Pattern, 9.
8. Judge, Social Pattern, 9.
9. Judge, Social Pattern, 14. Hatch intentionally prefers the term "republic," meaning that the polis governed by a constitution, to the term polis, because in the NT the meaning of the word polis "is sometimes inconsistent with its republican connotation" (Social Pattern, 14).

three dominant social patterns (the Republican *politeia*, the household, and unofficial associations) which were readily available for Christians to claim their space in the life of the Graeco-Roman polis.

Another important contributor to the study of early Christianity within its Graeco-Roman environment is Arthur D. Nock. As can be seen from the very title of one of his prolonged essays ("Early Gentile Christianity and Its Hellenistic Background"[10]) Professor Nock laid great emphasis on the Hellenistic influence on the form and content of early Christianity. In his study, Nock touches upon one peculiar feature of the nascent Christian movement – its claim to exclusiveness, a feature which has some bearing on Paul's warnings against the "enemies of the cross" in Philippians 3:18-20:

> Other causes would contribute to the ascendancy of the new religion, as for instance its *exclusiveness*. One mystery-cult did not exclude adhesion to another; at most it would claim to be the authentic and oldest form of worshiping a godhead. The Christian refusal to allow other worship would convey a conviction of sure knowledge which was and is psychologically effective.[11]

Another significant contribution to the study of early Christianity was made by Wayne Meeks through his publication in 1983 of *The First Urban Christians*.[12] In many respects it remains one of the most thorough analyses of the social world of Pauline Christianity. Writing from the perspective of social history, Meeks attempts to answer a simple question: "What was it like to become and be an ordinary Christian in the first century?"[13] His answer provides many insightful correctives, among which is his more balanced view of the social profile of early Christianity.[14]

---

10. Pp. 49-133 in Essays on Religion and the Ancient World (ed. Zeph Stewart; Cambridge, MA: Harvard University Press, 1972).
11. Nock, "Early Gentile Christianity," 132 (emphasis added).
12. Wayne Meeks, The First Urban Christians: The Social World of the Apostle Paul (New Haven: Yale University Press, 1983).
13. Meeks, Urban Christians, 2.
14. "Pauline congregation generally reflected a fair cross-section of urban society" (Meeks, Urban Christians, 73).

Of special interest for our study is Meeks' analysis of the four basic societal models (the household, the voluntary association, the synagogue, and the philosophic/rhetorical school) in their relation to the formation of Pauline churches.[15] His basic conclusion is that all four models "provide examples of groups solving certain problems that the Christians, too, had to face although "none of the four . . . captures the whole of the Pauline *ekklēsia.*"[16]

I would like to delineate three particular issues, which in Meeks' view characterize the difference between the Christian *ekklēsia* and other societal institutions. First of all, like A. Nock, Meeks stresses that Christian groups "were exclusive and totalistic in a way that no club nor even pagan cultic association was."[17] Second, "Christian groups were more inclusive in terms of social stratification and other social categories than were the voluntary associations." Third, there is "almost complete absence of common terminology for the groups themselves or for their leaders."[18] Through our study of both voluntary associations and of the Christian *ekklēsia* at Philippi we are going to probe whether these statements are in fact accurate.

Gerd Theissen is another ardent proponent of the socio-historical approach to NT study.[19] The German edition of his *Social Reality* is contemporaneous with Meeks' publication of *The First Urban Christians*. This is to say that both scholars work in cooperation and appreciation of each other's work. Thus Theissen, for example, shares with Meeks two specific characterizations of the early Christians. First of all, many of the followers of Jesus were people of "dissonance status."[20] They were people of different social orders (slaves, freedmen, foreigners, women) whose prospects of

---

15. Meeks, Urban Christians, 75-84.
16. Meeks, Urban Christians, 84. There are indications of Meeks' favoritism towards the household, which "remains the basic context within which most if not all the local Pauline groups established themselves" (Urban Christians, 84).
17. Meeks, Urban Christians, 78.
18. Meeks, Urban Christians, 79.
19. Here I refer primarily to his Social Reality and the Early Christians: Theology, Ethics, and the World of the New Testament (trans. Margaret Kohl; Minneapolis: Fortress, 1992). See also his illuminating article, "The Social Structure of Pauline Communities: Some Critical Remarks on J.J. Meggitt, Paul, Poverty and Survival," JSNT 84 (2001): 65-84.
20. Theissen, "The Social Structure," 67. Cf. Meeks' "status of inconsistency" in Urban Christians, 55.

attaining positions of power and authority were practically non-existent. To use Meeks' expression: "Their achieved status [was] higher than their attributed status."[21] Second, the followers of Jesus "were stamped by the fact that they were a socially deviant minority."[22] Deprived of the possibility of being fully integrated within society, their "dissonance status" left these people intentionally marginalized. In this regard Christianity presented itself as an excellent alternative for self-realization and upward mobility for the underprivileged members of society.

Theissen further expands his thoughts by referring to Alföldy's well-known societal pyramid,[23] within which there was a place for the peculiar phenomenon of the *familia Caesaris* (see Figure 1). This was a group of people who were "bound to the emperor by especially close ties of loyalty and were set apart from the normal societal structure."[24] Now within that same societal pyramid there is found a place for an alternative to the *familia Caesaris*, namely, the *familia Christi*. The fundamental difference between the two families is their totally different object of allegiance. As the members of the *familia Caesaris* owe their allegiance to Caesar, so the members of the *familia Christi* owe theirs to the Lord Jesus Christ. Christianity was able to offer "power to the powerless, possessions for the people who possess nothing, wisdom for the uneducated."[25] What is also probably true is that not all of those who constitute the alternative societal phenomenon of the *familia Christi* were ready to renounce their former allegiance to Caesar.

Among the many positive contributions made by Theissen, there are assessments of early Christianity that require additional consideration. Thus, for example, he joins Meeks in the assertion that "Christianity required a profound transformation of behavior and attitude."[26] As any Gentile who wanted to become a Jew had "to condemn what he previously reverenced"[27]

---

21. Meeks, "The Social Context of Pauline Theology," Int 36 (1982): 271.
22. Theissen, "The Social Structure," 67.
23. See Geza Alföldy, The Social History of Rome (trans. D. Braund and F. Pollock; London: Croom Helm; Totowa: Barnes and Noble, 1985), 148.
24. Theissen, Social Reality, 269.
25. Theissen, *Social Reality*, 280.
26. Theissen, *Social Reality*, 263.
27. Theissen, *Social Reality*, 262.

so the Christians inherited "nonconformist patterns of behavior." Furthermore, Christians "refused to participate in the emperor's loyalty cult [because] they rejected occupations that were linked with idolatry, and they avoided eating meat from ritually slaughtered animals."[28] While these might all be accurate general statements, they do not account for the complexities and diversity of first century Christianity. As we shall see, there was great diversity among Christians towards their respective past. At least some of them continued to cherish "what was previously reverenced."

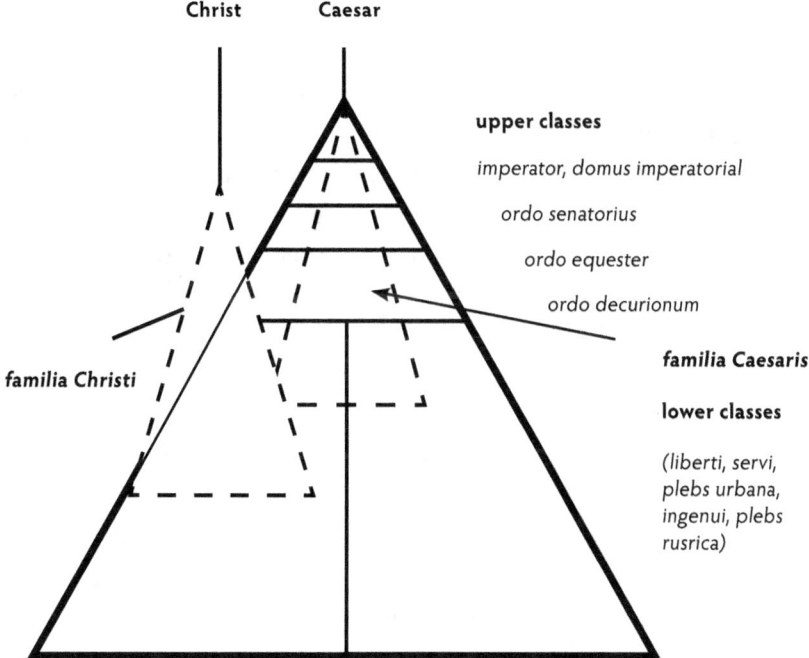

Fig. 1 *Familia Christi* within the Graeco-Roman societal pyramid.[29]

In 1993 Westminster/John Knox Press published *Christian Beginnings: Word and Community from Jesus to Post-Apostolic Times*,[30] edited by J. Becker who himself contributed a chapter on "Paul and His Churches." I will limit

---

28. Theissen, *Social Reality*, 281.
29. Adopted from Theissen, "The Social Structure," 74. Cf. idem, *Social Reality*, 271.
30. Trans. A.S. Kidder and R. Krauss.

myself to discussion of two major contributions of this essay. First of all, Becker gives his assessment of the Pauline churches "from the perspective of social history."[31] He suggests that "with regard to its sociological form one would have to describe [Christian community] as a private religious association in the form of the house church."[32] This is quite a remarkable statement in that the church combines in itself the features of both the household and the association. We are going to argue that both settings played their role in the formation of early Christianity at Philippi. Second, Becker likewise concedes that for a Gentile becoming a Christian meant a "radical change [of] no parallel."[33] The heightened apocalyptic expectations of the initial period seem to have complicated matters even more, for Christians, unlike Jews, did not seek to negotiate their existence with the outside world, assuming that the world was "no partner with which the church cooperates, [rather it was] exclusively [perceived as] an object of the church's mission [which would] soon perish unless it embraces the Christian faith."[34] By using the case of the misunderstood admonition of 1 Corinthians 5:9-10, Becker illustrates Paul's own predicament in drawing the line between withdrawal and/or involvement in social relations with outsiders.[35] Two other contributors to the same volume, Peter Lampe and Ulrich Luz,[36] argue that at least for some Christians assimilation to the surrounding culture was a viable option. It will be our contention in the coming discussion that Philippians 3:18-20 gives evidence of the confrontation between two models of Christianity, namely, the Pauline model, and that of a Christianity assimilated to Graeco-Roman culture.

Among other important contributors to our discussion I would like to mention Philip Harland who, following E. Hatch, attempts to study early Christian communities "as organizations in the midst of human society."[37]

---

31. Becker, "Paul and His Churches," 163.
32. Becker, "Paul and His Churches," 163.
33. Becker, "Paul and His Churches," 197.
34. Becker, "Paul and His Churches," 203.
35. Becker, "Paul and His Churches," 202.
36. Peter Lampe and Ulrich Luz, "Post-Pauline Christianity and Pagan Society," in *Beginnings of Christianity*, 242-80; esp. 269.
37. Philip Harland, *Associations, Synagogues, and Congregations: Claiming a Place in Ancient Mediterranean World* (Minneapolis: Fortress, 2003), 179.

In particular he opposes a certain tendency within scholarly circles to depict early Christianity (and Judaism) as being always exclusivistic and sectarian.[38] His more nuanced and balanced assessment of the primary evidence allows him to conclude as follows:

> Associations, synagogues, and congregations were small, non-compulsory groups that . . . [drew] their membership from several possible social network connections within the *polis*. All could be either relatively homogeneous or heterogeneous with regard to social and gender composition; all engaged in regular meetings that involved a variety of interconnected social, religious, and other purposes, one group differing from the next in the specifics of activities; all depended in various ways on commonly accepted social conventions such as benefaction for financial support . . . and the development of leadership structures; and all could engage in at least some degree of external contacts, both positive and negative, with other individuals, benefactors, groups, or institutions in civic context.[39]

In Harland's view the sectarian approach to early Christianity proceeds from a fraudulent methodology which assumes "a uniform picture of congregations" and an equally "artificially uniform picture of associations."[40] In so doing scholars do not take into account the more complex and diverse realities behind both Christian and Graeco-Roman assemblies. The sectarian depiction "obscures the more varied nature of evidence for Pauline and other groups."[41] Following Wilson's definition of a sect, namely, that a sect is a "minority religious movement within the context of [other] dominant religious traditions,"[42] Harland does not contest the "deviant" or distinctive character of Christian groups. Nor does he doubt whether they were at times in tension with some aspects of social life. What he does question is

---

38. See Harland's discussion in *Associations*, 182-212.
39. Harland, *Associations*, 211.
40. Harland, *Associations*, 181.
41. Harland, *Associations*, 184.
42. Bryan Wilson, *Magic and the Millenium* (London: Heinemann, 1973), 11.

the legitimacy of overemphasizing the ideas of exclusivity and separation at the expense of obscuring other data which testify to more complex dimensions of the relations of any given group to society.[43]

1.2.2 Scholarly Tendecies in Reading Philippians

With regard to the study of Philippians I would like to delineate three general scholarly tendencies. First, there is a growing tendency toward seeing the letter to Philippians as a compositional unity.[44] It is an important point for our future discussion, for we are going to argue that the question of the opponents (Phil 3:18-20) is a part of Paul's overall argument in Philippians 1:27 – 4:3.

---

43. Harland, *Associations*, 192.
44. Cf. L. Gregory Bloomquist, *The Function of Suffering in Philippians* (JSNTSS 78; Sheffield: JSOT Press, 1993), 97-116; William J. Dalton, "The Integrity of Philippians," *Bib* 60 (1979): 97-102; David E. Garland, "The Composition and Unity of Philippians," *NovT* 27 (1985): 141-73; Paul A. Holloway, *Consolation in Philippians: Philosophical Sources and Rhetorical Strategy* (Cambridge: Cambridge University Press, 2001), 7-33; Robert Jewett "The Epistolary Thanksgiving and the Integrity of Philippians," *NovT* 12 (1970): 40-53; T.E. Polard, "The Integrity of Philippians," *NTS* 13 (1966-67): 57-66; Jeffrey T. Reed, "Philippians 3:1 and the Epistolary Hesitation Formulas: The Literary Integrity of Philippians, Again," *JBL* 115 (1996): 63-90; idem, *A Discourse Analysis of Philippians: Method and Rhetoric in the Debate over Literary Integrity* (JSNTSS 136; Sheffield: Sheffield Academic Press, 1997); Duane F. Watson, "A Rhetorical Analysis of Philippians and Its Implications for the Unity Question," *NovT* 30 (1988): 57-88.

There are at least three arguments that are advanced by the proponents of the integrity of the letter: a) from the point of view of external evidence the hypothesis that Philippians is a compilation of letters is untenable. "There is no evidence, in all of its long history of interpretation, that it was ever considered as anything but a single letter" (Dalton, "Integrity," 101). Gordon Fee adds to this that there are no analogies to the "cut and paste" approach to letter-writing in antiquity (*Paul's Letter to the Philippians* [NICNT; Grand Rapids: Eerdmans, 1995], 22); b) lexical and thematic parallels likewise point in favor of the unity of the letter (Bloomquist, *Function of Suffering*, 102-3; Garland, "Composition and Unity," 158-59). Especially striking is the way the distinctive vocabulary of 2:5-11 recurs within the whole of chapter 3. Likewise the themes of unity (1:27-28; 2:2; 3:16), same-mindedness (1:27; 2:2, 5; 3:15; 4:2), suffering (1:29-30; 3:10-11), humility (2:1-11; 3:1-11), and joy (1:4, 18, 19; 2:2, 17, 18, 28; 3:1; 4:1, 4, 10) are repeated throughout. As W. Dalton remarks: "If a regular pattern of words and ideas is repeated in a way which reveals the inner movement and meaning of the text, then we have a new fact which the hypothesis of division will find hard to explain" ("Integrity," 99); c) finally, the epistolary conventions and the rhetorical structure of the letter undeniably testify to the unity of Philippians (see especially Bloomquist, *Function of Suffering*, 104-17; Reed, *Discourse Analysis*, 178-295; Watson, "Rhetorical Analysis," 84-88). To give just one example, Garland argues that Paul, in using the literary device known as *inclusion*, intended the letter to be seen as a cohesive whole (Garland, "Composition and Unity," 160-62).

Second, there is a tendency to read Philippians on its own terms. Recent scholarly work thus seeks to undo the propensity of two towering NT authorities of the mid-twentieth century, William Schmithals[45] and Helmut Koester,[46] to read Philippians through the grid of Galatians or 1 Corinthians. We concur with Wendy Cotter who argues that,

> since Paul writes to each particular community with attention to its special concerns, its membership and cultural orientation, his statements to one community, no matter how similar to the vocabulary and imagery in another letter to another community, cannot be used as proof of similar situations and similar enemies.[47]

It should be admitted that the same historical and cultural milieu of the Graeco-Roman world does not preclude similar traits in the development of Christianity at different locations of the Roman Empire. For example, we shall notice the similarly important role of the household in the formation of Christian communities both at Corinth and Philippi. However, in studying Philippians we will see examples of local idiosyncrasy (such as the terminology ἐπίσκοποι and διάκονοι) which reflect the peculiar circumstances of the Christian beginnings in that city.

Third, there is a tendency toward reading Paul within the realities of the first century Graeco-Roman city. This is especially relevant with regard to the issue of Paul's opponents in Philippians 3:18-20, where the scarcity of information has often provoked unwarranted, fanciful theological reconstructions,[48] as if Paul were writing to twentieth century theologians,

---

45. William Schmithals, "Die Irrlehrer des Philipperbriefes," *ZTK* 54 (1957): 297-341; ET, "The False Teachers of the Epistle to the Philippians," in *Paul and the Gnostics* (W. Schmithals; trans. J.E. Steely; Nashville: Abingdon, 1972), 65-122.
46. Helmut Koester, "The Purpose of the Polemic of a Pauline Fragment (Philippians iii)," *NTS* 8 (1961-62): 317-20.
47. Wendy Cotter, "Our Politeuma Is in Heaven: The Meaning of Philippians 3.17-21," in *Origins and Method: Towards a New Understanding of Judaism and Christianity: Essays in Honour of John C. Hurd* (ed. Bradley H. McLean; Sheffield: JSOT Press, 1993), 95.
48. Cf. some of the theories which identify Paul's opponents of Phil 3:18-20 as: a) gnostic libertines of a particular Jewish-Christian brand (W. Schmithals); b) gnostic Christian missionaries of Jewish origin and background (H. Koester); c) heretical libertinists with

not to poorly educated people primarily of the artisan class in first century Philippi. It would be wise, following the advice of W. Cotter, to probe all possible reconstructions against the "usual situation found on the first-century street."[49]

1.2.3 Pertinent Bibliography

In our survey we should mention several more bibliographic sources pertinent to the study of Philippians. In terms of epigraphic and inscriptional evidence for Philippi of fundamental importance remains the publication of the French scholar Paul Collart,[50] which is more recently enriched and expanded by Peter Pilhofer's exhaustive catalogue of the inscriptions from Philippi.[51] For the study of the religious background and of the role of women in the cultic practices at Philippi I find especially helpful the studies by Lucas Bormann,[52] Lilian Portefaix,[53] and Valerie Abrahamsen.[54] The work by Davorin Peterlin[55] provided some useful insights for understanding the internal conflict and its ramifications for the unity of the church at Philippi. In many ways I capitalize on the works of Craig S. De Vos,[56]

---

gnostic tendencies (Robert Jewett, "Conflicting Movements in the Early Church as Reflected in Philippians," *NovT* 12 [1970]: 362-90); d) judaizing Christians in pursuit of religious and moral perfectionism (Chris Mearns, "The Identity of Paul's Opponents at Philippi," *NTS* 33 [1987]: 194-204); or e) epicurean-type individuals "who do not organize their life according to faith in God's providence" (Karl Sandnes, *Belly and Body in the Pauline Epistles* [SNTSMS 120; Cambridge: Cambridge University Press, 2002], 149).

49. Cotter, "Our Politeuma," 96.

50. Paul Collart, *Philippes, ville de Macedoine depuis ses origins jusqu'a la fin de l'époque romaine* (2 vols.; Paris: Boccard, 1937).

51. Peter Pilhofer, *Philippi, Band II: Katalog der Inschriften von Philippi* (WUNT 119; Tübingen: Mohr Siebeck, 2000); cf. also his first volume *Philippi, Band I: Die erste christliche Gemeinde Europas* (WUNT 87; Tübingen: Mohr Siebeck, 1995).

52. Lucas Bormann, *Philippi: Stadt und Christengemeinde zur Zeit des Paulus* (NovTSup 78; Leiden: Brill, 1995).

53. Lilian Portefaix, *Sisters Rejoice: Paul's Letter to the Philippians and Luke-Acts as Seen by First-Century Philippian Women* (ConBNT 20; Stockholm: Almqvist & Wiksell, 1988).

54. Valerie Abrahamsen, *Women and Worship at Philippi: Diana/Artemis and Other Cults in the Early Christian Era* (Portland: Astarte Shell, 1995).

55. Davorin Peterlin, *Paul's Letter to the Philippians in the Light of Disunity in the Church* (NovTSup 79; Leiden: Brill, 1995).

56. Craig S. De Vos, *Church and Community Conflicts: The Relationships of the Thessalonian, Corinthian, and Philippian Churches with Their Wider Civic Communities* (SBL DS 168; Atlanta: Scholars Press, 1999).

Mikael Tellbe,[57] and Peter Oakes.[58] The first two authors provided some helpful clues for the identity of Paul's opponents and the origins of the πολίτευμα terminology in Philippians 3:18-20. Peter Oakes' study was especially useful in reading Philippians within Paul's anti-imperial polemics. Besides the commentary by Gordon Fee (n. 44), already mentioned, we will also interact with other valuable commentaries on Philippians.[59]

1.3 Voluntary Associations and the "Enemies of the Cross": The Thesis of the Dissertation

This leads us then to a discussion of one of the key questions of this dissertation, namely, who are the "enemies of the cross" (3:18)? While I appreciate the many valuable contributions made by scholars named above, I do not find their solutions to the identity of these "enemies of the cross" satisfactory especially because they do not account for the harshness of Paul's characterization of them.

---

57. Mikael Tellbe, *Paul between Synagogue and State: Christians, Jews, and Civic Authorities in 1 Thessalonians, Romans, and Philippians* (ConBNT 34; Stockholm: Almqvist & Wiksell, 2001).
58. Peter Oakes, "Philippians: From People to Letter" (Ph.D. diss., University of Oxford, 1995); idem, *Philippians: From People to Letter* (Cambridge: Cambridge University Press, 2001).
59. Francis W. Beare, *Philippians* (London: A. & C. Black, 1973); Markus N. A. Bockmuehl, *The Epistle to the Philippians* (BNTC 11; Peabody, Mass.: Hendrickson, 1998); J.F. Collange, *The Epistle of Saint Paul to the Philippians* (London: Epworth, 1979); Stephen E. Fowl, *Philippians* (THNTC 11; Grand Rapids: Eerdmans, 2005); Joachim Gnilka, *The Epistle to the Philippians* (NTSR 17; New York: Herder and Herder, 1971); Gerald F. Hawthorne, *Philippians* (WBC 43; Waco: Word) 1983; H.A.A. Kennedy, *The Epistle to the Philippians* (EGT 3; Grand Rapids: Eerdmans, 1983); I. Howard Marshall, *The Epistle to the Philippians* (EC; London: Epworth, 1992); Ralph P. Martin, *Philippians* (Grand Rapids: Eerdmans, 1980, c. 1976); Richard R. Melick, *Philippians, Colossians, Philemon* (NAC 32; Nashville: Broadman, 1991); Peter T. O'Brien, *The Epistle to the Philippians: A Commentary on the Greek Text* (NIGTC; Grand Rapids: Eerdmans, 1991); Carolyn Osiek, *Philippians, Philemon* (ANTC; Nashville: Abingdon, 2000); John Reumann, *Philippians: A New Translation with Introduction and Commentary* (AB; New Haven : Yale University Press, 2008); Moisés Silva, *Philippians* (BECNT 11; Grand Rapids: Baker, 1992); Bonnie B. Thurston, et al., *Philippians and Philemon* (Collegeville: Liturgical Press, 2004); Marvin R. Vincent, *A Critical and Exegetical Commentary on the Epistles to the Philippians and to Philemon* (ICC; Edinburgh: T & T Clark, 1897); Ben Witherington, *Friendship and Finances in Philippi: The Letter of Paul to the Philippians* (NTinC; Valley Forge, Pa: Trinity Press International, 1994).

In the current study I follow the lead of those scholars who locate the key to the "enemies'" identity in the Hellenistic term πολίτευμα understood as a voluntary association.⁶⁰ A possible clue that points in this direction is found in the inverted order of the phrase ἡμῶν γὰρ τὸ πολίτευμα ἐν οὐρανοῖς ὑπάρχει (3:20). The emphatic phrase "but *our* πολίτευμας suggests that Paul is in polemical conversation with his opponents whom he labels as the "enemies of the cross," and who spoke of a different πολίτευμα.⁶¹

It is our contention that Paul's "enemies" were indeed members of a local πολίτευμα (club, guild, association) which secured their existence within the overarching social framework of the Graeco-Roman *polis*. Voluntary associations (also known as πολιτεύματα) – a widely spread and popular phenomenon especially among the underprivileged people of the Roman Empire – served as an effective means of religious innovation and of the introduction of new cults and, in this way, provided implicit models for the formation of early Christian communities as well as competition for their loyalty. Organized around the devotion to a particular deity (often combined with the devotion to the ruling emperor), voluntary associations secured their existence within the socio-political structures of the empire. By withdrawing from worshiping gods, Christians threatened to tear this structure apart, thus inviting the prospects of social ostracism and suffering.

Thus I argue that in Philippians 3:18-20 Paul exhorts the Philippians to distance themselves from the deviant group of Christians whose membership in a local voluntary association (πολίτευμα) compromised their ultimate allegiance to the heavenly πολίτευμα, or governing authority, lodged in its crucified Lord and Savior Jesus Christ, and thus made themselves the "enemies of the cross of Christ." The major point of disagreement with Paul was neither their adherence to Jewish customs nor their Epicurean type libertinism but rather their different set of allegiances. It is this ideological feature that made them so dangerous in the eyes of Paul. His opponents were members of a πολίτευμα different from Paul's and continued to pledge

---

60. See Cotter, "Our Politeuma," 96-97; De Vos, *Church and Community Conflicts*, 273-75; Tellbe, *Paul between Synagogue and State*, 271.
61. Cf. Paul C. Böttger, „Die Eschatologische Existenz der Christen: Erwägungen zu Philipper 3: 20," *ZNW* 60 (1969): 244-63.

their allegiance to a different κύριος and σωτήρ, i.e., to the Roman emperor (Phil 3:20).

1.4 Outline of the Dissertation

In chapter 2 we are going to get acquainted with voluntary associations, a widely spread and important social institution of the Graeco-Roman world. We will assess the primary sources with regard to the issues of membership, organizational structure, and the social and religious functions of voluntary associations. Within the discussion of the religious functions of voluntary associations, special attention will be given to the role of the imperial cult in uniting the peoples of the empire under the bond of loyalty to the emperor. We are going to argue that in a highly stratified Roman society voluntary associations were a viable option for socializing and for personal self-realization, especially for the marginalized social groups like slaves, foreigners, and women. Although a mainly unofficial, grass-root phenomenon, voluntary associations, through the incorporation of emperor worship, legitimized their existence within the socio-political universe of the Roman Empire.

In our consideration of Philippi (chapter 3) we will try to find out how this Roman colony was similar or different to other cities of the Roman Empire. We will get acquainted with the demographic, socio-economic, political and religious features of the city. It will be our contention that, although from the point of view of its size and location, Philippi was of less significance than other cities of the empire (e.g., Thessalonica, Corinth, Ephesus), its special colonial status, the presence of the significant number of settled Roman veterans, and the clear display of the imperial cult emphasize the heightened political tenor of the city, and its clear pro-Roman stance.

In chapter 4 we will study the available epigraphic evidence for the presence of religious and professional associations at Philippi. Of special interest will be the evidence for the presence of devotion to the emperor in such associations.

The findings of chapters 2 and 4 will be further related to the study of the Christian community at Philippi in chapter 5. We are going to argue that Paul's ministry took place within the format of the household and of the professional *collegia*. Furthermore, from the point of view of membership, the active role of women, organizational structure, and other parameters, the Christian *ekklēsia* at Philippi, at least for the eye of an outsider, bore a strong resemblance to a religious voluntary association. The disagreement between the two leaders of the church (Euodia and Syntyche) and the multiplicity of the leadership titles (ἐπίσκοποι and διάκονοι) also suggest the competitive relationship between different household groups.

Finally, in chapter 6 we are going to present an argument that the opponents in Philippians 3:18-20 are a deviant group of Christians who retain their membership in a voluntary association (πολίτευμα). This supposition will be substantiated by: a) lexical study of the term πολίτευμα which was used of voluntary associations; b) structural analysis of Philippians 1:27 – 4:3 which suggests that Paul's concern for a different "walk" of the opponents is directly related to the different "thinking" between the leaders of the church. The Philippians' lack of response to Paul's previous warnings might be an indication that the opponents' model was an attractive alternative especially in view of the prospects of suffering for Christ; and c) analysis of the polemical description of the opponents, which in our view fits best the context of the socializing practices within voluntary associations. We are going to argue that Philippians 3:18-20 is an example of intentionally exaggerated polemics on the part of Paul to make his point: the opponents are dangerous people; imitation of them will lead to ultimate destruction. The danger proceeds from the ideological component (religious devotion to the emperor) associated with the socializing practices of the opponents.

In the second half of chapter 6 we are going to consider Paul's counter arguments against the opponents. We are going to propose that Paul utilizes the term πολίτευμα to his own advantage. As the term was used for the designation of a governing body within a *polis*, Paul refers to the πολίτευμα in heaven, behind which lurks the notion of the "heavenly Jerusalem" (Gal 4:25). It is to this governing body that Christians are accountable and pledge their allegiance. Second, certain terminology, such as "equality with God" (2:6), the worship motif (2:9-11), and the terms κύριος and σωτήρ (3:20), indicate Paul's engagement in anti-imperial polemics against those who, through their membership in voluntary associations, continue to pay homage to a different κύριος and σωτήρ, namely, the emperor. Finally, Paul's counter argument is directed against the opponents' deficient view of discipleship which denies the necessity of suffering with Christ. For Paul κοινωνία in Christ's sufferings is an essential part of being a follower of the crucified Jesus.

CHAPTER 2

Voluntary Associations within a Graeco-Roman City

Voluntary associations are essentially phenomena of the Hellenistic era.[1] Although historically they are known to have been in existence from a much earlier period,[2] their full-scale proliferation took place after Alexander the Great. The inscriptional evidence is available "virtually from every locale in the ancient world and from every period from the fourth century BCE

---

1. On the issue of voluntary association see Richard S. Ascough, "Greco-Roman Philosophic, Religious, and Voluntary Associations," in *Community Formation in the Early Church and in the Church Today* (ed. Richard N. Longenecker; Peabody, Mass.: Hendrickson, 2002), 3-19; idem, "Voluntary Associations and the Formation of Pauline Christian Communities: Overcoming the Objections," in *Vereine, Synagogen und Gemeinden im Kaiserzeitlichen Kleinasien* (ed. Andreas Gutsfeld and Dietrich-Alex Koch; Tübingen: Mohr Siebeck, 2006), 149-83; Albert Baumgarten, "Graeco-Roman Voluntary Associations and Ancient Jewish Sects," in *Jews in the Graeco-Roman World* (ed. Martin Goodman; Oxford: Clarendon Press, 1998), 93-112; Andrew D. Clarke, *Serve the Community of the Church: Christians as Leaders and Ministers* (Grand Rapids: Eerdmans, 2000), 59-77; Frederick W Danker, "Associations, Clubs, Thiasoi," *ABD* 1:501-3; Nicholas Fisher, "Roman Associations, Dinner Parties, and Clubs," in *Civilization of the Ancient Mediterranean: Greece and Rome* (ed. Michael Grant and Rachel Kitzinger, New York: Scribner's, 1988), 2:1199-225; John S. Kloppenborg, "Edwin Hatch, Churches and Collegia," in *Origins and Method: Towards a New Understanding of Judaism and Christianity: Essays in Honour of John C. Hurd* (ed. Bradley H. McLean; JSNTSS 86; Sheffield: JSOT Press, 1993), 212-38; idem, "Collegia and *Thiasoi*: Issues in Function, Taxonomy and Membership," *Voluntary Associations in the Graeco-Roman World* (ed. John S. Kloppenborg and Stephen G. Wilson; London: Routledge, 1996), 16-30; Stephen G. Wilson, "Voluntary Associations: An Overview," in *Voluntary Associations in the Graeco-Roman World* (ed. John S. Kloppenborg and Stephen G. Wilson; London: Routledge, 1996), 1-15.
2. Gaius' commentary on the Law of the Twelve Tablets contains references to the precursors of voluntary associations in the laws of Solon in sixth century BCE Athens. Cf. *Digesta* 47.22.4.

to the later Roman Empire." Their phenomenal popularity undoubtedly testifies to the special role that voluntary associations played in "mediating various kinds of social exchange"[3] in both Hellenistic and Roman societies.

Certain political and economical factors contributed to the spread of voluntary associations throughout the Graeco-Roman world. Michael Rostovtzeff was one of the first to point out that voluntary associations had a special appeal to those who "did not belong to the body of citizens of the particular city." The massive dislocation of people of the post-Alexandrian era signified for many of them the loss of ties with the family, tribe or *polis* and thus created a need for a new social arrangement. As the deterioration of the Greek ideal of the *polis* did not supply the same kind of stimulus or possibilities for active participation in political life, so, for many, especially for the resident aliens, "associations [became] a kind of substitute for city life."[4] Moreover, the aloof impersonal character of Roman religion turned people in search of more personal religious experience. Insofar as Graeco-Roman associations provided an "opportunity for evolution of new religious ideas,"[5] they became instruments of religious innovation and means for the introduction of new cults.[6]

"Voluntary association" is a modern term used in place of many ancient designations of the different types of informal groups of antiquity (κολλήγιον, θίασος, σύνοδος, συνέδριον, κοινόν, ἐκκλησία, πολίτευμα, etc.).[7] The term "voluntary" means that membership was not automatically assumed (e.g., by virtue of birth, as in the case of the household) but rather was a matter of choice. Second, the term "voluntary" is used in counter-distinction to other types of involuntary or "official" associations.

---

3. Kloppenborg, "Collegia," 17.
4. Michael I. Rostovtzeff, *Social and Economic History of the Hellenistic World* (Oxford: Clarendon Press, 1941), 2:1064.
5. Arthur D. Nock, "On the Historical Importance of Cult Associations," *CR* 38 (1924): 105.
6. Cf. Baumgarten, "Graeco-Roman Voluntary Associations," 109.
7. See Ascough, "Voluntary Associations," 14; idem, "Overcoming the Objections," 155-59; cf. S. Wilson, "Voluntary Associations," 1. Of special importance for our future discussion is the designation of voluntary association as πολίτευμα, the term Paul uses in Phil 3:20.

The distinctions between the two are of a legal and social nature.[8] The official associations (usually known as sacerdotal *collegia* or sacred *solidates*) were established either by imperial edict or senatorial act. These institutions drew their constituency from among the elite members of Roman society and they frequently played an important role in governmental structures. By contrast, voluntary (unofficial) associations sprang up sporadically and had no role within the official structures. They were tolerated rather than encouraged. Voluntary associations were populated primarily (but not exclusively) by non-elite members: freedmen, slaves, *peregrini*, etc.[9]

In the current chapter we are going to assess the primary epigraphic evidence regarding voluntary associations with the purpose of defining the issues of membership, organizational structure, and the different functions of voluntary associations within the Graeco-Roman city.[10] We are going

---

8. Cf. Kloppenborg, "Collegia and *Thiasoi*," 16. Cf. E. Hatch's statement: "Then, as now, many men had two religions, that which they professed and that which they believed: for the former there were temples and State officials and public sacrifices; for the latter there were associations: and in these associations, as is shown from extant inscriptions, divinities whom the State ignored had their priests, their chapels, and their rituals" (*Early Christian Churches*, 28).

9. It should be noted that the distinction between the two types of associations should not be overstated, because "membership in a synagogue, family cult, or trade guild may have been for different reasons more or less obligatory" (S. Wilson, "Voluntary Associations," 1).

10. Among other evidence we will refer to the following inscriptions:
   a) an inscription of a religious cult of Zeus from Philadelphia in Lydia (*SIG* 3.985; late 2nd – early 1st century BCE). We will refer to it as the Philadelphia inscription. The text of the inscription with translation is published by S. Barton and G. Horsley in the article, "A Hellenistic Cult Group and the New Testament Churches," *JAC* 24 (1981): 7-41;
   b) a papyrus (*PLond* 2193; dated in the 1st century BCE) contains the statutes of a religious association of Zeus Hypsistos in Philadelphia (Egypt). The text of the inscription with translation is published by Colin H. Roberts et al., "The Guild of Zeus Hypstistos," *HTR* 29 (1936): 39-88;
   c) the so-called Agrippinilla inscription (mid 2nd century CE) found on a marble base of a sculpture near the city of Torre Nova (Italy) lists the 402 names of the Dionysiac association. The inscription is for the first time published with translation by Bradley H. McLean in his article, "The Agrippinilla Inscription: Religious Associations and Early Church Formation," in *Origins and Method: Towards a New Understanding of Judaism and Christianity: Essays in Honour of John C. Hurd* (ed. Bradley H. McLean; JSNTSS 86; Sheffield: JSOT Press, 1993): 239-70. For future references we will use the following abbreviation: *IAgrip*;
   d) the by-laws of the Bacchic worshipers (Iobacchoi association) at Athens inscribed on a column (*IG* 2.2 1368; 2nd century CE). The English translation is published in M.N. Tod, *Sidelights on Greek History* (Oxford: Blackwell, 1932), 89-91;

to argue that voluntary associations were a viable option for many, especially the socially disadvantaged, to realize their potential as social beings. Voluntary associations recreated in many ways the life of the *polis* in its egalitarian version. It was the place where many social barriers were invalidated. When the Christian gospel reached the cities of the Mediterranean world there was an available model for the early Christians to adopt for the development of their community. The findings in this chapter will have an important bearing on the following discussion of voluntary associations at Philippi and especially on the analysis of the Christian *ekklēsia* in that city.

2.1 Religious and Professional Associations

In our study we are going to limit our consideration of voluntary associations to two primary types: private religious associations and professional associations.[11]

A primary purpose for private religious associations was religious worship which was practiced outside of the larger, recognized mysteries and cults of the day. Although a number of associations met in public spaces, and some even met as private religious associations within a larger public cult, their primary location was domestic. In the Philadelphia inscription it is specifically stated that the meetings of the association took place in the οἶκος of a certain Dionysius.[12] Private religious associations attracted their members based on their commitment to a particular deity or deities. In general, however, in the syncretistic atmosphere of the Hellenistic

---

e) an inscription (*CIL* 14.2112= *ILS* 7212; CE 136) from Lanuvium (Italy) spells out the by-laws of a burial association of Diana and Antinous (we will refer to it as the Lanuvium inscription). The English translation is published in Naphtali Lewis and Meyer Reinhold, eds. *Roman Civilization: Selected Readings*, Vol. 2: *The Empire* (RCSS; New York: Columbia University Press, 1951), 273-75.

11. Ascough, "Voluntary Associations," 12. We need to keep in mind however that in all probability there was a wider variety of types of associations. Cf. the classification of voluntary associations by Harland in *Associations*, 28-53. Besides the two types suggested by Ascough, Harland also delineates associations by their household ethnic (geographical), and neighborhood (locational) connections. Because in our research we are not trying to identify a specific type of the opponents' association at Philippi, we will limit our inquiry to Ascough's classification.

12. *SIG* 3.985: lines 5; 15; 24; 33; 53.

period, commitment to a particular deity was not exclusivist in character and was not always the primary reason for joining the association. Thus in the Philadelphia inscription we read: "In this place have been set up altars of Zeus Eumenes, and of Hestia his coadjutor, and of other savior gods, and Eudaimonia, Plutus, Arete, Hygieia, Agathe Tyche, Agathos Daimon, Mneme, the Charitae and Nike."[13] Later in the inscription we find the dedication to Agdistis "the very holy guardian and mistress of this *oikos*."[14] As B. McLean further points out, "membership was not determined by ideological commitment to [a particular deity] but rather by pre-existing bonds and networks."[15] The name of M. Gavius Squilla Gallicanus (*IAgrip*: col. 1, line 4), a highly influential senatorial official on the list of the Agrippinilla inscription, was as strong an incentive to join the association as the devotion to the patron deity, Dionysius.

Professional voluntary associations, or guilds, brought together people from a wide range of professions existing throughout the Graeco-Roman world. As Ascough remarks, "There are, in fact, very few professions not represented in the extant records of the professional voluntary associations of antiquity."[16] Although occupation was a central unifying principle, we should not discard the religious aspect of these associations. In this sense they were *religious* associations too. Each professional association claimed the patronage of a deity or deities which often were associated with a particular profession. Invocation of a deity[17] and participation in festivals and rituals were central to the communal life of an association. The gender exclusive character of some professional associations is explained mostly by the specifics of labor involving either male or female workers. While some of the religious associations were at times exclusive (like the all-male Silvanus association or predominantly female Diana association from Philippi), their exclusivity is not a commentary on gender-prejudice, but rather is explained by the orientation of the deity worshiped to supply specific male or

---

13. *SIG* 3.985: lines 9-11.
14. *SIG* 3.985: line 51.
15. McLean, "Agrippinilla Inscription," 270.
16. Ascough, "Voluntary Associations," 13.
17. Cf. the Philadelphia inscription: "When coming into this *oikos*. . . swear by all gods. . ." (*SIG* 3.985: line 15).

female needs. Overall, as we shall see shortly there is a remarkable openness (especially in religious associations) toward being gender-inclusive.

The Roman colony of Philippi was one of the places where voluntary associations (both religious and professional) existed and thrived. We will consider the available epigraphic evidence in the next chapter.

2.2 Membership

With regard to membership many of the associations reveal a remarkable degree of openness and inclusiveness toward people of different social standing. To be sure we should not over optimistically impose modern categories on ancient realities, yet in many ways (as follows from the epigraphic evidence) many such associations were in fact egalitarian-type societies. For example, the slave-members of the Lanuvium burial association are promised to be buried on a par with other members, even in cases when "master or mistress unreasonably refuses to relinquish his body."[18] The Philadelphia inscription with its strict moral code nevertheless does not differentiate members (real or potential) on the grounds of gender or social status: "When coming into this *oikos*, let men and women, free people and slaves swear by all the gods."[19] The line is repeated toward the end of the inscription: "May she [Agdistis, the holy guardian] create good thoughts in men and women, free people and slaves, in order that they may obey the things written here."[20] Reference to the "monthly sacrifices"[21] might be an indication that only those residing permanently in the area of Philadelphia could have been the members.

The 402 names found on the Agrippinilla inscription provide a wealth of information on its members' social prosopography. Almost 80% of the names are of Greek origin with the remaining 20% belonging to Roman origin.[22] One quarter of the Greek names (141 names) are attested elsewhere

---

18. *CIL* 14.2112: page 2, lines 3-4.
19. *SIG* 3.985: line 15.
20. *SIG* 3.985: lines 53-54.
21. *SIG* 3.985: line 55.
22. For the detailed analysis, see McLean, "Agrippinilla Inscription," 249-57. The high

as the names applied to slaves,[23] which strongly suggests that many of the association's members were slaves or freedmen of the Gallicanus family. The use of the *cognomina* (not *praenomina*) of the Roman names suggests that "the scope of the association is wider than the members of a single *familia*."[24] It also means that there were no slaves among the Roman members of the association.[25] Women constituted almost one third of the members (110 names). If the inscription bore the names only of the financial contributors to the statue, the actual percentage of female members of the association might have been even higher.

The requirements for membership varied greatly from one association to another, from some cases of its being a pure formality to other cases where an elaborate initiation was required.

> At one end of the scale, rules of behavior meant no more than the regulation of communal activities – which was as far as many *collegia* went – but at the other end it could extend to a comprehensive ethical vision for life as a whole… And while in some groups the initial process of entry was sufficient to open up full membership, in others (Mithraism is a classic example) there were carefully delineated stages through which members progressed.[26]

Membership required taking on certain financial and other obligations. Membership fees were paid to cover the operational costs and other types of expenditures (festivals, banquets, burial of members). The by-laws of the Lanuvium association spell out two clear requirements: first, "read the

---

percentage of Greek names in the association in the vicinities of Rome is explained by the fact that the Gallicanus family originally resided on the island of Lesbos, but then subsequently moved to Roman Campagna with the members of the household joining them in the relocation.

23. Linda C. Reilly, *Slaves in Ancient Greece: Slaves from Greek Manumission Inscriptions* (Chicago: Ares, 1978).

24. McLean, "Agrippinilla Inscription," 255.

25. "In the Imperial period the slaves in Roman households were named by adding a slave's praenomen to the full *tria nomina* of his owner" (McLean, "Agrippinilla Inscription," 255).

26. Wilson, "Voluntary Associations," 9.

by-laws carefully before entering, so as not to find cause for complaint later"[27]; second: "pay an initiation fee of 100 sesterces and an amphora of good wine."[28] Membership also required a monthly fee of five asses.[29] Although, the Philadelphia inscription does not contain any explicit financial/material obligations, the reference to "the monthly and annual sacrifices"[30] might imply that it was the responsibility of the members to supply all that was necessary for them. In some cases money went toward the upkeep of buildings or the erection of statues (like the one dedicated to Agrippinilla) and inscriptions or to help the needy members.

Membership also required compliance with the rules and regulations of the association. These were aimed primarily at limiting the disorderly behavior, which seems to have been a common place among the members of associations.[31] The very mention in the regulations of the Iobacchoi association of the "horses"[32] (bouncers), whose responsibility was to restrain the disorderly, tells us of the scope of the problem. The Lanuvium by-laws likewise provide some of the guidelines for managing a potential conflict ("It was voted further that if any member desires to make any complaint or bring up any business, he is to bring it up at a business meeting"),[33] as well as disciplinary measures for obstructing order:

> Any member who moves from one place to another so as to cause a disturbance shall be fined 4 sesterces. Any member, moreover, who speaks abusively of another or causes an uproar shall be fined 12 sesterces. Any member who uses any abusive or insolent language to a *quinquennalis* at a banquet shall be fined 20 sesterces.[34]

---

27. *CIL* 14.2112: page 1, line 19.
28. *CIL* 14.2112: page1, lines 20-21.
29. *CIL* 14.2112: page1, lines 21.
30. *SIG* 3.985: line 55.
31. See Philip Harland, "Spheres of Contention, Claims of Pre-eminence: Rivalries among Associations in Sardis and Smyrna," in *Religious Rivalries and the Struggle for Success in Sardis and Smyrna* (Waterloo: Wilfrid Laurier University Press, 2005), 53-63.
32. *IG* 2.2 1368, line 145.
33. *CIL* 14.2112 , page 1, line 23.
34. *CIL* 14.2112 , page 2, lines 25-28.

A similar note is heard in the regulations of the Zeus Hypsistos association from Egypt: "All are to obey the president and his servant in matters pertaining to the corporation, and they shall be present at all command occasions."[35] The rather detailed regulation regarding fighting, for example, ("if anyone begins a fight, is found disorderly, sits in someone's seat, or is insulting or abusing someone else"[36]) is an explicit commentary on the inner rivalry which took place during social events. At the same time we cannot help but marvel at the degree of civility with which matters of misbehavior were handled. Especially important was the corporate role of the association whereby disciplinary measures were decided, as in the Iobacchoi association, by vote:

> The person abused or insulted shall produce two members (*iobacchoi*) as sworn witnesses, testifying that they heard the insult or abuse. The one who committed the insult or the abuse shall pay to the common treasury 25 light drachmae. If someone comes to blows, let the one who was struck file a report with the priest or the vice-priest, who shall without fail convene a meeting; the members shall make a judgment by vote as the priest presides.[37]

A somewhat unusual precondition for membership in the Philadelphia Zeus association was a strict moral code concerning the sexual purity of both men and women.[38] The direct responsibility of members was to look after each other, and in case some sexual activity took place, they were "not to conceal it or keep silent about it."[39] The transgressors would not be allowed to enter the *oikos* again and they would bring upon themselves hate

---

35. *PLond* 2193, lines 10-12.
36. *IG* 2.2 1368, line 60.
37. *IG* 2.2 1368: lines 62-90.
38. "Apart from his own wife, a man is not to have sexual relations with another married woman, whether free or slave, nor with a boy nor a virgin girl; nor shall he recommend it to another. . . . A free woman is to be chaste and shall not know the bed of, nor have sexual intercourse with, another man except her own husband" (*SIG* 3.985: lines 27-28; 35-36).
39. *SIG* 3.985: line 32.

and punishments from the gods.[40] Although this may have been more of an exceptional case, the existence of such a moral code should caution us against the prejudiced and stereotypical portrayal of associations as having been the hotbed of immorality and other vices. The disciplinarian restrictions within associations are an important point to remember when we discuss morally reprehensible actions which allegedly took place during feasting times in Philippi.

Another important point, already briefly mentioned, is that membership in voluntary associations generally did not require an exclusive commitment to one particular association or deity.

> In principle there was usually nothing to stop a person belonging to or being the patron of more than one guild or mystery cult, each of which may have honored a different deity. Equally there is evidence that shows that some cult centres, for example Mithraea, were not averse to honoring deities other than the one who was their chief object of devotion.[41]

An inscription from Athens (2nd century BCE) names Simon of Poros as the new charter member of the Dionysiac club who was at the same time an adherent of the Mother of the Gods association.[42] Another inscription from Pergamon (106 CE) lists the same man, L. Aninius Flaccus, as a member of both the Dionysiac cult and of the association devoted to the god Augustus and the goddess Roma.[43] There are strong indications that some of the Jews combined their allegiance to the synagogue with membership in the professional guilds. An epitaph (190-220 CE) of Publius Aelius Glykon from Hierapolis contains the provisions for members of the guilds of purple-dyers and carpet-weavers to take care of his grave on particular

---

40. *SIG* 3.985: lines 32, 50-51.
41. Wilson, "Voluntary Associations," 10. Cf. also Richard Ascough, *Paul's Macedonian Associations: The Social Context of Philippians and 1 Thessalonians* (WUNT 2.161; Tübingen: Mohr Siebeck, 2003), 87-91.
42. *IG* 2.2 1325; 1326, 2948.
43. *IPergamon* 374.

Jewish holidays.[44] It seems to imply at least two things: a) Publius' affiliation with the local synagogue; b) at least some of the members in both associations were Jews.[45] A chief physician and a leader of the association of physicians at Ephesos, Julius, entrusted a Jewish group to take care of his grave.[46] In the coming discussion we will see that there were similar tendencies at Philippi. We will consider two inscriptions which testify that a certain Roman official who was also a high priest of the imperial cult was a co-sponsor of the Serapis association.

The evidence for multiple affiliations is further strengthened by some of the associations' attempts to lay exclusive claims on their members. The already-cited regulation of the guild of Zeus Hypsistos in Egypt forbade the devotees "to make factions or to leave the brotherhood of the president for another."[47] A similarly strong prohibition is found in the edict (404-359 BCE) which instructs the members of the *therapeutai* of Zeus in Sardis "not to participate in the mysteries of Sabazios – with those who bring the burnt offerings – and the mysteries of Agdistis and Ma."[48] The very legislation re-enacted in the late second century by Marcus Aurelius and Lucius Verus, which specifically prohibited membership in more than one association,[49] points to the fact that shared membership was more commonplace rather than an exception. This is an important point to keep in mind for our future discussion. For the evidence for multiple affiliations within voluntary associations suggests that a similar dynamic might have taken place within nascent Christianity. At least for some Gentiles becoming a member of a Christian *ekklēsia* did not imply an exclusive commitment to one particular group.

---

44. *IHierapJ* 342 = *CIJ* 777: "[Publius Aelius Glykon Zeuxianos Aelius] left behind 200 denaria for the grave-crowning ceremony to the most holy presidency of the purple-dyers . . . to take a share on the sixth day of the month during the Festival of Unleavened Bread. Likewise he also left behind 150 denaria for the grave-crowning ceremony to the association of carpet weavers, so that revenues from the interest should be distributed, half during the Festival of Kalends… and half during the Festival of Pentecost."

45. See an extended discussion in Harland, *Associations*, 207-9.

46. *IEph* 1677 = *CIJ* 745

47. *PLond* 2193, lines 13-14.

48. *ISardH* 4 = *NewDocs* 1:3

49. Digest 47.22.1.2: *non licet autem amplius quam unum collegium legitimum habere.*

2.3 Organizational Structure

The great geographical dispersion, ethnic and cultic variety and, mostly unofficial, autonomous character of voluntary associations preclude any attempts to identify some uniform structure and terminology for these organizations. Rather we can almost expect to encounter a variety of organizational models and structures which were often conditioned by local particularities.[50] There was a remarkable degree of flexibility in the association's ability to transform its structures in response to a crisis arising either internally or outside the group.[51]

In this regard the Philadephia inscription is of interest because there is a conspicuous absence of any references to a structure or hierarchy of offices. It can be assumed that Dionysius, who hosts the meetings of the association in his *oikos*,[52] plays some prominent role, yet he obviously does so without any formal title. From the inscription it also follows that the members of the association were supposed to be involved in some sort of monitoring of each other's moral conduct[53] with no special offices appointed for that task. This lack of formal organizational structure might be an indication of the cult's being in the state of infancy.[54]

The Agrippinilla inscription, to the contrary, displays a long list of 22 different titles from the most prestigious roles of priests and priestesses to the new initiates of the association. As is clearly seen from the inscription, the structure of the Dionysiac association was centered around the members of the senatorial family of M. Gavius Squilla Gallicanus. Pompeia Agrippinilla (*IAgrip*: col.1, dedication); the priestess (ἱέρεια) of the association (to whom the inscription is dedicated), was the wife of Gallicanus. Another Gallicanus mentioned (*IAgrip*: col. 1, line 5), was probably the father of M. Gavius Squilla. Both served as priests (ἱερεῖς). Two other men with the same name Macrinus (*IAgrip*: col.1, lines 1, 6), possibly Agrippinilla's

---

50. Kloppenborg, "Churches as *Collegia*," 232.
51. Ascough, "Voluntary Associations," 14.
52. *SIG* 3.985: line 5.
53. *SIG* 3.985: lines 23-25; 28-31.
54. Barton and Horsley, "A Hellenistic Cult Group," 22.

close relatives,[55] were appointed as *heros* (ἥρως)[56] and a priest respectively. Agrippinilla's daughter Cornelia Cethegilla (*IAgrip*: col. 1, line 2) was the torchbearer, the second position (!) in the association's hierarchy. It follows that the Roman *familia* constituted an important foundational element of many voluntary associations.

S. Wilson likewise points to a "considerable overlap"[57] in organization and practice between associations, households and other "small-group" format assemblies (including Jewish synagogues and Christian gatherings), for the simple reason that most of them had their meetings in houses. While this was probably true with regard to the majority of associations whose membership averaged two or three dozen members,[58] the case of Agrippinilla's Dionysiac association convinces us that "the growth in membership of family-based religious associations was not limited by the size of private dwellings, nor by the consanguinity with the founding *familia*."[59]

Although voluntary associations were in many ways egalitarian-type societies there was no mistaking who was in control. Not surprisingly it was the people of wealth and influence that played key roles in the associations' life, presiding at meetings and acting as patrons. The procedures of appointing leading officers differed from one association to another. It is also true that "in many instances, we have no indication of how officers were designated."[60] The guild of Zeus Hypsistos elected (by lot, or vote?) its president for a one-year period.[61] The Lanuvium burial association exercised an annual rotation of leadership, although the mechanism of the

---

55. Cf. McLean, "Agrippinilla Inscription," 248.
56. As McLean explains, the term ἥρως is connected with an archaic notion of the god Dionysus as being the bull-god and his worshipers as "cowherds." It is used in the inscription for the designation of the leader of the association. Cf. McLean, "Agrippinilla Inscription," 244, n. 3.
57. Wilson, "Voluntary Associations," 13.
58. Cf. Wilson: "It is estimated that most associations were relatively small in number, typically fifteen to twenty… Their size would have been constrained by the places in which they met. Many of them – churches, synagogues, *collegia*, schools – met in the room of a house, often that of their patron or one of their wealthier members" ("Voluntary Associations," 13).
59. McLean, "Agrippinilla Inscription," 257.
60. Kloppenborg, "Churches as *Collegia*," 232.
61. *PLond* 2193: lines 5-6.

rotation is not specified.[62] The Iobacchoi association elected officers either by lot or through the direct appointment by the priest.[63] Still in other cases it was probably the prerogative of the founder/donor to stay in the office or to appoint the people that he or she wanted. The Philadelphia inscription might be an example of this kind of leadership. By appealing to the divine authority ("to this man Zeus gives ordinances"[64]), Dionysius, the householder and patron of the association, assumed the leadership role for good. At least there are no indications to the contrary. In the case of the Agrippinilla association, undoubtedly the matters of leadership were in the hands of the leading family.

A position of leadership obviously meant an access to power and privilege. The members of the guild of Zeus Hypsistos are instructed to "obey the president and his servant."[65] In the Iobacchoi association it was sufficient for the officer in charge to lay down his *thyrsus* (reed or wand) on the person who acted in a disorderly way so that he would be dismissed.[66] In the Lanuvium association the chief officers, the so-called *quinquennalis*, were exempt from certain obligations and had a double share in all distributions.[67] More importantly, however, the position of leadership brought with it the coveted elevated social status within associations and, in case of a larger group, even within a wider social context. The case of the Agrippinilla association is a clear example of the kind of incentives that people of wealth and influence gained from being patrons of the association. After all, it was in their personal interest to have more than four hundred men and women in their social network of benefaction.

> Associations . . . resembled the whole social context they found themselves in and imitated it as best as they could. Like everyone else, they sought status; and like the members

---

62. *CIL* 14.2112: page 2, lines 14.
63. "The officer in charge of good order shall be chosen by lot or be appointed by the priest" (*IG* 2.2 1368: line 135).
64. *SIG* 3.985: line12.
65. *PLond* 2193: line 10.
66. *IG* 2.2 1368: line 136.
67. *CIL* 14.2112, page 2, line 19.

of many other kinds of groups . . . they also sought a range of further satisfactions not felt or attainable in the undivided urban population.[68]

An inevitable prize for being a leader lay in his/her financial or material commitments to sustain the proper functioning of the association.[69] An example of such a commitment is found in the Lanuvium inscription:

> Masters of the dinners in the order of the membership list, appointed four at a time in turn, shall be required to provide an amphora of good wine each, and for as many members as the society has, a bread costing 2 asses, sardines to the number of four, a setting, and warm water with service.[70]

Similarly the president of the guild of Zeus Hypsistos had to "make for all the contributors one banquet a month in the sanctuary of Zeus."[71] Some of the associations (especially religious ones) preferred rotating offices for a simple reason that "their members were so poor that they were unable to afford the expenses for the office." The professional associations, however, preferred long-term offices because their leaders were able to pay expenses for the office.[72]

It should be noted that leadership roles in voluntary associations were not an exclusive prerogative of men. It follows from the Agrippinilla inscription that almost one-third of different titles and functions were allotted to women. What is of special importance is that women were represented at the highest level in the association's hierarchy: Agrippinilla's daughter Cornelia (*IAgrip*: col. 1, line 2) was the torchbearer and Agrippinilla herself

---

68. Ramsey MacMullen, *Roman Social Relations, 50 B.C. to A.D. 284* (New Haven: Yale University Press, 1974), 77.
69. Consider a letter of resignation by a patron of an association in Egypt: "To Thrax, the president, and to the fellow members of the association, from Epiodoros. Since I am impoverished and unable to act ad benefactor to the guild, I ask that you accept my resignation. Farewell" (*PKar.* 575, cited in Ascough, "Voluntary Associations, 15).
70. *CIL* 14.2112: page 2, lines 14-16.
71. *PLond* 2193: lines 8-9.
72. Theissen, "Social Structure," 77.

was the priestess of the association. This seems to be consistent with the general trend in the first and second centuries CE toward women's more active involvement in the high-priestly offices of various civic cults. Thus, for example, in the inscription dated in the middle of the first century CE found in Magnesia we read: "The *boule* and the *demos* honored Juliane, daughter of Eustratos, . . . the high priestess of Asia, who was the first woman to serve as high priestess of Asia, . . . because of (her) excellence."[73] According to the analysis by S. Friesen, toward the end of the second century CE almost half of all high priests in Asia were women.[74]

It will be of special importance for us to know that in Macedonia women likewise played an important role in cultic activities. An inscription from Thessalonica contains the testament of a "priestess Evia of Prinophoros"[75] of a Dionysiac association. She was also a patron of the association for she "bequeath[ed] for the perpetuation of [her] memory two plethra of vineyard, together with the adjacent irrigation ditches . . . "[76] Quite remarkably, out of fourteen inscriptions containing references to the imperial cult priests at Philippi, six contain the names of women-priestesses: Cornelia Asprilla, daughter of Publius;[77] Julia Modia;[78] Julia Auruncina, daughter of Gaius;[79] Maecia Auruncina Calaviana, daughter of Gaius;[80] Octavia Polla, daughter of Publius;[81] and the name of a woman which was not preserved in the inscription.[82] Valerie Abrahamsen, in her study of rock reliefs at Diana's sanctuary at Philippi, concluded that out of a total of two hundred

---

73. *I.Mag.* 158.
74. Steven Friesen, "Networks of Religion and Society at Ephesus: Men and Women in Provincial Highpriesthood" (paper presented at the annual meeting of the Archeology of the NT World Group of the SBL, San Francisco, 1992).
75. *IG* 10.2 1 260; also published in Charles Edson, "Cults of Thessalonica (Macedonica III)," *HTR* 41 (1948): 167-68.
76. *IG* 10.2 1 260 (lines 5-8).
77. *CIL* 3. 651.
78. Published in Patrick Weber and Michel Sève, "Un monument honorifique au forum de Philippes," *BCH* 112 (1988): 468.
79. Weber and Sève, "Monument honorifique," 468.
80. Weber and Sève, "Monument honorifique," 470.
81. Weber and Sève, "Monument honorifique," 470.
82. Published in P. Collart, "Inscriptions de Philippes," *BCH* 57 (1933): 347.

carvings, at least forty represent women priestesses.⁸³ We will find similarly active roles for women among the followers of the Dionysiac association at Philippi.

Among the many titles used within associations, of special interest are those that point to an overlap between pagan and Christian usage. In this regard the use of the titles ἐπίσκοπος and διάκονος (exactly the same titles used by Paul in Phil 1:1) will be a matter for our future consideration. After all, Christianity "did not have to invent the notion of a religious society distinct both from the family and the *polis* or state."⁸⁴ As we shall see, the Christian *ekklēsia* at Philippi as an association-like assembly shared organizational features with non-Christian groups of the time.

2.4 Social Function of Voluntary Associations

The social function of voluntary associations is an important constituent part of the city's social life in general.⁸⁵ With the deterioration of the

---

83. Valerie Abrahamsen, "Women at Philippi: The Pagan and Christian Evidence," *JFSR* 3 (1987): 21.
84. Kloppenborg, "Churches as *Collegia*," 213.
85. Cf. de Vos, *Church and Community Conflicts*, 28-35. The very spatial organization of the Roman cities reflected its social orientation. Roman cities (and Greek cities too) were usually built according to a regular grid-plan around one of many of Roman roads. Near the center of the grid was a relatively large open area (*agora* or *forum*) surrounded by colonnades, shops, temples and civic buildings. In the vicinity of the *forum* there were usually located market buildings which regularly drew a crowd of buyers and shoppers. Markets, especially for the lower classes, were improvised social gathering points. The many temples and shrines besides their pure religious function likewise fulfilled an important social function in that the surrounding gardens, diners, art galleries, and shops served as meeting places, repositories of valuables, and a place for beggars. Romans inherited from the Greeks the practice of building facilities for leisure and entertainment, although they made significant modifications to them. For the Greeks, baths were merely an appendage to the *gymnasium* (a place for physical and intellectual education of wealthy young males), but for the Romans that which was an appendage became the focal point of the social gathering (J. Dominic Crossan and Jonathan L. Reed, *In Search of Paul: How Jesus's Apostle Opposed Rome's Empire with God's Kingdom* [New York: HarperSanFrancisco, 2004], 189). In a sense, the baths epitomized the social life of a Roman city. Baths, or better bath complexes, contained hot, warm, and cold pools, libraries, lecture halls, massage-rooms, barber shops, etc. Frequent religious and other kind of festivals were another important part of the cities' social life. The occasions for celebration were many: e.g., commemoration of a particular god, or the founding of that god's temple, seasonal religious and family festivals, etc. Such events usually mobilized the whole population

polis the household became the "primary social universe"[86] within which Graeco-Roman society existed and evolved.[87] Especially in Roman times the household gradually evolved into a complex system of inner and outer connections of allegiances and obligation, which upheld internal kinship and external ties of friendship. Yet by the first century CE the household itself was not without problems. For many people, displaced due to military or economic reasons, the very notion of the household lost its meaning. They were aliens in the cosmopolitan world. Still for others belonging to the household it meant "forever being frustrated by the subordinate position they occupied within the household framework."[88] For these reasons the voluntary association, a widely spread informal institution, became a viable option for socializing for people of different social standing.

John Kloppenborg summarized the social attractiveness of voluntary associations as follows: "The association afforded each member a say in who joined the group and how the group was run, fellowship and conviviality, and perhaps the opportunity to become an officer or magistrate – in short, to participate in a *cursus honorum* to which he or she could never aspire outside of the association."[89] Not the least of the reasons that people joined associations was "the basic and instinctive desire of most people to socialize with whom they share things in common . . . [including] love of

---

to take an active part in a full-blown celebration. The temples were decorated, sacrifices offered, processions were held, markets were set, souvenirs sold. Celebrations were accompanied by music and drama performances, mimes and dancers, chariot races, gladiatorial contests. The high point of the festival was the feast normally laid on at public expense. The feast usually was held in the temples or forum with the statue of a god set as a visible sign of the god's communion with the people. Participation in the festivals was "a personal religious duty and delight, a major social activity, and a means of demonstrating allegiance to the state" (De Vos, *Church and Community Conflicts*, 35).

86. William Lane, "Social Perspectives on Roman Christianity During the Formative Years from Nero to Nerva: Romans, Hebrews, 1 Clement," in *Judaism and Christianity in First-Century Rome* (ed. Karl P. Donfried and Peter Richardson; Grand Rapids: Eerdmans, 1998), 208.

87. Cf. Bruno Blumenfeld: "As public political life shrinks and sheds it relevance, the *oikos* expands its sphere and increases in significance; it itself becomes a *polis*" (*The Political Paul: Justice, Democracy and Kingship in a Hellenistic Framework* [JSNTSS 210; London: Sheffield Academic Press, 2001], 113).

88. Robert J. Banks, *Paul's Idea of Community: The Early House Churches in Their Historical Setting* (Grand Rapids: Eerdmans, 1988), 7.

89. Kloppenborg, "Collegia," 18.

eating and drinking in good company."⁹⁰ Following an ancient ideal of a good family, the members of voluntary associations shared together space, time, and meals.⁹¹ In fact, eating and drinking was for some members the primary purpose for the association's existence: "A major element in the life of the association was the sacrificial feast and common meal held at regular intervals."⁹²

According to Philo's references, some of these associations were notoriously known for excessive drinking parties.⁹³ A funerary association of Aesculapius and Hygeia in Rome (153 CE) was known for the periodic banquets which were accompanied by the distribution of bread, wine and money given to the association by its benefactors.⁹⁴ On three different occasions the by-laws of the Lanuvium association mention "an amphora of good wine": it was required of a new member,⁹⁵ of a freed slave,⁹⁶ and of the master of the feast.⁹⁷ One of the responsibilities of the president of the guild of Zeus Hypsistos was to make sure that the wine supply would not run out.⁹⁸ No wonder there was a need for bouncers to restrain the disorderly!

What should not escape our attention is that the social dimension of feasting in antiquity was inseparably connected with the religious one. We shall return to this issue in our future discussion.

Another essential social function of voluntary associations was in fostering and promoting patronage. Crossan and Reed call patronage the "moral

---

90. Cf. Wilson, "Voluntary Associations," 14.
91. Cf. Strabo: "Eating together at the same table, drinking libations together, and lodging together under the same roof" (*Geog.* 9.3-5).
92. Hans-Joseph Klauck, *The Religious Context of Early Christianity: A Guide to Graeco-Roman Religions* (Minneapolis: Fortress, 2003), 44. Cf. Dennis Smith: "The most common club activity. . . the club banquet, . . . was usually the primary activity in which the club members participated as a group" ("Meals and Morality in Paul and His World," in *SBL 1981 Seminar Papers* [ed. Kent H. Richards; San Francisco: Scholars Press, 1981], 323).
93. Cf. Philo, *Flacc.* 136; *Spec. Leg.* 2.145-46; *Vita Cont.* 40-47. We are going to deal with these references in our future discussion.
94. *CIL* 6.10234. A wealthy woman by the name Marcellina contributed to the association 25,000 sesterces in commemoration of her deceased husband. Each member was awarded from 1-6 denarii for taking part in such banquets.
95. *CIL* 14.2112: page 1, line 20
96. *CIL* 14.2112: page 2, line 7.
97. *CIL* 14.2112: page 2, line14.
98. *PLond* 2193: line 21

glue of ancient public life [which] permeated every level of the society, from gods to emperors, emperors to countries, aristocrats to cities, and, indeed, from any have to have-not."[99] In fact the Roman imperial system in many ways succeeded as the emperor assumed the role of the supreme benefactor of the nation. "Augustus was able to consolidate power and set up a system in which "the inaccessibility of the center except through personal links" deepened and nourished the patronal structure of the society, and to cast himself as *pater patriae*, chief benevolent father figure of the entire Mediterranean world."[100] While the essence of patronage is the relationship between two individuals,[101] patronage within voluntary associations reveals an "intermediate form,"[102] whereby the relationship is set between one dominant person and a *group* of social inferiors.

Voluntary associations proved to be an ideal setting for the creation of "a network of fictive kinship which served to structure relationships and nurture loyalties."[103] The abundance of family-like terms (μήτηρ,[104] πατήρ,[105] ἀδελφοί[106]) used in the associations point to their function as surrogate families creating a fictive kinship especially for those who did not belong to a family or had to abandon one. "It is true that their [associations'] small size, intimate relations, and convivial gatherings could have been substitutes for family and clan; and opportunities to lead and organize, together

---

99. Crossan and Reed, *In Search of Paul*, 297.

100. Carolyn Osiek, "*Diakonos* and *Prostatis*: Women's Patronage in Early Christianity," *HvTSt* 61 (2005): 349.

101. Richard Saller delineates three essential characteristics of Roman patronage: a) there is reciprocal exchange of goods and services; b) the relationship is personal and of some duration; c) the relationship is asymmetrical, i.e., it is the relationship between two individuals who are not social equals. Patronage was an effective instrument for the weak to influence the powerful. The client could expect to gain some economic or political benefits. The patron in return could expect loyalty, public support, votes, and the other things of this nature. See *Personal Patronage under the Early Empire* (Cambridge: Cambridge University Press, 1982), 1: 127-128; 191-92.

102. Osiek, "*Diakonos* and *Prostatis*," 351.

103. McLean, "Agrippinilla Inscription," 266.

104. *IG* 1. 604.

105. *CIL* 14.70; *Ditt.*³1111. 15.

106. *TAM Suppl* 3.201; *OGIS* 51; *P.Paris* 42.

with conferred grades, ranks and titles, could have satisfied needs that were not met in the outside world."[107]

As was argued before, it was often the prospect of expanding one's social network through access to an influential patron, rather than an ideological commitment, that stimulated people to join the association. The benefit was not always material gain but rather the possibility of enhancing the prestige and honor of an association. In this way the patronal system was often the cause of the inner rivalry between associations to gain favor with an influential patron.[108] Especially telling are the attempts of certain groups through the setting up of monuments or through correspondence to gain the benevolence of an emperor (or emperor-to-be).[109]

Out of many examples of the patron-client relationships within associations, I would like to emphasize the role of women as patrons for it, I believe, will have some direct bearing on the role of women in the Christian *ekklēsia* at Philippi.[110] There is ample epigraphic evidence for women benefactors in voluntary associations. A second century BCE inscription from Megapolis (Peloponnesus) honors a priestess of Aphrodite, Euxenia, for "[she built] a sturdy wall around the temple . . . for the goddess, and a house for public guests."[111] There is another interesting case of a female benefactor by the name of Tation from Kyme who, at her own expense, either built or remodeled a synagogue. The wording of the inscription ("The Jews honor her"[112]), as well as her family name (daughter of Straton son of Empedon), suggest that she was not Jewish. A fuller's guild from

---

107. Cf. S. Wilson, "Voluntary Associations," 13.
108. See Harland, "Spheres of Contention," 55-59.
109. An association in Smyrna set up a monument in honor of Hadrias (*ISmyrna* 622) and maintained correspondence with Marcus Aurelius and Antonius Pius (*ISmyrna* 600).
110. The role of women as benefactors both on public and private levels is a well-attested phenomenon in the ancient world: "Women . . . seem to have encroached upon the traditionally sacrosanct, male-dominated spheres of public life and city politics. Many public offices and liturgies performed by men were also performed by women. Women were also active from an early period onwards as "spontaneous" benefactors; they competed with men in building of temples, theatres, public baths, and in many other type of benefactions" (Riet Van Bremen, "Women and Wealth," in *Images of Women in Antiquity* [ed. Averil Cameron and Amélie Kuhrt; London: Croom Helm, 1983], 225). See Osiek, "*Diakonos* and *Prostatis*," 347-70.
111. *IG* 5.2 461.
112. *NewDocs* 1:111.

Pompei erected a dedicatory statue with an inscription in commemoration of the benefactions of the priestess and patroness of the guild Eumachia.[113] The decree of the Lycian city of Telmessos (1st century CE) celebrates the προστάσια by the name of Junia Theodora, a native Lycian woman, who, by living in Corinth, distinguished herself with deeds of hospitality and mediation.[114] Another important civic patron, Sergia Paullina, hosted a burial society in a house in Rome.[115] On the list of women benefactors is also Agrippinilla. The very dedication of the inscription points to her important role not only as priestess but also to her being a pre-eminent patron of the association. In fact, the functions of priestess and benefactor by necessity went together, for "the holding of a priesthood often involved spending large sums of money on festivals, banquets and games in honor of the gods, and it was common enough for priests to take on the building or restoring of a temple."[116] The evidence for women's active roles as benefactors in the Graeco-Roman world will support our further supposition that women converts to Christianity at Philippi likewise were involved as leaders and patrons.

Finally, we should mention briefly one more important social function of voluntary associations in that practically all of them functioned as *collegiums tenuiorum*, i.e. as burial societies, guaranteeing their members a decent funeral and execution of the bequest. We can refer to the already-cited regulation of the Lanuvium association which promised the burial of the slave members on a par with other members.[117] A similar regulation is found in the by-laws of the Iobacchoi association: "If any Iobacchus die, a wreath shall be provided in his honor not exceeding five denarii in value, and a single jar of wine shall be set before those who have attended the funeral."[118]

---

113. *CIL* 10.810-13.

114. *NewDocs* 6:24-25.

115. *CIL* 6.9148. Consider some other names of women benefactors: Fradia Roscia Calpurnia Purgilla (*CIL* 8.14470); Caecilia Sexti f. Petroniana Aemiliana (*AE* 1931.42); Egnatia Certiana (*CIL* 9.1578); Laberia Hostilia Crispina (*AE* 1964.106).

116. Van Bremen, "Women and Wealth," 225.

117. *CIL* 14.2112: page 2, lines 3-4.

118. *IG* 2.2 1368, lines 160-63.

Concluding this part of the discussion we can concur that, for many especially marginalized and displaced people, voluntary associations constituted their social identity. In the alienated world of the uneven opportunities for social advancement, membership in such associations provided the sense of belonging, fostered camaraderie, and communal solidarity.

2.5 *Relating to Imperial Rome*

In view of the spontaneous and uncontrolled character of voluntary associations, the relationship with the Roman state was at times quite uneven.[119] This was especially true during the period of political instability of the late Roman Republic.[120] The early imperial period likewise was characterized by the changing attitudes, at times favorable and at times restrictive, toward associations. Augustus, concerned for the restoration of public order and peace, reinforced specific restrictions on the associations which, in his view, were of a potential threat: "Numerous leagues, too, were formed for the commission of crimes of every kind, assuming the title of some new guild . . . Therefore to put a stop to brigandage, [Augustus] . . . disbanded all guilds, except such as were of long standing and formed for legitimate purposes."[121]

Despite the many efforts to eradicate the associations, "epigraphy made plain the fact that professional, athletic, literary, dining and cultic associations flourished in every city of the empire."[122] The subversive potential of voluntary associations was in fact quite limited. This was due to the fact

---

119. Cf. Hatch: "The State feared lest the honyecombing of the empire by organizations which in their nature were private, and so tended to be secret, might be a source of political danger: but the drift of the great currents of society towards associations was too strong for even the empire to resist" (*Early Christian Churches*, 27). On the history of Roman restrictions of voluntary associations, see Wendy Cotter, "The Collegia and Roman Law: State Restrictions on Voluntary Associations, 64 BCE – 200 AD," in *Voluntary Associations in the Graeco-Roman World* (ed. J. S. Kloppenborg and S. G. Wilson; London: Routledge, 1996), 74-89.
120. In 64 BCE the Roman Senate banned associations for being potentially seditious. See Asconius, *Pis.* 7.
121. Suetonius, *Aug.* 32.
122. Kloppenborg, "Churches and *Collegia*," 213.

that, as was previously mentioned, most associations averaged 15-20 people.[123] As can be seen in the correspondence between the governor Pliny and the emperor Trajan, Rome would be quite nervous and suspicious if the number of members exceeded 150 people.[124] Second, most associations were of local character, and thus had limited possibilities for establishing a network of relationships with other associations.[125] Although there were associations which were trans-local (e.g. the Dionysian mystery cult), "once established, local cults remained largely autonomous and could take quite divergent forms from one locality to another."[126] Third, Rome had the ability to "shrewdly harness"[127] associations to serve its own economic and political interests. Without the help of the professional associations (*collegium* of merchants, grain shippers, and the kind) Rome would never have solved the extremely difficult problem of transporting large and bulky masses of goods (grain) for public consumption. Needless to say, these associations "would never have [been] recognized . . . had it not been for their utility to the state."[128]

Among other associations which enjoyed the protective hand of Rome were the associations of carpenters, rag dealers, and timber cutters, who normally served as firefighters (except in Rome).[129] Likewise in the area of politics Rome found a way to utilize associations "as a means of reinforcing

---

123. See note 119. Cf. Meeks, *Urban Christians*, 31. The correspondence between the governor Pliny and emperor Trajan reveals a concern on the part of the governor with regard to the size of the *collegium*.

124. See Pliny the Younger, *Ep.*10.33.

125. Clarke, *Serve the Community*, 71. See the article by R. Ascough in which he contests the view that Christian groups in this regard were any different from voluntary association ("Translocal Relationships among Voluntary Associations and Early Christianity," *JECS* 5 [1997]: 223-41).

126. Wilson, "Voluntary Associations," 3.

127. Clarke, *Serve the Community*, 72.

128. Michael I. Rostovtzeff, *The Social and Economic History of the Roman Empire* (Oxford: Clarendon Press, 1926; 1957), 158. In his earlier cited *Social and Economic History of the Hellenistic World*, 2:1064. Rostovtzeff claims that "the government [during the Hellenistic period] looked favorably on this spontaneous growth of corporative life, . . . and gave them a legal status and granted them some important privileges such as the right of owning property."

129. Cf. Kloppenborg, "Collegia," 24.

the dominant social order."¹³⁰ In other words, the potentially subversive character of the associations was converted for the good of the empire. The formation of associations around influential patrons, like M. Gavius Squilla Gallicanus of the Agrippinilla association, as well as the successful utilization of religion (particularly of the imperial cult), helped engage associations in the socio-political discourse of the empire (see the following discussion). By paying homage to the ruling emperor, the members of the voluntary associations legitimized their place within Graeco-Roman society at large.

2.6 *The Religious Function of Voluntary Associations*

The religious function of voluntary associations is related to the broader issue of the role of the religion in Roman society.¹³¹ From the very beginning, the Roman perception of the gods was strictly functional. Romans perceived themselves living in a mysterious world in which all of the natural processes were divinely activated and controlled. The worship of the gods was a natural necessity for the preservation of the well being of an individual and society as a whole. Thus early on there grew a close functional link between religion and state. The former existed for the promotion and endorsement of the latter and vice versa.¹³² There was no place for a personal

---

130. A. Clarke, "Serve the Community," 72.
131. See on the subject: Mary Beard et al., *Religions of Rome*, vol. 1: *A History* (Cambridge: Cambridge University Press, 1998), esp. 167-210; idem, *Religions of Rome*, vol. 2: *A Sourcebook* (Cambridge: Cambridge University Press, 1998); John Ferguson, "Classical Religions," in *The Roman World* (ed. John Wacher; vol. 2; London: Routledge, 2002), 749-60; W. Warde Fowler, *Roman Ideas of Deity in the Last Century before the Christian Era: Lectures Delivered in Oxford for the Common University Fund* (Freeport: Books for Libraries, 1969); Peter Garnsey and Richard Saller, *The Roman Empire: Economy, Society and Culture* (Berkeley: Universtity of California, 1987), 163-77; R. Ogilvie, *The Romans and Their Gods in the Age of Augustus* (London: Chatto & Windus, 1969); Jo-Ann Shelton, *As Romans Did: A Sourcebook in Roman Social History* (2ⁿᵈ ed.; New York: Oxford University Press, 1998), 359-430; Paul Zanker, *The Power of Images in the Age of Augustus* (trans. Alan Shapiro; Ann Arbor: University of Michigan Press, 1988).
132. This proved however to be the "weakest link" of the Roman religion. Already Varro (in Augustine's rendering) admits that the gods of the State are simply human institutions (see Aug. *Civ. Dei*.4.4). That is their very existence depends upon the worship established

religion or deity. Roman society essentially viewed each of its members as a social being whose vocation was to seek, through the worship of gods, the "welfare of the city." The state encouraged and sponsored the construction of temples; the priests oversaw the participation of the people in religious ceremonies and festivals as sure signs of their loyalty to the state. It is important that Roman religion did not imply the existence of a separate community within Roman society, but rather identified that community with the whole of the society.

An important religious novelty of the Roman era was the introduction of the imperial cult.[133] Similar to the way that the Greek honorific tradition was tailored by the ruling elite for the legitimization of the status quo,[134] the imperial cult became "a medium through which the web of power and influence was constructed and maintained on the city, provincial, and imperial level."[135] The imperial cult moved into the very center of the public discourse of urban life. Through temples, altars and statues (often placed in

---

by the State. No wonder that many of the original Roman gods perished from neglect during the general decline of religion in the Late Republic.

133. On the issue of the imperial cult see Glen W. Bowersock, "The Imperial Cult: Perceptions and Persistence," in *Jewish and Christian Self-Definition* (ed. Ben F. Meyer and E.P. Sanders; vol. 3; Philadelphia: Fortress Press, 1983), 171-82; Allen Brent, *The Imperial Cult and the Development of Church Order* (Leiden: Brill, 1999), 1-72; M. Charlesworth, "Some Observations on Ruler-Cult Especially in Rome," *HTR* 28 (1935): 5-44; M. Clark, "*Spes* in the Early Imperial Cult: 'The Hope of Augustus,'" *Numen* 30 (1983): 80-105; Dominique Cuss, *Imperial Cult and Honorary Terms in the New Testament* (CHECLT; Switzerland: Fribourg University Press, 1974); John Ferguson, "Ruler-Worship," in *The Roman World* (ed. J. Wacher; vol. 2; London: Routledge, 2002), 766-79; Duncan Fishwick, *The Imperial Cult in the Latin West: Studies in the Ruler Cult of the Western Provinces of the Roman Empire* (EpaROdLR 108; Leiden: Brill, 1987); Steven J. Friesen, *Imperial Cults and the Apocalypse of John* (Oxford: Oxford University Press, 2001); Erik M. Heen, "Phil 2:6–11 and Resistance to Local Timocratic Rule: *Isa Theo* and the Cult of the Emperor in the East," in *Paul and the Roman Imperial Rule* (ed. Richard A. Horsley; Harrisburg, Pa.: Trinity Press International, 2004), 125-53; Donald L. Jones, "Christianity and the Roman Imperial Cult," in *ANRW*, II.23.2, 1023-54; Alistair Kee, "The Imperial Cult: the Unmasking of an Ideology," *SJRS* 6 [1985]: 112-28; H. Kennedy, "Apostolic Preaching and Emperor Worship," *Exp* 7 (1909): 289-307; Hans-Joseph Klauck, *The Religious Context of Early Christianity: A Guide to Graeco-Roman Religions* (trans. B. McNeil; Edinburgh: T&T Clark, 2000): 250-330; S.R.F. Price, *Rituals and Power: The Roman Imperial Cult in Asia Minor* (Cambridge: Cambridge University Press, 1984); idem, "Gods and Emperors: The Greek Language of the Roman Imperial Cult," *JHS* 104 (1984): 79-85.

134. Heen, "Philippians 2:6-11," 128-29.

135. Heen, "Philippians 2:6-11," 126.

baths, gymnasia, theaters, private homes) the emperor made himself visible to his subjects.[136] The imperial cult epitomized the socio-political life of the *polis* in two ways. On the one hand, it was controlled and promoted by the local elites to their own advantage; on the other it "helped construct an ideology of empire, an ideology that was anchored in the depiction of the emperor as a god, that is, the high patron of the empire."[137]

It is important to see the imperial cult deeply imbedded in the overall Graeco-Roman religious universe. The genius of Roman political thinking revealed itself in successful alteration of the foundational Roman story whereby the imperial family was incorporated into the Olympian branch of the pantheon, thus providing a link to the "mythic narratives of the origins of the world."[138] Due to this strategy "the *Sebastoi* were placed at the height of power alongside other gods in a realm separate from, though in interaction with, humans and human communities."[139]

Among the many occasions (festivals, emperor's birthday, military victories) and forms (street processions, oaths of loyalty, prayers and hymns) the imperial cult was celebrated at the regular gatherings of the voluntary associations. P. Harland points to the two interrelated types of imperial-related activities in voluntary associations. First, there was participation in honoring emperors through the existing networks of benefaction.[140] An example of such participation is found in an inscription from Macedonia (Acanthus) dedicated by Roman merchants to Caesar Augustus: "To Emperor Caesar Augustus, god, son of god. By the city and the association of Roman merchants and those dwelling with them."[141] An association of fishermen

---

136. Warren Carter, *The Roman Empire and the New Testament: An Essential Guide* (Nashville: Abingdon, 2006), 77.

137. Heen, "Philippians 2:6-11," 133.

138. Friesen, *Imperial Cults*, 123. Friesen in particular refers to the sculptured panels of the Sebastion at Aphrodisias, which depict the emperors as "a latter-day branch of the Olympians, offspring of Venus/Aphrodite." As he further explains, "this practice did not give the imperial family a cosmogonic role; it simply explained the dynasty's connection to the beginnings."

139. Harland, *Associations*, 133.

140. Philip Harland, "Honouring the Emperor or Assailing the Beast: Participation in Civic Life among Associations (Jewish, Christian and Other) in Asia Minor and the Apocalypse of John," *JSNT* 77 (2000): 111.

141. Published in M. Tod, "Macedonia. Inscriptions," *ABSA* 23 (1918-19): 67-97.

in Ephesus dedicated a new fishery toll-office to the emperor Nero, his mother and wife.[142] There in the inscription (125 CE) of the Dionysiac devotees in Ephesus and Smyrna who also worshiped νέος Διόνυσον (a new Dionysus), i.e., the emperor Hadrian, as their patron.[143] A variation on the same objective (honors paid to emperor) was paying homage to the highly ranking officials (like M. Gavius Squilla Gallicanus) who by playing the key roles of patrons or high priests engaged voluntary associations in the upholding of the Roman socio-political universe. Thus, for example, a Dionysiac association and the young men's association from Pergamon honored C. Antius Aulus Julius Quadratus, the proconsul of Asia in around 109 CE, and a relative of Julia Severa.[144] There is another brief inscription[145] from the ancient cite of Beroia in Macedonia in which a man by the name Domitius Euridikos is called both an official (μακεδονιάρχης) of the provincial Synhedrion in Beroa and the high priest (ἀρχιερεύς) of the κοίνον of the Macedonians. As Edson has argued, the full title of the high priest of that association must have been ἀρχιερεύς τῶν Σεβαστιῶν καὶ ἀγωνοθέτης (high priest of the Augustus and Agonothete).[146] Undoubtedly, Domitius' role as an official and a priest of the imperial cult ensured Rome of his being an instrument of Roman imperial politics.

The second type of imperial-related activity was the cultic activity proper within associations in honor of the emperor or his family. The very names of some of the associations suggest that the members of the imperial household were chosen as patron deities and were recipients of the regular cultic honors: the "friends of the Sebastoi" (*philosebas[toi]*) at Pergamon (*IPergamonAsklep* 84); the "friends of the Agrippa" (*philagrippai*) from Smyrna (*ISmyrna* 331; *IG* 6 374); the Tiberians (*Tibeireioi*) from Didyma (*IDidyma* 50.1a. 65). The guild of shippers from Nicodemia (Bithynia) dedicated its sanctuary to Αὐτοκράτορι Οὐεσπασιανῷ Καίσαρι Σεβαστῷ

---

142. *IEph* 20 = *NewDocs* 5:5.
143. *SEG* 6.59 (54-59 CE), also published in W.H. Buckler and J. Keil, "Two Resolutions of the Dionysiac Artists from Angora," *JRS* 16 (1926): 245-46.
144. *IGR* 4. 643, re-edited by William M. Ramsay, *The Social Basis of Roman Power in Asia Minor* (Amsterdam: Adolf M. Hakkert, 1967), 33.
145. *EAM* 38, also published in Edson, "Cults of Thessalonica," 196.
146. Edson, "Cults of Thessalonica," 196. Cf. also J. Cormack, "High Priests and the Macedoniarchs from Beroa," *JRS* 33 (1943): 39-44.

(*TAM* 4.22; 70-71 CE). There are several inscriptions from Asia Minor which provide examples of the inclusion of emperor worship in the associations: in Ephesus the emperor worship was included into the Demeter mysteries (*SIG* 2.820); in the same city the emperor was worshiped in the Dionysiac association along with many other gods and goddesses (*GIBM* 3.600); an association of hymn-singers from Pergamon celebrated the birthday of Divus Augustus during the three-days festival on September 21-23, and also on the first day of each month (*IPergamon* 374).[147]

It should be noted that the imperial cult had a prominent place within religious life in the Roman colony of Philippi. First, this relates to the official cult setting. A number of inscriptions recovered at the two sanctuaries, east and west of the forum, testify to the fact that both sanctuaries were dedicated to emperor worship. There are at least fourteen Latin inscriptions in which an active role of *flamines divi Augusti* and *sacerdotes divae Augustae* is emphasized.[148] There is also ample evidence for the presence of the *seviri Augustales*, officially sponsored religious associations, who were actively involved in emperor worship.[149] Most importantly there is some evidence for the inclusion of the imperial cult into the cultic practices of voluntary (religious) associations. One particular inscription mentions Marcus Velleius, a *liberti* of Marcus who was both a member of the woodcutters' guild (*dendrophorus*) and an *Augustalis*.[150] In another inscription, published by P. Collart,[151] Lucius Valerius Priscus, a *decurion*, an *eiranarch* and a *magistrate*, is praised by the worshipers of Serapis and Isis for the organization of the gladiatorial contest. A similar kind of relationship between a Roman official and representatives of cultic groups is seen in two other inscriptions published by P. Lemerle[152] (cited in full in chapter 4). Both are dedicated

---

147. Cf. H. Pleket, "An Aspect of the Emperor Cult: Imperial Mysteries," *HTR* 58 (1965): 337.
148. See Bormann, *Philippi*, 43-44. We already mentioned the significant number of women priestesses in the official cults (see pp. 41-42).
149. Bormann lists eight inscriptions with references to *seviri Augustales* (*Philippi*, 45-46).
150. Published in Paul Lemerle, "Incscriptions latines et grecques de Philippes. I. Inscriptions latines," *BCH* 58 (1934): 466 (for the text of the inscription see chapter 4).
151. P. Collart, "Inscriptions de Philippes," *BCH* 62 (1938): 429 (for the text of the inscription see chapter 4).
152. P. Lemerle, "Inscriptions latines et greques de Philippes (suite)," *BCH* 59

to the same man, Quintius Flavius Hermadion, a γυμνασιάρχος and an ἀρχιερεύς of the Imperial cult who is praised as εὐεργέτης by the worshipers of Serapis.

Philip Harland stresses the importance of what he calls "the grassroots or spontaneous nature" of the honors and rituals which "served to legitimate the authority and ideology of Roman rule within a developing ideology or worldview of the *polis*."[153] The ritual actions within the context of the imperial cult were "not simply an outward and meaningless statement of political loyalty, . . . [but rather] a symbolic expression of a worldview held in common by those participating."[154] Participation in the imperial cult reinforced the sense of belonging to the overall new cosmic framework, and "made a statement regarding the place of that group or community within the societal and cosmic order of things."[155] "The group could be viewed as playing a part in the overall maintenance of fitting relations within the

---

(1935): 140.

153. Harland, *Associations*, 135.

154. Harland, *Associations*, 133. Harland contests what he calls "the traditional view" expressed by a number of scholars (Bowersock, Fishwick, Nock, Nilsson) for whom imperial cults "were not well integrated within religious life" (p. 119). For example, Fishwick states that emperor worship was "a purely mechanical exercise, a conventional gesture affirming membership in the state and sympathy with its aims, a duty to be hurriedly performed before turning to the particular worship in hand" ("Provincial Ruler Worship in the West," *ANRW* II.16.2: 1253). In rebuttal Harland evokes an influential study of religion by Clifford Geertz, *The Interpretation of Cultures: Selected Essays by Clifford Geertz* (New York: Basic, 1973). Geertz understands religion as "a cultural system of symbols or inherited conceptions, analogous to language, which communicates meaning" (cited in *Associations*, 132). Religion as a system of symbols functions to maintain "both the way of life (ethos) and the worldview of a particular group, community, or society" (*Associations*, 133). A religious symbol for Geertz formulates "a basic congruence between a particular style of life and a specific… metaphysic" (cited in *Associations*, 133). In this regard Harland underlines the important role of ritual which for Geertz sustains "the interplay between social experiences and worldview" (cited in *Associations*, 133). "In a ritual, the world as lived and the world as imagined, fused under the agency of a single set of symbolic forms, turn out to be the same world" (Geertz, *Interpretation of Cultures*, 112; cited in Harland, *Associations*, 133). Furthermore, Harland, following Price (*Rituals and Power*, 239-48), argues that modern distinctions between politics and religion "do not fit the ancient context, where the social, religious, economic, and political were intricately interconnected and often inseparable" (p. 120). Likewise, a similar modern dichotomy between "private" and "public" religious experience should not be imposed on the ancient evidence. "Piety and religiosity were often more concerned with the performance of rituals within group or community settings in order to maintain fitting relations between communities and gods rather than with the inner feelings of the individual" (p. 120).

155. Harland, *Associations*, 135.

webs of connections that linked individuals (of all social strata), groups, civic or provincial communities, imperial functionaries, and the gods."[156]

At the time of Paul's letter to the Philippians the imperial cult *was not* forcefully imposed on the subjects of the empire.[157] Yet already at that time it was not *participation*, but rather *non-participation*, which mattered. The celebration of the imperial cult reinforced the sense of belonging to the overall new cosmic framework. Failure on the part of Christians (and Jews) to participate in honoring the emperor threatened to tear that cosmic framework apart.[158] In other words, by refusing to worship the emperor Christians were at odds with the whole of the Roman religious system and thus were perceived as a potential "cause of those natural disasters and other circumstances by which the gods punish individuals, groups, and communities that failed to give them their due."[159]

---

156. Harland, *Associations*, 135.

157. Rather than being a Roman imposition "from above," the imperial cults (especially on the provincial level) were often initiated "from below." Behind such initiatives there often lay "a shrewd political calculation" (Heen, "*Isa theō* and the Cult of the Emperor," 132) of those who expected to receive favor for their loyalty. Thus the imperial cult was utilized as an effective tool in ongoing competition between cities to win the favor and benevolence of Rome. Cf. Friesen: "Cities found new ways to compete with each other within the imposed structures of Roman imperialism, seeking favorable positions within the imperial hierarchies" (*Imperial Cults*, 55).

158. As Price stated: "In the persecutions of the Christians the cult of the emperor was less important than the cult of gods" (*Rituals and Power*, 221). In view of this, Donald Jones' assessment that, "from the perspective of early Christianity, the worst abuse in the Roman Empire was the imperial cult" ("Christianity and the Roman Imperial Cult," *ANRW* II.23.2: 1023) should be regarded as an unnecessary overstatement.

159. Harland, *Associations*, 243. A similar concern is expressed by the Gentiles toward Jews: "If the Jews (says [Apion]) be citizens of Alexandria, why do they not worship the same gods with the Alexandrians?" (Josephus, *C. Ap.* 2.65; cf. *Ant.* 12.125-126). Cf. Tertullian's statement: "They [the pagans] think the Christians the cause of every public disaster, of every affliction with which the people are visited. If the Tiber rises as high as the city walls, if the Nile does not send its waters up over the fields, if the heavens give no rain, if there is an earthquake, if there is famine or pestilence, straightway the cry is, 'Away with the Christians to the lion!'" (*Apol.* 40).

Conclusion

We have concluded our consideration of voluntary associations in the ancient Mediterranean world. We conclude from the epigraphic evidence that voluntary associations were quite a unique phenomenon in that these grass-root organizations, although imitating the social structures of the *polis*, went further in questioning the validity of the social structures of society. They created in many regards egalitarian types of communities which provided for many marginalized social groups (slaves, *liberti*, women) an opportunity for self-realization and social advancement.

An important conclusion of our research is that voluntary associations were an intricate part of the socio-political universe of the Roman Empire. They often were formed around a household, and actively promoted the system of patronage. We have seen an important role that women played in both leadership capacities and in exercising the patronal functions in the associations. We will see a similar prominent role of women in the Christian community at Philippi.

Another important conclusion is that in the ancient world devotion to a particular deity was not of an exclusive character. Devotion to more than one deity, or membership in more than one association, was more a norm than an exception. Often it was an opportunity to enhance one's social standing through joining the network of benefaction, not religious devotion, which prompted people to join associations. We will utilize this point to argue that a similar stimulus might have been effective for the Christian converts at Philippi.

The syncretistic atmosphere of the time helped embrace and make prominent the imperial cult within voluntary associations. Paying homage to the ruling emperor was one of the most natural ways for the ordinary people to express their gratitude for the benefits of the *Pax Romana* and secure their legitimate space within Graeco-Roman society. This is an important point, for we are going to argue further that it was continuing devotion to the emperor within a Christian circle at Philippi that troubled Paul so much. What was perceived by some Gentile converts to Christianity as a quite natural combination of the religious loyalties was totally inadmissible for Paul.

CHAPTER 3

The Roman Colony of Philippi

According to Acts 16:11,[1] sometime in the early fifties of the first century CE, Paul crossed over the Aegean Sea from the city of Troas in Asia Minor to Neapolis, and thereby ventured onto the European continent proper. The first city where Paul's ministry led to the founding of a Christian community was Philippi (Acts 16:12-40), a Roman colony located about 10 miles northwest of Neapolis (see map 1).

What was Philippi like? How was it similar or different to other cities of the Roman Empire? In the current chapter we will get acquainted with the key characteristics of the city of Philippi, such as its demographic, socio-economic, political and religious features. We are going to argue that Philippi, while being a relatively small provincial city, at the same time displayed its clearly pro-Roman character and pride in being a privileged Roman colony. It is in places like Philippi that the imperial cult was an important means of expressing loyalty and gratitude for the *Pax Romana*. It will be our contention in the following chapters that the essence of Paul's disagreement with those whom he calls "the enemies of the cross" in Philippians 3:18-20 was the issue of continued devotion to emperor worship.

---

1. On the historical reliability of Acts see the comments in chapter 5.

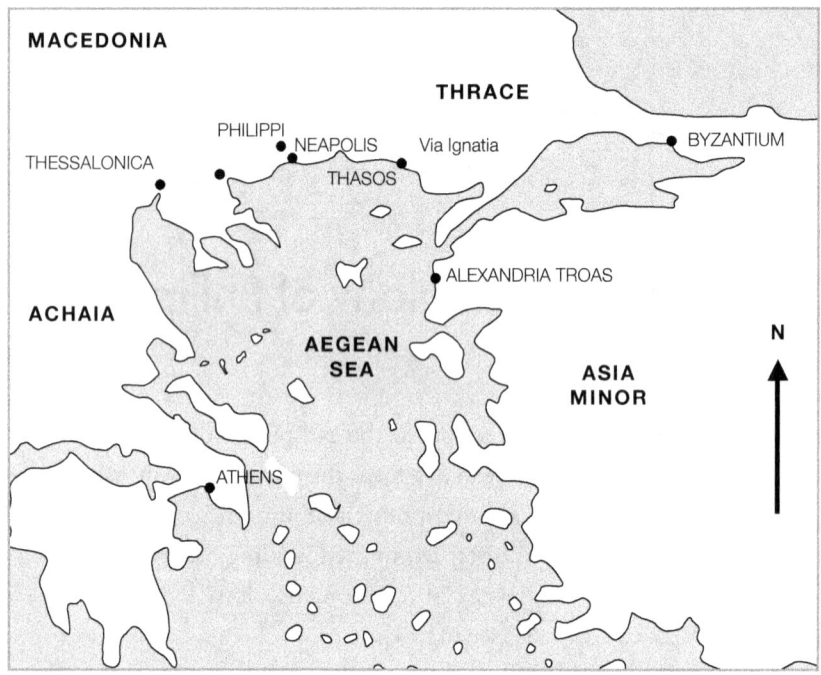

Map. 1. Macedonia and the neighboring areas

3.1 Historical Overview

The Roman period in the life of the ancient Macedonian city of Philippi[2]

---

2. The ancient site of Philippi was located at the far eastern end of a large fertile plain of Datos in Central Macedonia. Philippi, protected by hills from the north and marshes from the south, with plenty of fertile soil, situated on the strategic route, was destined to play a significant role in history. In 360 BCE the Thasians from the nearby island of Thasos, led by a certain exiled Athenian by the name of Kalistratos, founded a settlement and named it Krenides which means a site "with many springs." Appian states: "Philippi is a city that was formerly called Datos, and before that Krenides, because there are many springs bubbling around a hill there" (*B. Civ.* 4.105). In 356 BCE the colonists sought the protection of Philip II of Macedonia from the constant invasions of the local Thracian tribes. It did not take Philip, who at that time was seeking to extend his kingdom to the East, long to realize the strategic importance of the site, which played a role as the "gateway between Europe and Asia" (Appian, *B. Civ.* 4. 106). After renaming the place after himself, Philip undertook a whole range of important measures, which eventually made Philippi a stronghold of the Macedonian kingdom. The city was fortified with new walls; a theater was built, and some of the surrounding marshes were drained and thus became excellent agricultural land. The intensified exploration of the Pangaion hills rich with minerals, especially gold and silver, brought an additional one thousand talents of revenue into the king's treasury (Diodorus Siculus, 16.8.6; Strabo, *Geog.*7). Actually,

begins in 148 BCE when the Romans occupied Macedonia. The city was included in the first of the four districts into which the province was divided under the Roman administration.³ To this period is ascribed the construction of the *Via Egnatia* (initiated by and named after the governor Gnaeus Egnatius), which became the major road connecting the Adriatic and Aegean seas.

The crucial year, which really became a landmark in Philippi's history, was 42 BCE, when Antony and Octavian defeated the forces of Cassius and Brutus in a historic battle which took place outside the western wall of the city.⁴ Immediately after that Antony renamed the city *Antoni Iussu Colonia Victrix Philippensium*⁵ and settled some of his veterans there.⁶ Yet

---

the first Macedonian golden coins known as *Philippeioi* were struck from Philippi's gold (Diodorus Siculus, 16.8. 7). The significance of the city (especially with the exhaustion of the mines) gradually declined during the following Hellenistic era.

    For the bibliography on Philippi see ch. 1; also: *Philippi at the Time of Paul and after His Death* (ed. Charalambos Bakirtzis and Helmut Koester; Harrisburg, Pa.: Trinity Press International, 1998); Holland L. Hendrix, "Philippi (Place)," *ABD* 5:313-17; D. Lazarides, "Philippi (Krenides)," *PECS*: 704-5; Fanoula Papazoglou, "Macedonia under the Romans," in *Macedonia: 4000 Years of Greek History and Civilization* (ed. M.B. Sakellariou; Athens: Ekdotike Athenon, 1983), 192-207.

3. Livy, 45.29; cf. Acts 16:12.

4. Appian, *B. Civ.* 4.105-38; Dio Cassius, 47.35-49; Plutarch, *Brut.* 38-53; Strabo, *Geog.* 7.41.

5. Collart, *Philippes*, 227.

6. The Latin word *colonia* derives its meaning from the noun *coloni* ("tillers of the soil," "peasants") and originally was used with regard to a group of settlers established by the Roman state. At first *colonia* was used in the process of consolidation of the Roman state within the limits of the Italian peninsula. Yet as the years and centuries passed, the practice of colonization proved to be one of the most effective tools of Roman territorial and cultural expansion. The very fact that *colonia civium Romanorum* survived for more than 500 years speaks in favor of the great effectiveness of this institution primarily because of its ability to adapt to changing political realities. The founding of colonies was undoubtedly connected with Roman military advances. An original purpose of the colonies to either hold the earlier inhabitants in subjection or to repel the inroads of the enemies was later enhanced by the economic interests of Rome. The colonies organized from around 100 BCE to AD 30 could be categorized primarily as *coloniae militares*, which means that they were established on the conquered territories and settled by the veteran soldiers. Roman colonization reached its highest point during the reign of Augustus who founded about seventy-five new colonies. On his own admission Augustus "established colonies of soldiers in Africa, Sicily, Macedonia, the two Spains, Achaia, Asia, Syria, Gallia Narbonensis, and Pisidia" (*Res Gestae* 28.2). Augustus estimates that altogether there were about 300,000 soldiers whom he settled in the colonies and all of to whom he "assigned land or gave money as [rewards] for military service" (*Res Gestae* 3.3). On the issue of Roman policy of colonization, see Susan E. Alcock, *Graecia Capta*:

about eleven years later (30 BCE), after Antony had been defeated in the battle at Actium by his former ally Octavian, the colony was reorganized under the new name *Colonia Iulia[7] Augusta[8] Philippenses* and settled with an additional group of war veterans.[9] There is no general agreement on the number of settlers but since an average settlement during the Caesarean and Triumviral period numbered between two to three thousand men, we can assume comparable numbers for Philippi.[10]

3.2 Demographic Situation

Philippi was a colony of a relatively small size. It is generally agreed that the population of Philippi of Paul's time was around 10,000 *urbs*.[11] When compared with the population of the two other colonies visited by Paul,

---

The Landscapes of Roman Greece (Cambridge: Cambridge University Press, 1996); Peter A. Brunt, *Italian Manpower 225 B.C.-A.D. 14* (Oxford: Oxford University Press, 1987); Lawrence Keppie, *Colonization and Veteran Settlement in Italy 47-14 BC* (London: British School at Rome, 1983); Barbara Levick, *Roman Colonies in Southern Asia Minor* (Oxford: Clarendon Press, 1967); John C. Mann, *Legionary Recruitment and Veteran Settlement During the Principate* (IAOP 7; London: Institute of Archeology, 1983); Edward T. Salmon, *Roman Colonization under the Republic* (Ithaca, N.Y.: Cornell University Press, 1970).

7. Strabo, *Geog.* 7, frg. 41; Pliny the Elder, *HN.* 4.42; Diodorus Siculus, 51.4.6. Brunt, *Manpower*, 234-35 argues that the colony was named *Iulia* in honor of Julius Caesar, not as some suppose (e.g., Fee, *Philippians,* 25, n.70) after Octavian's daughter Julia.

8. The epithet "Augusta" was added after 27 BCE.

9. Octavian settled both his supporters and those of Antony's side who were dispossessed from their lands in Italy and moved to Philippi and other places as a compensation for their losses (Dio Cassius, 51. 4. 6).

10. Cf. Brunt, *Italian Manpower*, 236, 261; Mikael Tellbe, *Between Synagogue and State*, 213; Bormann, *Philippi*, 22 n.67, suggests 1000 settlers.

11. The rationale provided by scholars is somewhat different. Pilhofer (*Philippi,* 74) comes up with the number of 5,000–10,000 based on the capacity of the local theater (about 8,000 seats); for some reason Paul E. Davies suggests 50,000 seats ("The Macedonian Scene of Paul's Journeys," *BA* 26 [1963]: 100). Oakes considers this approach rather "precarious" because "theater-size could reflect the hoped-for prestige of a city rather than its present population" (*Philippians,* 45). He himself comes up with the number of 10,000 based upon the population density of Pompeii. He also suggests an additional 5,000 of those living in the vicinity of the city and 21,000 for the rest of the *territorium* (*Philippians,* 45). DeVos assumes the density of the population to be around 200-250 people per hectare and from that comes up with the number of inhabitants for Philippi between 9,000–11,500 (*Church and Community Conflicts*, 33-34, 238-39).

Thessalonica (40,000-50,000 people)[12] and Corinth (100,000-130,000 people),[13] the conclusion becomes self-evident: the smaller size of Philippi implied a higher degree of awareness with regard to the life of the community and its individual members.

Peter Oakes gives a helpful description of the two major ethnic designations: the "Romans" (i.e., the Roman citizens) and "Greeks" ("non-citizens who were largely Greek-speakers").[14] To the first category belonged, first of all, the descendants of the original settlers of Italian origin. They were the privileged category of Roman citizens, some of whom played key roles in the political structures of the colony. Some were wealthy landowners, yet undoubtedly there were some even in this category who belonged to the category of the poor. To the "Romans" also belonged other Roman citizens (retired soldiers, traders, peasants) who moved into the city after its initial colonization. Quite a significant number of "Romans" constituted *liberti* – the freed slaves of the colonists along with their freeborn children. Our analysis of the social prosopography will confirm a significant percentage of *liberti* among the members of voluntary associations (ch. 4) and of the Christian *ekklēsia* (ch. 5). Finally, this category also included a small number of influential and wealthy native Greeks who were granted Roman citizenship.[15]

---

12. DeVos, *Church and Community Conflicts*, 129.

13. DeVos, *Church and Community Conflicts*, 185. Alcock suggests slightly lower numbers for Corinth – 80,000-100,000 people (Alcock, *Graecia Capta*, 160).

14. Oakes, *Philippians*, 71-74.

15. Sometimes general statements like "the citizens of this city [Philippi] were Roman citizens" (O'Brien, *Philippians*, 4), or "the privilege of citizenship [was] conferred upon the whole colony of Philippi" (Banks, *Paul's Idea of Community*, 39) might give the misleading impression that all the inhabitants of the colony were Roman citizens. Rome utilized the policy of enfranchisement as a powerful incentive in dealing with the conquered nations. It was not uncommon in the Republican period to extend Roman citizenship to whole provinces and territories; however, in the period of the early *Principate,* the granting of citizenship became increasingly a matter of individual merit rather than a collective enterprise. Historians point out the marked change in Augustus' policy of enfranchisement after 27 BCE. Thus Suetonius relates the emperor's concern for the purity of the Roman race from any contamination by foreign or servile blood (*Aug.*40.3). However, when the need strikes, the concern for purity of the race may have to wait. This can be best illustrated by Octavian's practice of enlisting legions from the provincials. Whereas military service was the supreme prerogative of Roman citizens, yet in the times when Italy itself was exhausted by civil strife to the extent that conscription became quite unpopular, the emperor allowed the recruitment of provincials, granting them the franchise on

The second ethnic category of the "Greeks" included some of the Macedonian and Thasian descendants of the early colonists of the 4th century BCE. Although there was no doubt a massive depopulation of the area, especially in the aftermath of the events of 42 BCE,[16] it is reasonable to assume that at least some of their descendants remained. The discovery of a number of inscriptions[17] with Latinized Thracian names and their religious practices, along with the Thracian names of the villages in the area, allows us to conclude that there was a marginalized settlement of Thracians. The "Greeks" also comprised a group of Hellenistic immigrant workers[18] as well as a substantial number of slaves from the Greek-speaking East. Finally, the Hellenized Jews would have fit into the category of the "Greeks"; however, the evidence for their presence at Philippi is conspicuously absent.[19]

---

enlistment. To this category belonged first of all the so-called *castris*, the sons of the illicit unions between the soldiers and *peregrinae* women. Whereas from birth they bore the status of their mothers, yet at their enlistment they were granted Roman citizenship. To this category also belonged a vast number of provincial soldiers enlisted in the auxiliary units. However, in this case the enfranchisement was automatically bestowed and was usually granted upon the soldier's discharge after 15-25 years of service.

With regard to the situation in the Roman *coloniae* the sharp distinction between the colonists (Roman citizens) and the *incolae* ("inhabitants" or "natives") remained intact. The historical records do not support the view of the universal enfranchisement of the colonies' native population. As we shall see further, the colonists, though maintaining the role of the ruling élite, did not in all probability constitute the majority of the population. There were, though, some other ways of obtaining Roman citizenship. First of all, through the manumission of slaves there was a growing number of the *libertae* in the colonies. Second, as was mentioned before, there was a significant change with regard to the status of the children born from the illicit unions between soldiers and native women. In the later *Principate* the sons of the legionnaires born from such unions were granted citizenship upon their birth, not from the time of their enlistment in military service (as in the Augustus' times). There was also always reserved the possibility of obtaining Roman citizenship for the wealthy local elite especially in the case of their involvement in the local government. The important point here is that granting the status of Roman *colonia* did not involve an automatic transfer of Roman citizenship to the indigenous population. See A. N. Sherwin-White, "The Roman Citizenship. A Survey of Its Development into a World of Franchise," *ANRW* 1.2:23-58.

16. Ancient historians convey the information that in the battle at Philippi two legions of Macedonians fought on the side of Brutus (App., *B. Civ.* 3.79; 4.75; Plut., *Brut.* 24), which allows us to assume that at least some of them were from Philippi. Even if some of them survived in the battle their families and relatives were forced to flee the area as a result.

17. Collart, *Philippes*, 297.

18. In favor of this supposition is the presence of different oriental cults in Philippi.

19. As L. White remarks, "Indeed, apart from Acts itself, there is very little evidence (either literal or archeological) for Jewish activity at Philippi" ("Visualizing the "Real"

Generally, the evidence for Jewish activity in Philippi belongs to a much later date, namely, the 3rd-4th century CE, to which period probably belongs a marble inscription confirming the presence of a Jewish synagogue in the city.[20] Among the reasons for the scarce Jewish representation in the 1st century CE is the relatively recent beginning of Philippi: the colony was refounded "in precisely the same period when the position of Jewish communities in other Hellenistic cities was being ratified."[21]

Based on the archeological evidence and sociological analysis of the Roman imperial society Peter Oakes comes to an interesting conclusion: Roman citizens possibly comprised only 40% of the city's population, with the remaining 60% allotted for Greek-speaking non-citizens.[22] Although there is an overwhelming dominance of Latin inscriptions over those in Greek,[23] Oakes argues that the majority of the inscriptions found belong to a later period (2nd to 3rd century CE). He also points to the fact that the inscriptions were found in the predominantly Roman quarters of the city (forum, gymnasium, baths). The character of the inscriptions (honorific epitaphs) reflects mostly political, not numerical factors, yet "what matters for population estimates is no-elite evidence."[24]

Peter Oakes' sociological reconstruction, which attempts to provide a reasonable range of possibilities for the social stratum of Philippi's population, although commendable, is not without problems.[25] He himself chooses a questionable methodology, which allows dealing with a lack of evidence by projecting data from the second century CE onto the earlier

---

World of Acts 16: Toward Construction of a Social Index," in *The Social World of the First Christians: Essays in Honor of Wayne A. Meeks*. [ed L. Michael White and O. Larry Yarbrough; Minneapolis: Fortress, 1995], 247).

20. See Chaido Koukouli-Chrysantaki, "Colonia Iulia Augusta Philippensis," in *Philippi at the Time of Paul and after His Death* (ed. Charalambos Bakirtzis and Helmut Koester; Harrisburg, Pa.: Trinity Press International, 1998), 28.

21. White, "Visualizing Acts 16," 249.

22. Oakes, "Philippians," 75-77; idem, *Philippians*, 40-50.

23. Among the inscriptions found in Philippi 421 were in Latin and only 60 in Greek (Levick, *Colonies*, 161).

24. Oakes, *Philippians*, 39.

25. Consider, for example, the critique of P. Oakes by C. DeVos, *Church and Community Conflicts*, 241-44.

period.²⁶ Oakes argues, for example, for the majority of Greek-speaking population on the grounds that those who built the forum used Greek letters for the alignment markers on the bricks.²⁷ DeVos dismisses this argument as meaningless, because the builders were predominantly from among slaves, and the construction area in the forum belongs to the second century CE.²⁸ The predominance of the Greek inscriptions in the sanctuary of Isis points to its popularity with the Greek-speaking population, but does not say anything about the number of the cult's followers. There is, for example, evidence of twenty six Latin inscriptions that come from people of Thracian origin.²⁹ The main problem with Oakes' reconstruction is his underestimation of the Greek *liberti*, most of whom appear to have been "strongly Romanized."³⁰ The Latin inscription from Philippi reveals the names of the 69 members of the Silvanus association, almost all of whom bore the tripartite Roman names. Yet, one third of the names betray their Greek or non-Roman origin.³¹

Although in time the strong Roman component of the population was undoubtedly diluted by the influx of settlers of different ethnic origin, with the result that not all the inhabitants of Philippi were Roman citizens, the prevalence of Latin language over the Greek, the prominent place of the imperial cult and other displays of political loyalty to Rome (see 3.4) seem to suggest a significant percentage of Roman citizens at Philippi in the first century CE.

3.3 Socio-Economic Features

It is reasonable to suppose that the social pyramid of the city reflected the general trend of Greco-Roman society of the period.³² Given the nature of

---

26. Oakes, *Philippians*, 39.
27. Oakes, "Philippians," 65.
28. DeVos, *Church and Community Conflicts*, 242.
29. Collart, *Philippes*, 301, n.5; Portefaix, *Sisters Rejoice*, 68 n. 89, 69 n.110.
30. DeVos, *Church and Community Conflicts*, 242.
31. For the text of the inscription and further discussion, see ch. 4.
32. Three major factors determined one's place in the social structure of Roman society: a)

the colony, the Romans were destined to occupy the positions of power and prestige. The original social stratification of Philippi would have included army officers, praetorians, and soldiers, as well as some *liberti*, natives and slaves.

The top of the societal pyramid in Philippi was occupied by the ruling elite who constituted from 3 to 5 percent of the city's population.[33] This category included high-ranking officers,[34] wealthy colonists, as well as a few indigenous wealthy people.

Quite a significant percentage (30-40 percent) of the indigenous population comprised the broad category of the service group which included artisans, traders, construction workers, etc. By the middle of the first century this category was balanced by the inclusion of the Roman *liberti* and colonists who would by that time have lost their land. This social stratum is of importance for us for at least for two reasons. First of all, it is this category of people which would be among the most likely prospects for

---

wealth; b) freedom; and c) Roman citizenship. The top of the social pyramid was occupied by a few (less than one percent of the population) extremely wealthy and influential people of senatorial and equestrian ranks. The Roman middle class comprised a whole range of social stratum from representatives of local elite and army officers to well to-do traders, artisans, and farmers (30%-40%). The next place on the social ladder was taken by slaves (up to 30%), and finally at the bottom were the large mass of the destitute poor. See Joe-Ann Shelton, *As the Romans Did*, 4; Oakes, *Philippians*, 46-49; MacMullen, *Relations*, 88-99.

33. Robin Lane Fox, *Pagans and Christians* (San Francisco: Harper and Row, 1986), 57; Oakes, *Philippians*, 47.

34. Most obviously the veterans were the first (but not only) ones to be enrolled as local officials. Besides the prospect of getting farm land, the desire for an enhanced social status was just as powerful an incentive for the colonists. It is generally agreed that an average allotment of land for a veteran soldier in the Imperial period was about 50 *iegura* = 3 acres (Salmon, *Colonization*, 20-24, 145; Brunt, *Manpower*, 295-96; Keppie, *Settlement*, 91-96). Yet the junior officers, centurions and tribunes were awarded up to 100 *iegura* and more. The membership in a city council required material wealth equivalent to 100,000 *sesterces*. As Keppie points out (*Settlement*, 106) only those of the settlers whose allotments were 100 *iegura* and higher could qualify for the office. Thus the initial distribution of land already presupposed the further social stratification of the community. Those of larger allotments could afford living in the city and be involved in the local government by employing other farmers (often the previous owners of the property) and slaves (cf. Dio Cassius, 48.9). In time they had better prospects of acquiring new property from the less fortunate colonists and become influential landowners. Those with the smaller allotments most probably had to settle down in the *territorium* and work on their land themselves or utilize slaves. Some of them, in the case of unfortunate circumstances, might lose their land and eventually find themselves on the lowest level of social pyramid, i.e., among the city's poor.

membership in the professional associations. In fact in the next chapter we are going to present the evidence for the existence at Philippi of the associations of woodcutters, purple-dyers, gravediggers, and gladiators. Second, Paul himself, being an artisan by trade (Acts 18:3), had a better chance to reach out to the people who were "committed to talk to strangers,"[35] i.e., to the small shop owners, craftspeople, and traders. It is of significance that, according to Acts 16, among the first converts to Christianity is a businesswoman by the name of Lydia.

Farmers constituted another significant portion (20-25 percent) of the city's population. What distinguished Philippi from other colonies and underscored its "real" colonial status was its mostly agricultural character.[36] Whereas the distribution of land had been one of the primary objectives in colonization, in many other places (e.g., Corinth, and Pisidian Antioch) trade and commerce supplanted agriculture as the major economic factor.[37] Colonization signified the arrival of a new social class of Roman landowners and peasant colonists obviously at the expense of displacing their Greek counterparts.[38] The original distribution of land was followed in the first century by its subsequent redistribution and its concentration in the hands of a few wealthier landowners. Thus the initial prevailing percentage of the Greeks employed by the Romans as farmers and servicemen was later replenished by a number of Roman settlers who now lost their land and had either to rent it from a landowner, or to fill a slot allotted to the city's poor.

---

35. Oakes, *Philippians*, 58.

36. Collart, *Philippes*, 275; Oakes, *Philippians*, 70.

37. Undoubtedly, because of the *Via Egnatia*, trade contributed its dividends into the city's economy, yet not as significantly as agriculture did. Papazoglou comments with regard to the whole region of Macedonia: "Macedonia has a lot of arable and excellent pasture; it is, therefore *a priori* likely that, even under the empire, when urban life had reached its peak of development, Macedonia was essentially a rural area" ("Macedonia," 200).

38. Although in some cases Rome acquired land by compensating the previous owners, in the case of Philippi it is reasonable to assume that, because the area had been won by conquest, the land was considered as one of the spoils of war, and thus readily available for distribution among the settlers (Salmon, *Colonization*, 148). It very well may be that in his later years Augustus attempted to amend this by spending 260 million *sesterces* for the purchase of land in provinces underscoring that he was "the first and the only one . . . to have done this" (*Res Gestae* 16.1). In this regard, Salmon makes the following comment: "[A]s Augustus, he had considerable difficulty in living down the misdeeds he had perpetrated as Octavian" (*Colonization*, 138).

Another significant percentage of the colony's population was allotted to slaves. Ramsay MacMullen[39] estimates that up to a quarter of Italy's population were slaves. In the provinces their percentage was around ten percent. Because of the significant Roman presence in Philippi it is fair to suppose a somewhat higher percentage of slaves than on average for the provinces – around twenty percent of the colony's population.[40] It is sometimes mistakenly assumed that slaves covered the very bottom of the social pyramid. Whereas it is true that they were deprived of any rights of their own, yet they experienced some degree of social and economic protection from their masters. In this sense they were much better off than the city's beggars and those who were destitute. Slaves were a peculiar social phenomenon in that they were actually scattered throughout the social stratum of the society: from Caesar's household to artisans and farmers. In Philippi we can envision a similar situation with the majority of slaves belonging to the servile groups, but also being among those who worked on the fields and in servitude to the local elite. It is worth being reminded that gradual manumission of slaves brought in an additional number of *liberti*.

At the bottom of the social pyramid, as was just stated, were the free poor. It should be admitted that the boundary line between the poor and the rest of the service group is not clearly delineated. Almost all other categories, besides the local elite, could face the prospect of going broke. This category included a whole range of people from beggars to small business people whose income was consistently below subsistence level. The poor is the most difficult category to trace with regard to the exact numbers: the poor could not afford paying for their names to be remembered in ages to come. Scholars are able to come up with some hypothetical figures based on records which go back to medieval Europe.[41] Peter Oakes suggests that in Philippi the percentage of the poor was in the area of 20 percent.[42]

---

39. MacMullen, *Social Relations*, 92. Garnsey and Saller (*Empire,* 83) opt for even higher percentage of slaves (up to 30%) in Rome.

40. Oakes, *Philippians*, 48.

41. Cf. MacMullen: "In fourteenth and fifteen-century Europe, . . . one person in three lived in habitual want" (*Social Relations,* 93).

42. Oakes, *Philippians,* 47.

3.4 Political Profile

Philippi was a distinctively Roman colony. Whereas in other places (e.g., in Ephesus), Rome ruled through the medium of wealthy Greeks, in Philippi it was an exclusive prerogative of the Romans themselves. Philippi was only one of four colonies in Macedonia which had been granted the highest status of the Roman provincial municipality – the *ius Italicum*.[43] This status gave the Roman citizens additional privileges (exemption from taxes, tributes, and duties) and protection of the Roman law.[44] Philippi was Rome in miniature, starting from the constitutional legislation and administration of the colony and ending with the way people spoke and dressed.

The above-mentioned numerical superiority of the Latin inscriptions definitely points to the persistent dominance of the Latin language at Philippi. Whereas, for example, in Corinth, a colony with an equally strong Roman element, Latin was gradually supplanted by Greek,[45] in Philippi it remained one of the most conspicuous signs of Roman domination for almost three hundred years. Roman civic inscriptions along with the inscriptions on coins[46] were constant reminders to the non-citizens of their alien status. Peter Oakes summed this up: "The Greeks would have lived in a city where they were surrounded by Latin."[47] It is true that people all over the Roman Empire were the subjects of Caesar, yet they were also the citizens of their cities (especially in the Greek East) who retained much of their wealth, status, and rights for local self-government. In this sense the Roman influence was much more acute for the non-citizens in Philippi.

The status of a Roman colony meant that the city "possessed special importance, that it was esteemed by the emperor and deemed worthy to be

---

43. Papazoglou, "Macedonia," 197; Tellbe, *Between Synagogue and the State*, 214.
44. Roman citizens were entitled to the right of purchase, ownership and transfer of property, and tax exemption, as well as the right to civil lawsuits and vote (Salmon, *Colonization*, 141.)
45. Alcock, *Graecia Capta*, 169. A similar phenomenon of the decline of the Latin language in Asia Minor is traced by Levick (*Roman Colonization*, 130-62).
46. Coins minted in Philippi bore well through the third century the original designation of the city as a Roman colony (Abrahamsen, *Women and Worship*, 11).
47. Oakes, *Philippians*, 74.

the residence of Roman citizen-soldiers."[48] Ever since Octavian's triumph over his last competitor, Antony (30 BCE), Philippi became a visual symbol of the *Victoria Augusta*.[49] Roman administration of the city operated in the name of the *Imperator divus* and the head of the city's council was at the same time a high priest of the imperial cult. Early on the cult of Augustus, of his wife Livia, and other members of the imperial family occupied a prominent place in the city's religious life.[50] This has been firmly established through the numerous artifacts and inscriptions discovered in archeological digs. Thus the remains of the statues of Augustus and of other emperors of the Julio-Claudian dynasty were found in the forum. Several inscriptions, dated from the second half of the first century, found in two temples next to the forum, clearly testify that both were dedicated to the worship of the emperor.[51]

Philippi's religious institutions likewise were structured after Rome's pattern. The fourteen inscriptions, mentioned in chapter 2, testify to the existence of the *flamines divi Augusti* and *sacerdotes divae Augustae* who were consecrated to the cult of Julius Caesar, Augustus, Claudius, and Vespasian.[52] Eight other inscriptions contain references to particular colleges of priests at Philippi, *seviri Augustales* and *dendrophorus Augustales*, who were devoted to the cult of the emperor.[53]

---

48. Tellbe, *Between Synagogue and the State*, 213. For the following material I am mostly indebted to this author.

49. Several inscriptions found at Philippi celebrated the *Victoria Augusta, Quies Augusta*, and the *Fortune* and *Genius* of the colony. The Philippian coins of the first century CE carried the inscription *VIC(toria) AUG(usta)*, and *COL(onia) PHIL(ippensium)* on the reverse. See Bormann, *Philippi*, 32-36.

50. Bormann, *Philippi*, 32-67. Actually the ruler cult had a longstanding tradition in Philippi and was originated by the city's founder, Philip II of Macedonia.

51. Tellbe, *Between Synagogue and the State*, 215.

52. Collart, *Philippes*, 238, 265; Bormann, *Philippi*, 42-44.

53. The priestly colleges named after Augustus (*solidates Augustales*) were founded in CE 14 after the death of the emperor. Their important distinction from other priestly colleges was that *Augustales* were open to freedmen. They afforded a successful *libertus* the means by which he could receive honors comparable with those accorded to *decurions* and *magistrates*. One of them by the name of P. Hostilius Philadelphus is mentioned on an inscription from Philippi as a member of the *seviri Augustales*. See Kloppenborg, 16-17; Collart, *Philippes*, 270, 412; Bormann, *Philippi*, 45-46.

Although it is true that the significance of Philippi as a military outpost gradually subsided,[54] it nevertheless continued to be a guardian of the empire, a reminder of its military might. Most of all, colonies like the one at Philippi were responsible for the dissemination of Latin language and Roman culture and religion throughout the empire.[55] It is this special bond of allegiance to Rome and to the emperor in particular which some of the converts to Christianity might have found difficult to overcome, or did not deem it necessary to overcome. We will return to this issue later in our discussion.

3.5 Religious Profile

As we discussed the political profile of Philippi, we have already inevitably intruded into the area of religion as it was related to the worship of the emperor. Politics and religion, as is well known, go hand in hand. As we are going to explore in the next chapter the evidence for the existence of religious associations at Philippi, here we will limit ourselves to several general observations. First of all, the religious situation in first century Philippi is characterized by the diversity of the cults and deities worshiped. This diversity was the result of a prolonged period of coexistence and adaptation of the native Thracian and Macedonian gods to their Greek, Roman, Syrian, and Egyptian counterparts.[56] In general the more cosmopolitan character of the urban population always presupposed a greater religious variety when compared to the rural tendency to stick with the traditional ancestral cults. Undoubtedly, by daring to navigate in the syncretistic wa-

---

54. The military functions of the colonies were gradually transferred to the army units which were stationed in specially fortified camps and forts (Salmon, *Colonization*, 149-150). Most probably there was no significant influx of new veterans except for those few who would return to Philippi as their homeland. J.C. Mann points out the usual trend among veterans to settle down either at the frontier districts where they served, or back in their homeland. The latter option had an advantage in that a veteran did not have to start "from scratch" in a totally new environment but continued in a business inherited from his parents; see *Legionary Recruitment*, 18-19.

55. "Augustus was more responsible for the diffusion of the Latin language and of Roman practices generally than anyone else in history" (Salmon, *Colonization*, 144).

56. For the summary of the deities worshiped at Philippi see Appendix 1.

ters of the Graeco-Roman religious world, Paul was in for trouble. In this regard, Luke's comment on Paul being "deeply distressed to see that the city [Athens] was full of idols" (Acts 17:16) probably accurately relays Paul's own disposition. Religious exclusivism, as over against inclusivism, in our assessment constituted the focal point of Paul's disagreement with some Christians at Philippi.

Second, amidst this religious diversity the imperial cult was one dominant voice, to which everybody else had to listen and accommodate themselves accordingly. We already mentioned the two recovered sanctuaries, east and west of the forum in Philippi, which were dedicated to emperor worship. With a significant number of veteran soldiers who were always considered as the most loyal and traditional supporters of the civic cults, it must have been important for other cults and associations in the city to accommodate themselves in support of the official status quo. In fact, as the inscriptions testify, many of the local gods of Roman, Greek and Egyptian origins (Mercury, Jupiter, Silvanus, Cybele and Isis) were integrated into the worship of emperors.[57] This was also true with regard to trade and business life. Thus Mercury, the god of trade and the patron of business-people, was closely associated with the cult of Augustus.[58] In the city with its clear pro-Roman stance, the imperial cult was one of the most natural ways for the citizens to express their loyalty and appreciation for the benefits of Roman rule. This obviously set the stage for the growing tension between the followers of Jesus and the rest of society. Their conspicuous withdrawal from participation in the public cult created an ambiguous situation which begged for an explanation.

---

57. Bormann, *Philippi*, 54-60, 64-65.
58. Bormann, *Philippi*, 51-52. This might help us better understand the rationale behind the sharp reaction against Paul's preaching at Philippi as it is related in the book of Acts. Paul was accused of disseminating "customs that [were] not lawful for . . . Romans to adopt or observe" (Acts 16:21). As Tellbe further explains, the preceding exorcism of the "pythonic spirit" (πνεῦμα πύθωνα; Acts 16:16) is most likely a reference to the spirit which empowered the Pythian prophetess at Delphi to be a mouthpiece for the god Apollo (*Between Synagogue and the State*, 237). It was said that Augustus was especially inspired by this god to the point of making him his special god and identifying himself with Apollo (see J.R. Fears, "The Cult of Jupiter and Roman Imperial Ideology," *ANRW* II. 17.1, 3-141). It is quite possible that Paul's preaching and actions were perceived as undermining the authority of the cult of Apollo and the closely associated imperial cult.

Third, the religious diversity at Philippi implies a variety of deities and settings for worship, including the existence of unofficial cultic associations. While it would have been natural for the ruling Roman élite to worship Roman gods, many *liberti* and slaves of non-Roman origin would be more open to worship other deities as well. As we shall see in the next chapter the existence at Philippi of the associations of Silvanus, Diana, Isis, and others testify to that effect.

Conclusion

The ancient Greek city of Philippi was destined to regain its significance after it was resettled by Roman veterans in the forties and thirties of the first century BCE. The privileged status of the *ius Italicum* had a long lasting effect on the outlook of the colony. From the prevalent number of Latin inscriptions and from the prominent place of the imperial cult it follows that in many ways Philippi was a pro-Roman city whose inhabitants prided themselves in being citizens of Rome. Whereas in other cities and colonies Rome ruled through the medium of wealthy natives, the administration over Philippi was in the hands of the Romans themselves. A distinguishable feature of Philippi was its mostly agricultural character. At the same time a significant percentage of the population (up to 40%) would have belonged to the service group (artisans, traders, construction workers). As was indicated earlier, this social category is of importance for our future discussion, for it most certainly points to the presence of professional associations at Philippi. Moreover, it is the people of this social stratum that would have been the object of Paul's outreach (himself an artisan by trade).

The religious diversity at Philippi was the result of the prolonged assimilation of the native Thracian and Macedonian gods to their Greek, Roman, Syrian, and Egyptian counterparts. We have pointed out that amidst this religious diversity the dominant voice was that of the imperial cult, with which others had to reckon. In the next chapter we will see examples of other cults incorporating the imperial cult in their worship. It is in a city like Philippi where emperor worship must have been considered as the most appropriate means for expressing gratitude for the benefits bestowed by the Roman emperor on the citizens of this Roman colony.

CHAPTER 4

Voluntary Associations at Philippi

In the current chapter we will examine the evidence that helps us to understand the character of voluntary associations at the Roman colony at Philippi. Although voluntary associations were a widely spread phenomenon, literary evidence for them is quite sporadic. As A. Clarke explains, this is partly due to the fact that "much of the available literary evidence derives predominantly from aristocratic circles, which in turn were more interested in reporting on public, than private activities."[1] The available literary evidence often reflects the élites' prejudice and disdain toward such groups.

The second major source of information about associations is the extant epigraphic material. Richard Ascough relates that there are at least seventy-five inscriptions related to voluntary associations in Macedonia dated from as early as the second century BCE through the early second century CE.[2] The diversity of the material evidence strongly suggests that associations of various types were as widely spread in Macedonia (and Philippi) as elsewhere in the Graeco-Roman world.[3]

For the study of the relevant material we will use Pilhofer's *Philippi, Band 2: Katalog der Inschriften von Philippi*, as well as Collart's still-invaluable volume on Philippi (*Philippes, ville de Macédoine*), and other primary source literature. Our study will be selective in character, i.e., we will try to present the evidence most appropriate to the first century period. When

---

1. Clarke, *Serve the Community*, 61. As he further explains, by producing legislative acts restricting the activity of voluntary associations Rome inadvertently supplied for us valuable sources of information.
2. Ascough, *Macedonian Associations*, 18.
3. Ascough, *Macedonian Associations*, 19.

citing inscriptions of a later date we will try to present the evidence for the existence of the cult in the first century milieu. Taking into account the sporadic and occasional character that many of these inscriptions have, and the poor chances of surviving over time, we cannot expect to get a full picture, but rather glimpses of historical evidence which will give us some understanding with regard to the existence and function of voluntary associations at Philippi. This is to say that the absence of the evidence should not automatically lead to the conclusion that some particular association did not exist. I have in mind in particular the absence of epigraphic evidence for the existence of veteran associations at Philippi, although their existence would have fit the profile of the city settled by veterans.

The epigraphic evidence testifies to the presence of both religious and professional associations at Philippi (although, as was argued earlier, both types of associations were formed around devotion to a deity). With a significant percentage of the population belonging to the artisan class, the existence of professional associations comes to us as no surprise. Likewise, the ethnic and religious diversity of the city presupposes the existence of various religious associations, as was the case throughout the Roman Empire.

The findings of this chapter will be used in our future discussion, for the presence of different types of voluntary associations at Philippi was a factor in how the early Christian community was organized and how it functioned.

4.1 Silvanus Association

We are going to consider, first, two Latin inscriptions which testify to the existence of the all-male association of Silvanus, a Roman god of woods and forests.[4] The inscriptions were discovered in the acropolis area of Philippi, north of the Via Egnatia, where a number of the "folk-religion"[5] groups

---

4. The inscriptions are published in *CIL*3.633.1-2 = Collart, *Philippes*, 403; Pilhofer, *Philippi*, 2:170-72, 176. For the English translation see V. Abrahamsen, "Christianity and Rock Reliefs at Philippi," *BA* (1988): 55, n.2, 3.

5. The term used by L. Portafaix of the Greek-Roman, Thracian, and Oriental cults (*Sisters Rejoice*, 71).

had their sanctuaries in an abandoned quarry. Although V. Abrahamsen[6] dates the construction of the Silvanus sanctuary in the second century CE, there are reasons to believe that the origins of Silvanus worship at Philippi go back to the Augustan era.[7]

Inscription #1[8]:

P(ublius) Hostilius Philadelphus | ob honor(em) aedilit(atis) titulum polivit | de suo, et nomina sodal(ium) inscripsit eorum

Col.1

qui munera posuerunt: (5) Domitius Primigenius statuam | aeream Silvani cum aede; | C(aius) <H>oratius Sabinus at templum tegend(um) | tegulas CCCC tectas; | Nutrius Valens sigilla marmuria (10) dua, Herculem et Mercurium. | Paccius Mercuriales opus cementic(ium) |* CCL ante templum, et tabula picta Olympum *XV; | Publicius Laetus at templum aedifi|candum donavit * L; (15) item Paccius Mercuriales at templum | aedificandum, cum filis et liberto, don(avit) | * L; item sigillum marmirium Liberi * XXV; |

Col. 2

|Alfenus Aspasius sacred. signum aer. Silvani cim basi; (20) item vivus * L mortis causae sui | remisit; *vacat* Hostilius Philadelphus inscin|dentibus in tempo petram excidit d(e) s(uo).

---

6. Abrahamsen, "Rock Reliefs," 49.
7. Thus Paul Davies suggests the origins of the Silvanus sanctuary in 20-30 CE ("The Macedonian Scene of Paul's Journeys," *BA* 26 [1963]: 101. H. Hendrix also suggests a 1st century date for the Silvanus sanctuary ("Philippi,"*ABD* 5: 316). Craig de Vos likewise argues that some of the names, especially on the second inscription, suggest a mid-first century CE setting (*Church and Community Conflicts*, 244, n. 41).
8. Text is from Pilhofer, *Philippi*, 2:176 [164/L001]. The English translation with minor alteration is based on Abrahamsen's translation.

(translation)

Publius Hostilius Philadelphus, on account of his public office of *aedile*, on his own expense polished this inscription and inscribed the names of the association (members)

Col. 1

who had deposited their fees. (5) Domitius Primigenius [gave] a copper statue of Silvanus with the temple. Gaius Horatius Sabinus, [gave] as the covering of the temple 400 covered rooftiles. Nutrius Valens [gave] (10) two marble images – Heracles and Mercury. Paccius Mercuriales [gave] 250 denarii for a work of concrete in front of the temple and 15 denarii for a painted board of Olympus. Publicius Laetus, furthermore, donated 50 denarii for building the temple. (15)

Likewise Paccius Mercuriales along with (his) son and freedman donated 50 denarii for the building of the temple, as well as 25 denarii for a marble image of Liber.

Col. 2

Alfenus Aspasius, priest, paid one denarii for a copper image of Silvanus with [its] base (20) while he was alive, which was remitted to him on account of his death. Hostius Philadelphus himself quarried the rock ascending into the temple.

Inscription #2[9] :

P(ublius) Hostilius P(ublii) l(ibertus) Philadelphus | petram inferior(em) excidit et titulum fecit, ubi | nomina cultor(um) scripsit et sculpsit, sac(erdote) Urbano, s(ua) p(ecunia).

---

9. The Latin text is from Pilhofer, *Philippi*, 2:170-72 [163/L002].

Publius Hostilius Philadelphus, freedman of Publius, at his own expense he cut out the rock below and the tablet upon which he wrote and sculpted the names of the members [of the association] under the priest Urbanus.

Inscription #2 is followed by a list of 69 members of the association (see Appendix 2). Both inscriptions were carved at the initiative and expense of Publius Hostilius Philadelphus, who although himself a *libertus*, might have been one of the patrons of the association. There is a strong indication that the association was formed around several family clans: the Domitius *nomen* is repeated six times;[10] the Atiarius *nomen*, five times;[11] the Plotius[12] and Publicuus[13] *nomina*, four times each; the Abellius,[14] Flavius,[15] Paccius,[16] Volattius[17] *nomina*, each three times; the Atilius,[18] Claudius, Velleius,[19] Vettius[20] *nomina*, each two times. Inscription # 1 twice mentions the contribution made by Gaius Paccius Mercurialis, the second time together with his son and the *libertus*. The names of Gaius Paccius Mercurialis and of his freedman (Gaius Paccius Mercurialis – *libertus*) are found on the membership list (col. 1, line 7; col. 3, line 50). Marcus Plotius Valens, with his two sons Plotianus and Valens (col. 2, lines 35-37), is another example of members of one family being members of the association. Moreover, we have in the membership list the names of three slaves, two of whom share membership in the association with their masters: Crescens Abelli (col. 1, line 12) is a slave of the Abellius family; Chrysio Pacci (col. 2, line 48) is a slave of the Paccius family.[21] Unlike the way in which the names

---

10. Col. 1: lines 18, 25; col. 2: line 42; col. 3: lines 61, 64, 70.
11. Col. 1: line 26; col. 2: lines 38, 46; col. 3: lines 66, 69.
12. Col. 2: lines 33, 35, 36, 37.
13. Col. 1: lines 11, 19; col. 2, line 33; col. 3: line 58.
14. Col. 1: lines 9, 20; Col. 3: line 59.
15. Col.1: line 13; Col. 2: line 41; Col. 3: line 56.
16. Col. 1: line 7; Col. 2: line 45; Col. 3: line 50.
17. Col. 1: line 4; col. 3: lines 57, 62.
18. Col. 2: lines 28, 29.
19. Col. 2: line 40; col. 3: line 54.
20. Col. 1: line 8; col. 2: line 47.
21. The owners of the third slave, Hermeros Metrodori (col. 1, line 6), are not found on

are inscribed on the Agrippinilla inscription, where the rank and the significance of each member is clearly discernible, the names of the members of the Silvanus association seem to be given at random, with the names of slaves often preceding that of their masters. Undoubtedly the members of the prominent Romans *gens*, such as Atilius, Domitius, Flavius, Claudius, and Valerius, played key roles in the association. There are at least three members whose elite *cognomina* points to their possibly prominent role: Ti(berius) Claudius Magnus (Col. 1, line 24), Fontius Capito (Col. 3, line 67), M(arcus) Glitius Carus (Col. 3, line 68).[22] There are at least 14 other men whose *cognomina* suggest that they were freeborn.[23] Twenty-four other names contain Greek *cognomina* or common servile *cognomina*, strongly suggesting that they come from a servile background.[24]

Overall the two inscriptions provide important information with regard to the social prosopography of the Silvanus association which possibly was contemporaneous with the Christian *ekklēsia* in Philippi. Although it is an exclusively male association, it united men of different social standing (freeborn, *liberti*, slaves) and ages (fathers and sons). What is of significance is

---

the membership list. Besides the names of the three slaves, there are four other names of so-called public slaves: Orinus *coloniae* (col. 1, line 10), Tharsa *coloniae* (col. 2, line 30), Phoebus *coloniae* (col. 2, line 31), Phoibus *coloniae* (col. 3, line 55).

22. For the analysis of Latin *cognomina*, see I. Kajanto, *The Latin Cognomina* (Helsinki: Societas Scientiarum Fennica, 1965). It is all the more surprising that we do not find their names of the list of the contributors (inscription #1).

23. Col. 1: Lucius Nutrius Valens iunior (line 5), Marcus Minucius Ianuarius (line 15), Col. 2: Gaius Atilius Niger (line 29), Publius Trosius Geminus (line 34); Marcus Plotius Valens (line 35), Marcus Plotius Valens filius (line 37), Lucius Atiarius Firmus (line 46); Col. 3: Gaius Valerius Firmus (line 52), Gaius Flavius Pudens (line 56), Lucius Volattius Firmus (line 57), Canuleius Crescens (line 65), Domitius Peregrinus (line 70); Col. 4: Iulius Candidus (line 71), Valerius Clemens (line 72).

24. Col.1: Gaius) Paccius Mercurialis (line 7), Caius Abellius Anteros (line 9), Publius Hostilius Philadelphus (line 16), Marcus Varinius Chresimus (line 14), Publius Herennius Venustus (line 17), Lucius Domitius Ikarus (line 18), Gaius Abellius Agathopus (line 20), Lucius Domitius Primigenius (line 25), Lucius Atiarius Thamyrus (line 26); Col. 2: Marcus Herennius Helenus (line 22), Lucius Laelius Felix (line 32), Marcus Plotius Valens (line 35), M(arcus) Plotius Plotianus (line 36), Lucius Atiarius Successus (line 38), Titus Flavius Clymenus (line 41), Lucius Domitius Callistus (line 42), Gaius) Paccius Trophimus (line 45), Marcus Publicius Primigenius (line 44), Publius Vettius Aristobulus (line 47); Col. 3: M(arcus) Alfenus Aspasius (line 51), A(ulus) Velleius Onesimus (line 54), Gaius) Abellius Secundus (line 59), Lucius Domitius Venerianus (line 61), Lucius Domitius Icario (line 64), Lucius Atiarius Moschas (line 66), Lucius Atiarius Suavis (line 69).

that almost all men bear tripartite Roman names, although their different *cognomina* point to a variety of backgrounds. What is also quite noticeable is an active *patronal* role of the *liberti* whose respective contributions are mentioned in inscription #1 (Publius Hostilius Philadelphus, Lucius Domitius Primigenius, Gaius Paccius Mercurialis). Especially significant is the role of Publius Hostilius Philadelphus, who sponsored the inscriptions to be carved in stone. The fact that he was elected for the public office of *aedile* speaks in favor of his being "well-connected"[25] within the local social network of patronage. This seems to correspond to a generally prominent place that *liberti* played in the political and economic spheres in Macedonia.[26]

4.2 Diana Association

Given the number of inscriptions and especially the large number of rock reliefs, the cult of Diana was probably one of the most popular cults at Philippi.[27] Although the available epigraphic material dates to the second century CE, the worship of this Roman goddess, albeit under different names, has a long history at Philippi. An original Thracian goddess Bendis was adopted by the colonists from Thasos under the name of Artemis, and then later, during Roman times, was worshiped as Diana.[28] All three goddesses were known as protectors of women during childbearing, and were also associated with moon, nature, and the underworld. These features explain the particular popularity of this cult with women. Earlier we referred to the study of rock reliefs by V. Abrahamsen, who concluded that out of a total of two hundred carvings found at Diana's sanctuary at Philippi, at

---

25. De Vos, *Church and Community Conflicts*, 245.
26. Cf. Papazoglou: "We know the names of dozens of [*liberti*] from dedications and epitaphs, and we also have lists of names which may be those of manumitted slaves. . . . Freedmen played a significant role in the economic life of the community, occupying themselves, as they did in most cases, with trade. It is especially worth noting that the overwhelming majority of freedmen were former slaves of Roman citizens" ("Macedonia," 200).
27. De Vos, *Church and Community Conflicts*, 248.
28. Portefaix, *Sisters Rejoice*, 75-95.

least forty represent women priestesses.[29] Following are some of the examples of the inscriptions dedicated to Diana:

Inscription #1[30]:

Galgestia Primilla pro filia De[a]ne v(otum) s(olvit) l(ibens) m(erito).

Galgestia Primilla has rightly paid off with pleasure (this) votive to Diana on behalf of (her) daughter.[31]

What is significant about this inscription is that a woman by the name of Galgestia Primilla seems to have been a Roman citizen.[32] Four other inscriptions also contain the names of Roman citizens: Licinius Valens,[33] Vatinius Valens,[34] and Rutilius Maximus,[35] Cassius Coronus.[36] At the same time another inscription devoted to Diana Minerva contains at least eight names of Thracian origin.[37] The same inscription lists Manta Zercedis as the priestess (*sacerdos*) of the cult.

Inscription #2[38]:

Cintis Polulae fil(ius) Sc|aporenus sibit et uxori su|ae Secu Bithi fil(iae) v(irus) f(aciendum) c(uravit) | dedu her(edibus) meis * LX, eut ex u|suris eius adaiant Rosal(ibus) | sub curat(ione)

---

29. Abrahamsen, "Women at Philippi," 21.
30. Pilhofer, *Philippi*, 2:188 (173/L575); Abrahamsen, "Rock Reliefs," 49.
31. Translation by Abrahamsen, "Rock Reliefs," 49.
32. Her name is listed under the *Cives Romani* category in Pilhofer, *Philippi*, 2:864.
33. Pilhofer, *Philippi*, 2:186 (170/L008); Abrahamsen, "Rock Reliefs," 49.
34. Pilhofer, *Philippi*, 2:185 (168/L006); Abrahamsen, "Rock Reliefs," 49.
35. Pilhofer, *Philippi*, 2:189 (174/L011); Abrahamsen, "Rock Reliefs," 49.
36. Pilhofer, *Philippi*, 2:194 (181/L018); Abrahamsen, "Rock Reliefs," 49.
37. Pilhofer, *Philippi*, 2:504 (519/L245); the inscription is also cited (without the list of names) in Portefaix, *Sisters Rejoice*, 84.
38. *CIL* 3.1.707; Collart, *Philippi*, 474, n. 3; Pilhofer, *Philippi*, 2:497 (512/L102); Portefaix, *Sisters Rejoice*, 83.

Zipae Mesti fil(i). | ad arb[i]terio eius s(upra) n(ominatus) e(st) Dianae | *vacat* *CCL. *Vacat.*

Cintus, the son of Polula, of Scaporenus, has made the following inscription for himself and for his wife Secis, the daughter of Bithus, during his lifetime. I have left my heirs sixty denarii, so that the interest from it might go to the *rosalia*, under the auspices of Zipas, the son of Mestus (deceased), in order to celebrate the funeral meal. In the same way, I have also left two hundred fifty denarii for Diana, under the auspices of the same person who is named above.

Here we have an example of a bequest by the husband and wife of Thracian origin for a dignified funeral and subsequent commemoration during the *rosalia* festival. This funerary rite was introduced at Philippi by the colonists from Italy.[39] Once a year the tombs were decorated with roses and offerings were burnt at the site. It is of significance that *rosalia* was particularly popular with the military personnel.[40]

The significance of the Diana cult for our study is that possibly along with the incipient Christian movement at Philippi we have an example of a vibrant religious community which embraced women and men, Roman citizens and non-citizens alike, and which touched upon the fundamental issues of life (childbearing) and life after death. In contrast to the Silvanus association, "the Diana cult was ruled primarily, if not solely, by women and women were its primary participants."[41]

---

39. Papazoglou "Macedonia," 206.
40. Cf. George Watson: "[Rosalia] had a prominent place at and [was] assigned a significant part in military ceremonies of all kinds" (*The Roman Soldier: Aspects of Greek and Roman Life* [Ithaca, N.Y.: Cornell University Press, 1969], 130).
41. V. Abrahamsen, "Christianity and the Rock Reliefs at Philippi," *BA* 51 (1988): 50. Diana being also the hunting goddess was venerated by the two other groups at Philippi: the praetorians and the gladiators (Portefaix, *Sisters Rejoice*, 72, n. 144).

4.3 Dionysiac Association

During the excavations at Philippi, underneath the public baths there was discovered a sanctuary of a Dionysiac association dating "to the first period of the Roman colony."[42] Inside the sanctuary there were recovered five Latin inscriptions, three of them dedicated to the triad Liber-Libera-Hercules, and the other two to Liber Pater.

Inscription # 1[43]:

Lib(ero) et Lib(erae) | Herc(uli) sacrum.| C(aius) Valer(ius) | Fortuna|tus cum | Marroni|a Eutych[ia] | ux[ore].

Consecrated to Liber and Libera (and) to Hercules. Gaius Fortunatus with his wife Marronia Eutychia.

Inscription # 2[44]:

ex imperio | Liberi et Liberae | et Herculis | nequis nequ|eve velit faciem | tangere, | nesi | siqui imperat|um fueret | ex imperio | Pomponia |Hilara posuit.

By the authority of Liber and Libera and Hercules. Nobody is to touch the face (of the stella?) unless it is commanded by the authority (of the deities?). Pomponia Hilara set this (stella) up.

---

42. Portefaix, *Sisters Rejoice*, 63. On the history of the excavation see Collart, *Philippes*, 367-68.
43. Collart, *Philippes*, 414, n. 1 (pl. 68/1); Portefaix, *Sisters Rejoice*, 100, n. 134; Pilhofer, *Philippi*, 2:344-45 (338/L333).
44. Collart, *Philippes*, 414, n. 1 (pl. 68/2); Portefaix, *Sisters Rejoice*, 100, n. 131; Pilhofer, *Philippi*, 2:345-46 (339/L338).

Inscription #3[45]:

Lib[ero] et Lib[era] et Her[culi], | thiasus Maenad[arum] | regianar[um] aq|[ua]m induxit [p(ecunia) s(ua)].

To Liber and Libera and Hercules by the *thiasos* of the *maenads* who at their own expense built a magnificent water (conduit).

Inscription # 4[46]:

Salvia | Pisidia | Lib(ero) | Pat(ri) MN.

Salvia Pisidia (consecrated) to Liber Pater 1000 sestertia.

Inscription # 5[47]:

Pisidia | Helpis | L(ibero) P(atri) v(otum) s(olvit) | l(ibens) a(nimo).

Pisidia Helpis discharges her votive offering to Liber Patri with much pleasure.

The cult of Dionysus-Bacchhus[48] was deeply rooted in Macedonia and attracted devotees from all social strata.[49] The god of agriculture, fertility, and wine, Dionysus was often equated with Liber (also known as Liber Pater) and his daughter Libera, whose very names emphasizes the "liberating" experience that the worshipers of the cult claimed to undergo in their rituals. It is interesting that on the three inscriptions devotion to Liber and

---

45. Collart, *Philippes*, 414, n.1 (pl. 68/3); Portefaix, *Sisters Rejoice*, 100, n. 129; Pilhofer, *Philippi*, 2:346-47 (340/L589).
46. Collart, *Philippes*, 415 n. 4; Portefaix, *Sisters Rejoice*, 100, n. 132; Pilhofer, *Philippi*, 2:346-47 (341/L267).
47. Collart, *Philippes*, 415 n. 4; Portefaix, *Sisters Rejoice*, 100, n. 133; Pilhofer, *Philippi*, 2:348 (342/L292).
48. Bacchus is the Roman adaptation of Dionysus. See Euripides, *Bacch.* 491.
49. Cf. Papazoglou, "Macedonia," 205.

Libera is coupled with the devotion to Hercules (Gr. "Heracles"), who was considered a national hero of the Macedonians.[50] The *maenads* (inscription #3) were the female worshipers of Dionysus who in ritual dances reenacted the nymphs' care of the infant Dionysus.[51] It is of special importance that the members of this ecstatic cult disclose such commendable examples of public service by investing their resources into building a water supply. Another noticeable detail is that four of the inscriptions contain the names of women: Marronia Eutychia (mentioned with her husband; inscription # 1); Pomponia Hilara (inscription # 2), Salvia Pisidia (inscription # 4), Pisidia Helpis (inscription # 5). The geographical references in the names of the three women suggest that they were liberated slaves.[52] Pomponia Hilara might have been a member of a distinguished Roman family of Pomponians, or a freedwoman of that family.[53] The very fact that the women of the *thiasos* of the *Maenads* sponsored the construction of the water supply, and also made personal contributions (like Salvia Pisidia),[54] suggests that "these women had a remarkable degree of economic independence, which can be explained by the fact that they enjoyed complete control over their money."[55]

4.4 Associations of Isis and/or Serapis

A number of inscriptions found in the Acropolis and elsewhere testify to the popularity of the Oriental healing gods Isis and Serapis. Although the available inscriptions are dated in the second-third centuries CE, the unearthed temple of the Egyptian gods at Philippi dates back to the Augustan

---

50. Cf. Papazoglou, "Macedonia," 205.
51. Diodorus Siculus 4.3.
52. Portefaix, *Sisters Rejoice*, 101. Marronia Eutychia probably came from the nearby Maroneia, while Salvia Pisidia and Pisidia Helpis originated from the Pisidia area in Asia Minor.
53. Portefaix, *Sisters Rejoice*, 100.
54. Inscription # 4 suggests that Salvia Pisidia contributed "MN" which stands for *milia nummum* and equals 1000 sestertia (not 1000 denarii as Portefaix claims [*Sisters Rejoice*, 101]), which is about 250 denarii (see Pilhofer, *Philippi*, 2:348).
55. Portefaix, *Sisters Rejoice*, 101.

era.[56] As Papazoglou contends, the cult of Isis and Serapis "took firmest root in Macedonia."[57] The local popularity of these cults is possibly explained by the fact that "the Egyptian gods were regarded as the protectors of Antony and his followers in the battle for authority over the Roman Empire."[58]

The first inscription was found outside the Isis temple, close to the eastern gate of the city and is carved on the altar stone:[59]

> Isidi Reg(inae) sac(rum) | ob honor(em) divin(ae) | domus pro salute | colon(iae) Iul(iae) Aug(ustae) Philippiens(is) | Q(uintus) Mofius Euhemer(us) | medicus ex imperio | p(ecunia) s(ua) p(osuit) idem subselia quattuor | loco adsig(nato) d(ecreto) d(ecurionum).
>
> Dedicated to Isis Regina for the honor of the imperial house, and for the well being of the *Colonia Iulia Augusta Philippensis*. Quintus Mofius Euhemerus, a physician, at his own expense and at the behest of Isis has erected this (inscription), as well as four benches in the same place, at the order of the city council.

There are at least two important aspects connected with the designation of Isis as the queen (Regina).[60] First, it points to the function of the goddess who, as a mighty ruler, conquers disease and death.[61] Second, Isis was often portrayed carrying a rudder and identified as Isis Tyche, the mistress of Fate

---

56. Portefaix, *Sisters Rejoice*, 72. The remains of the temple suggest that some of the expensive materials used for the decoration of the outside wall and for the flooring of the terrace were imported from outside Macedonia. This also suggests that at least some of the adherents of the cult were people who were well off (Collart, *Philippes*, 72, 74).

57. Papazoglou, "Macedonia," 205.

58. Portefaix, *Sisters Rejoice*, 114, n. 244.

59. Paul Collart, "Le sanctuaire des dieux égyptiens à Philippes," *BCH* 53 (1929): 83-84; Bormann, *Philippi*, 59; Pilhofer, *Philippi*, 2:132 (132/L303).

60. See the discussion in Portefaix, *Sisters Rejoice*, 72.

61. Cf. Diodorus Siculus: "As for Isis, the Egyptians say that she was the discoverer of many health-giving drugs and was greatly versed in the science of healing; consequently, now that she has attained immortality, she finds her greatest delight in the healing of mankind and gives aid in their sleep to those who call upon her, plainly manifesting both her very presence and her beneficence towards men who ask her help" (1.25.2-3).

who holds the future of people in her hands.⁶² There is clear indication of the ability of this Egyptian cult to penetrate and adapt to Roman soil. In the inscription, a man who bears a Roman tripartite name (a Roman citizen?), speaks and writes in Latin, a physician by education, is at the same time an adherent of Isis and a functionary of the local administration (he fulfills the order of the *decurionum*). The inscription clearly points to a special role of Isis as the protector of Philippi: the goddess is used for the legitimization of imperial rule and for the well being of the Roman colony. It is of significance that Isis and Serapis are hailed in a number of inscriptions as savior gods.⁶³

A similar blend of social function and religious devotion is found on another inscription:⁶⁴

> L(ucio) Valerio L(uci) f(ilio) | Volt(inia) Prisco | orn(anmentis) dec(urionatus) hon(orato) | dec(urioni) irenar(chae) IIvi(o) iur(e) d(icundo) muner|ario cultores | deo(rum) Serapis [et] Isidi[s].
>
> To Lucius Valerius Voltinia Priscus, son of Lucius, decorated with the decurions' honor, a decurion, an eiranarch, a magistrate, the organizer of the gladiatorial games. By the worshipers of the gods of Serapis and Isis.

In the inscription, a highly decorated Roman official, a member of a prominent Roman *gen*, with many important social obligations, is praised by the worshipers of Serapis and Isis as their benefactor. This inscription might be an example of a peculiar Philippian preoccupation with honorific titles.⁶⁵ In honoring Epaphroditus with five honorific titles (Phil 2:25) Paul might be playing against this social background.

---

62. Cf. Apuleius: ". . . know that I [Isis] alone may prolong thy days above the time that the fates have appointed and ordained" (*Met.* 11.6).
63. Cf. *IG* 11.4 1253; 1299.
64. P. Collart, "Inscriptions de Philippes," *BCH* 62 (1938): 428; Bormann, *Philippi*, 59.
65. For other epigraphic evidence revealing the same tendency see J. Hellerman, "Brothers and Friends in Philippi: Family Honor in the Roman World and in Paul's Letter to

There are two more inscriptions made by the worshipers of Serapis found at Philippi:

Inscription # 1[66]:

Ἀγαθῇ τύχῃ | Κ(οίντον) Φλάβιον Ἐρ|μαδίωνα τὸν | ἀξιολογώτα | [τὸ]ν οἱ θρησκευ|[ταὶ] τοῦ Σεράπι | [τὸ]ν εὐεργέτην | [μνή]μης χάριν.

To good Fortune. The worshipers of Serapis honor Quintius Flavius Hermadion as their benefactor.

Inscription # 2[67]:

Κο(ίντον) Φλάβιον Ἐρ|μαδίωνα υἱὸν | Κο(ίντου) Φλάβιου | Ἐρ|μαδίωνος | τοῦ κρα(τίστου) γυμνασιάρχου κα[ὶ] ἀρχιερέως, οἱ θρησκευτὲ τὸν ἴδιον | ἀγωνοθέτην τῶν μεγάλων Ἀσκληπείων.

To Quintius Flavius Hermadion, the son of the most excellent Quitius Flavius Hermadion, the gymnasiarch, and the chief priest, for organizing the great (festival) of Asclepieia. The worshipers [of Serapis].

The inscriptions are found engraved on two steles. A highly decorated Roman official (the most excellent gymnasiarch and the chief priest), Quintius Flavius Hermadion, and his son are praised by the Serapis association for their patronage. P. Lemerle, who first published the inscriptions, argues that the term ἀρχιερέως should be understood as referring

---

Philippians," *BTB* 39 (2009): 15-20.
66. Paul Lemerle, "Inscriptions latines et grecques de Philippes (suite)," *BCH* 59 (1935): 140; Collart, *Philippes*, 447; Bormann, *Philippi*, 60; Pilhofer, *Philippi*, 2:313 (307/G410).
67. Paul Lemerle, "Inscriptions latines," *BCH* 59 (1935): 141; Collart, *Philippes*, 448; Bormann, *Philippi*, 60; Pilhofer, *Philippi*, 2:318-19 (311/G411).

to his being a high priest of the imperial cult.⁶⁸ If that is the case, then we have an example of a symbiotic relationship between the imperial cult and other cults of the time. Another remarkable feature noticed by Lemerle is that the worshipers of Serapis took part in the festival of Great Asclepeia, not in the Serapieia festival, attested elsewhere, which would have been most naturally expected.⁶⁹ This could be taken as a sign of some syncretistic tendencies within the cult, especially because both Serapis and Asclepios were thought to be healing gods. There is still one more important observation. The second inscription, although recognizing the role of Quintius Flavius Hermadion, the son, in organizing (presiding at?) the games of the Great Asclepieia, nevertheless seems to be laying the major emphasis on the highly decorated father. Why? In this way the followers of Serapis undoubtedly sought to express their gratitude to the father for his faithful patronage which is now being continued in his son. This might be an example of an implicit "rhetoric of rivalry"⁷⁰ between associations for securing the continual support of benefactors.

4.5 Associations of the Thracian deities Sourgethes and Hero

A testamentary inscription, which contains references to two associations, formed around Thracian deities Sourgethes and Hero.⁷¹

> Αὐρή(λιος) Ζιπύρων | ἐτῶν Λν ἐνθάδε | κει Οὐαλ(ερία) Μαντάνα | τῷ εἰδίῳ ἀνδρὶ καὶ | αἰαυτῇ ζῶσα ἐποί|ησεν. ἐὰν δὲ τις | μεταρῇ τὸν βωμὸν | τοῦτον. δῶσι τῇ πώλι | X χίλια. καὶ δηλάτω|ρι X Φν. | Οὐαλερία Μοντάνα κα|τὰ κέλευσιν τοῦ ἀνδρὸς Αὐρη|λίου Ζιπύρωνος Δίζανος ἔδω|κα συνποσίῳ Θεοῦ Σουρεγέθου | πρὸς τὴν ἀγορὰν παρὰ τὸ ὡρο|λόγιν XΠN v. ἀφ'

---

68. Lemerle, "Inscriptions," 145. Cf. Bormann, *Philippi*, 60.
69. Lemerle, "Inscriptions," 146-47.
70. Harland, "Spheres of Contention," 53-63, esp. 61-63.
71. The inscription was published in Paul Lemerle, "Le testament d'un Thrace a Philippes," *BCH* 60 (1936): 336; recently by Pilhofer, *Philippi*, 2:134-35 (134/G441).

ὧν ἐκ τῶν τόκ[ων| π]αρακαύσωσιν κατὰ ῥόδοις. [ἐὰν| δὲ] μὴ
παρακαύσωσιν, δώσο[υσιν| πρ]οστείμου τὰ προγεγράμμ[ενα|
δι]πλᾶ τοῖς ποσιασταῖς Ἥρ[ωνος | πρὸ]ς τᾶ Τορβιανά.

Aurelius Zipuron, 30 years old lies | here. Valeria Montana made [this stella] for her husband and | for herself while she was still | alive. If anyone | should raise this funerary altar | give to the merchants | 1000 denarii | and to the informer 500 denarii. | Valeria Montana, according | to the will of her husband | Aurelius Zipuron Dizanus gave | 150 denarii to the association of the god Souregethes | which is by the marketplace beside the clock.| and out from the interest [received] | they should burn an offering on the day of the *rosalia*. | If they do not | light [an offering] they should give the double| of the amount written above | to the members of Heros association | which is near Torbiana.

The inscription may serve as an illustration of multiple affiliations discussed earlier, i.e., both Aurelius Zipuron and his wife Valeria Montana were members of two different associations. Probably they had reasons to doubt whether their last will would be followed up by the members of one association, so they had to come up with a "back-up" plan. It follows from the inscription that associations were financially stimulated to follow their members' bequests, especially in view of a competitive group watching over their shoulder. We will use this inscription as an example of the inter-group competition between different associations.

4.6 Association of Dendrophorus Augustalis

The existence of the woodcutters' association at Philippi is attested in the following inscription:[72]

---

72. The inscription was first published in Paul Lemerle, "Inscriptions latines et grecques de Philippes," *BCH* 58 (1934): 466-69; also by Collart, *Philippes*, 456, n. 2; more recently by Bormann, *Philippi*, 55; Pilhofer, *Philippi*, 2:326 (321/L377).

> [M(arcus) V]elleius M(arci) l(ibertus) . . . | [dendro]phorus Aug(ustalis), an(norum) I . . . | [sibi et V]elleiae Primigeniae u[xori. . .].
>
> Marcus Velleius, a *libertus* of Marcus… *dendrophorus Augustales* in the year of… he and his wife Velleia Primigenia…

Woodcutters were known as worshipers of Cybele (Magna Mater), the Phrygian goddess of mountains, fortresses, and wild animals.[73] What is peculiar in this inscription is that Marcus Velleius, being a devotee of Cybele, is at the same time a member of the *seviri Augustales*, an officially sponsored religious association, members of which were actively involved in emperor worship (see chapter 2). This is yet another important example of the adaptation of the imperial cult by the worshipers of other deities.

4.7 Association of the Purple-Dyers

The following inscription was found in 1872 by Stauros Mertzides and published subsequently in his book:[74]

> Τόν πρῶτον ἐκ πορ|φυροβάφ[ῶν Ἀν]τίοχον Λύκου | Θυατειρ[ιν]ὸν εὐεργέτ[ην] | καὶ [...] ἡ πόλις ἐτ[ίμησε]
>
> To the first among the purple-dyers, Antiochus, son of Lukus from Thyatira, a benefactor and… the city honored

---

73. Bormann, *Philippi*, 55.
74. See Οἱ Φίλιπποι (Constantinople, 1897), 186-89. S. Mertzides claimed that the inscription was subsequently destroyed. The authenticity of the inscription was doubted by Louis Robert in "Hellenica V, Inscriptions de Philippes publiées par Mertzidès," *Revue de Philologie* 13 (1939): 142, but affirmed by P. Lemerle, *Philippes et la Macédoine orientale à l'epoque chrétienne et byzantine* (BEFAR 158; Paris: Boccard, 1945), 28-29; and more recently by Pilhofer, *Philippi*, 1:180-1. The inscription is published in Pilhofer, *Philippi*, 2:693 (697/M580).

The presence of the purple-dyers in Philippi is also attested by a fragmentary Latin inscription which reads: [PU]RPVRARI[.[75] That the purple-dyeing business was known in Macedonia is corroborated by an inscription from Thessalonica:[76]

Ἡ συνήθεια τῶ|ν πορφυροβάφ|ων τῆς ὀκτω|καιδ/εκάτης | Μένιππον Ἀμιου | τὸν καὶ Σεβῆρον | Θυατειρηνὸν μνήμης | χάριν.

The association of purple-dyers from the Eighteenth [street/district?]. To Menippus, son of Amius, (also known as) Severus, from Thyatira. In memory.

The evidence for the purple-dyers' association at Philippi (if authentic) adds an additional point towards Luke's historical credibility. Lydia of Acts 16:14, a πορθυρόπωλις from Thyatira (cf. the inscription's Antiochus, son of Lukas also from Thyatira) and the leader of the household, might have been a member of this association.

4.8 Association of Grave-Diggers

An inscription carved on a stone was found in a ditch between Philippi and Kavalla.[77]

Μάντα ἰδίῳ τέκνῳ | Σουδίῳ Παιβίλα ἔ|των κς νν μνήμης χάριν. | καταλείπω δὲ κου|[π]ίασιν Καλπαπου|ρείτα(ι)ς Χ ρνν. παρα|καύσουσιν δὲ ἅπαξ | τοῦ ἔτους ῥόδοις.

---

75. *CIL* 3.646, published in Pilhofer, *Philippi*, 2:650 (646/L035). See the argument in Pilhofer, *Philippi*, 1:176, n. 6.

76. There is also an attested case of the purple-dyers association at Thessalonica (Pilhofer, *Philippi*, 1:176; *IG* 10.2 1.291).

77. The inscription was first published by Franz Cumont, "Notices épigraphizues. V. Inscriptions de Macédoine," *Revue de l'Instruction publique en Belgique*," 41 (1898): 338; also by Paul Perdrizet, "Inscriptions de Philippes: Les Rosalies," *BCH* 24 (1900): 306; Collart, *Philippes*, 286, n. 5; more recently by Pilhofer, *Philippi*, 2:26 (029/G215)

Manta in memory of her own son, Soudios Paibilas of 26 years. I bequeath to the gravediggers of Kalpapoureitia 150 denarii. They shall light (an offering) once a year during the rosalia.

An engraved figure of the Thracian Horseman points to the fact that this popular and indigenous Macedonian deity was worshiped by the members of the association. A sanctuary of the Thracian Horseman was recovered in Philippi.[78] The worship of this deity was "contaminated by local belief in an afterlife which represented the dead as heroes."[79] Of particular interest is the fact that along with some other deities the Thracian Horseman was venerated as σωτήρ (*CCET* 1.10). Paul's proclamation of the coming Savior and the concomitant future transformation (Phil 3:20-21) might have resonated well with the Philippian audience.

4.9 Association of Gladiators

On the doorposts of the theater at Philippi an inscription was recovered which testifies to the existence of the gladiators' association.[80]

> Μ(άρκος) Βελλεῖος Ζώσι[μος] | ἱερεὺς τῆς ἀνεικήτου Νεμν[εσε-] | ως ὑπὲρ φιλοκυνηγῶν τοῦ στέ[μ-]|μα vacat τος | τὰ ἀφυδ vacat ρεύ|ματα τῶ|ν θεῶν | ἐκ{κ} τῶν ἰ|δίων ἐ|ποίησ|εν

> Marcus Velleius Zosimus, priest of the invincible Nemesis, for [the association] of huntsmen has made the reliefs of the gods at his own expense.

The inscription is carved in marble with the goddess Nike holding a palm branch and standing on a globe in the lower part of the relief. It is

---

78. Pilhofer, *Philippi*, 1:33-34.
79. Papazoglou, "Macedonia," 205.
80. The inscription is published in Paul Collart, "Le théâtre de Philippes," *BCH* 52 (1928): 108-10; recently in Pilhofer, *Philippi*, 2:144-45 (142/G562).

one of three votive inscriptions which were found on the doorposts of the opening into the western *parados* of the theatre. Two of them contain a reference to φιλοκυνηγοί τοῦ στέμματος = lit. "lovers of chase of the wreath," an idiomatic expression for the guild of huntsmen.[81] Although the inscriptions are dated in the second century CE, the gladiators' fights with the animals were well known from much earlier times. As P. Davies testifies, "The theater . . . is surely one structure which Paul in the first century A. D. would see on his visits to Philippi." Already at that time it had "the underground passages [used] . . . for animals in their shows."[82] Thus it is possible that there was a gladiator's association contemporaneous with Paul's letter to Philippians.

Conclusion

In the current chapter we have considered the epigraphic evidence for the presence of voluntary associations at Philippi. The major conclusion is that voluntary associations, both religious and professional, were present in that Roman colony by the time the Christian gospel reached the city. We have seen a variety of inscriptions, some extensive, honorary inscriptions with detailed membership lists (like the Silvanus association); others, short funerary epitaphs for the deceased members of a family. The membership list of the Silvanus association provided insights with regard to the social prosopography of the association. This all-male association embraced people of different social standing (masters, liberti, slaves) and of different generations (father, sons). Almost one third of all members are representatives of the freeborn and, in some cases, influential Roman families. Coupled with the fact that the inscription is in Latin, it gives us reasons to believe that Roman citizens were actively involved in the life of voluntary associations. The inscriptions of the Silvanus association pointed to the active role of the liberti as one of the major sponsors of the association.

---

81. Cf. LSJ, 1936.
82. Davies, "Paul's Journeys," 101.

The Dionysus association presented a counter-balance to an exclusive all-male Silvanus association. We could not help but notice an active role of women as sponsors of some public projects (the construction of the water conduit) and as private donors for the needs of the association.

Several inscriptions presented an example of a Roman official's involvement in sponsoring the activities of the associations, either as a private admirer of a cult or as an active member of it. This is the case, for example of Quintius Flavius Hermadion, the gymnasiarch, and the chief priest who is praised by the Serapis association for sponsoring the Asclepian festival. The same is true with regard to a distinguished *Decurion*, Lucius Valerius Voltinia Priscus, who is praised by the association of Isis and Serapis for organizing the gladiatorial games. Still another example is Quintus Mofius Euhemerus, a physician and a devotee of the queen Isis, who, at his own expense, installed a stele to the Egyptian goddess and four benches (at the order of the city council).

Most importantly we have seen examples of mixed religious devotion within an association (like in the Dionysus association – devotion to Liber, Libera and Hercules) and active penetration of the imperial cult into the religious life of the associations. This is especially obvious in the case of Marcus Velleius, who was a devotee of Cybele/Mater (*dendrophorus*) and a member of *Augustales* association dedicated to the imperial cult. This is also true with regard to Quintius Flavius Hermadion, who was a benefactor of the Serapis association and at the same time was (as some argue) a chief priest of the imperial cult.

The findings of this chapter will be used further in our analysis, for it is our contention that the early Christians who came from a pagan background were open to utilizing the available structures for their community formation. From the limited information available to us from Paul's letter to the Philippians and the book of Acts we will see that there are similarities between the Christian *ekklēsia* and voluntary associations, especially in the areas of social prosopography, the active role of women, and organizational structure.

CHAPTER 5

Christian *Ekklēsia* at Philippi and Voluntary Associations: Discovering the Points of Correlation

In the current chapter we are going to argue that voluntary associations played an important role in the formation of the early Christian community at Philippi. The chapter consists of two major sections. In the first section we will try to describe the social context of Paul's ministry. We are going to argue that it was the format of the "small group"[1] setting (the household and professional *collegia*) in which his ministry took place. In the second section we will assess the available NT material with regard to the Philippian church's social prosopography, the role of women, its organizational structure, and similar factors. We are going to argue that, in the predominantly Gentile context of the Roman colony of Philippi, voluntary associations were the closest analogue for the early Christians to follow and structure their community.

The resemblance of the Christian *ekklēsia* to voluntary associations has its bearing on the identity of Paul's opponents in Philippians 3:18-20. Paul's fondness in the letter for the language of friendship discloses his

---

1. The term "small groups" is not to be confused with its modern religious usage. In using it we refer primarily to a setting which encompassed a relatively limited number of people (like the household or voluntary association) and fulfilled a similar social function, i.e., it defined the role and place of each member in the society at large. Cf. Bruce Malina: ". . . it [is] fair to say that early Christians formed groups that were essentially small, face-to-face groups within an incipiently face-to-face (agency controlled) society" ("Early Christian Groups: using small group formation theory to explain Christian organizations," in *Modelling Early Christianity: Social-Scientific Studies of the New Testament* [ed. Philip Esler; London: Routledge, 1995], 92).

familiarity with the well-known Graeco-Roman *topos*, also appropriated by many voluntary associations. This bond of friendship among the Christians at Philippi, however, is under the threat of being disrupted by inter-group rivalry. In our assessment, this rivalry is the reflection of the disagreement between the two leaders of houshold groups within the church, namely, Euodia and Syntyche. As we are going to argue in chapter 6, the essence of their disagreement goes back to the unresolved issue of Paul's "enemies of the cross."

5.1 *The social context of Paul's ministry*

The study of the social context of Paul's ministry undertaken by some scholars led them to question the assumption that Paul was much involved in street preaching and other forms of public mass appeal.[2] Rather, as is evidenced from the book of Acts[3] and from Paul's own letters his ministry took

---

2. Stanley K. Stowers, "Social Status, Public Speaking and Private Teaching: The Circumstances of Paul's Preaching Activity," *NovT* 26 (1984): 59-82; also Wayne Meeks, "The Social Context of Pauline Theology," *Int* (1982): 266-77.

3. The issue of the historical reliability of the book of Acts is a matter of a continuous debate between those who take Luke's narrative as being basically an eyewitness account (e.g., Martin Hengel, *Acts and the History of Earliest Christianity* [SCM, 1979], 59-68, esp. 66) and those who take it as novelistic fiction (e.g., Richard I. Pervo, *Profit with Delight: The Literary Genre of the Acts of the Apostles* [Minneapolis: Fortress Press, 1987], 21-24; Robert C. Tannehill, *The Narrative Unity of Luke-Acts: A Literary Interpretation* [2 vols; Minneapolis: Fortress, 1986], 1:7-8; 2:196-205). Still there are scholars who argue for a mediating position whereby some actual historical occurrences were stylized by Luke to fit his thematic intent (e.g., Philip F. Esler, *Community and Gospel in Luke-Acts: The Social and Political Motivations of Lukan Theology* [SNTSMS 57; Cambridge: Cambridge University Press, 1987], 14; Gerd Lüdemann, *Early Christianity according to the Traditions in Acts: A Commentary* [trans. John Bowden; Minneapolis: Fortress, 1987], 177-84, esp. 183; L. Michael White, "Visualizing the "Real" World of Acts 16: Toward Construction of a Social Index," in *The Social World of the First Christians. Essays in Honor of Wayne A. Meeks* (ed. L. Michael White and O. Larry Yarbrough; Minneapolis: Fortress, 1995), 234-61. See also important bibliography on the issue: David L. Balch, "The Genre of Luke-Acts," *SwJT* 33 (1990): 5-19; William F. Brosend, "The Means of Absent Ends," in *History, Literature and Society in the Book of Acts* (ed. Ben Witherington III; Cambridge: Cambridge University Press, 1996), 348-62; W. Ward Gasque, "The Historical Value of Acts," *TynB* 40 (1989): 136-57; Joel B. Green, "Internal Repetition in Luke-Acts," in *History, Literature and Society in the Book of Acts* (ed. Ben Witherington III; Cambridge: Cambridge University Press, 1996), 283-99; Stanley E. Porter, *Paul in Acts* (LPS; Peabody, Ma.: Hendrickson Publishers 2001). Much of the confusion is due to the attempts of

place within the "small groups" setting. It was primarily within the context of the household and that of the artisan's workshop that the Christian gospel was heard and appropriated.[4] Luke clearly indicates that Christian gatherings took place in private houses (Acts 2:46; 5:42; 8:3; 18:7). Most importantly meetings in private houses could only have taken place at the volition of the *paterfamilias*, i.e. only in case of the head of the household's conversion to Christianity.[5] Again, Luke tells us of several household conversions, two of which took place at Philippi (the household of Lydia, 16:15; and of the Philippian jailer, 16:31-34). There are good reasons for trusting Luke's account, for the same pattern is corroborated by Paul's own testimony (cf. 1 Cor 1:16; 16:15, 19; Rom 6:3-5; 16:10; Phlm 2).

> Christianity's decision to choose an organizational structure centered in the home provided that movement with a space that was exempt from external authority and especially suitable for pursuing its own development; it also made it possible

---

some scholars to impose the norms of modern historiography on ancient historiography. The view that Luke from the point of view of modern historiography was a "bad historian" does not mean that he "therefore [was] writing novels" (Porter, *Paul in Acts*, 17). In fact, there are reasons to believe that Luke was not bad a historian after all. At some key points (such as the role of households and artisans' workshops in spreading of Christianity) Luke and Paul seem to be on the same page.

4. Cf. David L. Balch, "Paul, Families, and Households," in *Paul in the Greco-Roman World: A Handbook* (ed. J.Paul Sampley; Harrisburg, Pa.: Trinity Press International, 2003), 258-92; Vincent P. Branick, *The House Church in the Writings of Paul* (Wilmington, Del.: Michael Glazier, 1989); Jürgen Becker, "Paul and His Churches," in *Christian Beginnings. World and Community from Jesus to Post-Apostolic Times* (ed. Jürgen Becker; trans. Annemarie S. Kiddler and Reinhard Krauss; Louisville: Westminster John Knox, 1993), 163-72; Abraham Malherbe, *Social Aspects of Early Christianity* (Philadelphia: Fortress, 1983), 60-91; Ronald F. Hock, "The Workshop as a Social Setting for Paul's Missionary Preaching," *CBQ* 41 (1979): 438-50; Floyd V. Filson, "The Significance of the Early House Churches," *JBL* 58 (1939): 105-12; Karl O. Sandnes, "Equality within Patriarchal Structures: Some New Testament perspectives on the Christian Fellowship as a Brother- or Sisterhood and a Family," in *Constructing Early Christian Families: Family as Social Reality and Metaphor* (ed. Halvor Moxnes; London: Routledge, 1997), 150-82; idem.,"The Role of the Congregation as a Family within the Context of Recruitment and Conflict in the Early Church," in *Recruitment, Conquest, and Conflict: Strategies in Judaism, Early Christianity, and the Greco-Roman World* (ed. Peder Borgen et al.; Atlanta, Ga.: Scholars Press, 1998), 333-46.

5. Cf. Sandnes, "The starting point of the churches was normally the conversion of the *paterfamilias*, who embraced the Christian faith together with his whole household" ("Patriarchal Structures," 153).

for Christianity to design worship and everyday life as an integral whole and according to its own ideas, with the additional advantage of being able to utilize an established network of close personal, economic, social, and religious relationships as an already existing infrastructure.[6]

There was a certain advantage in that Christians did not have to invent some alternative structure for organizing their fellowship.[7] To use a metaphorical image: the household provided the stage with decorations ready for the same actors (members of the household) to play new roles in the newly written Christian script. G. Dix, although writing of a slightly later historical milieu, thus expressed the usefulness of the Roman household for Christian worship:

> Here ready to hand was the ideal setting for the church's "domestic" worship . . . The chair of the *paterfamilias* became the bishop's throne; the heads of the families were replaced by the presbyters, and the clansmen by the laity. Virgins and widows and any others for whom it might be desirable to avoid the crowding in the *atrium* could be placed behind the screens of the *alae*. At the back near the door, where the clients and the slaves of the patrician house . . . had once stood at its assemblies, were now to be found the catechumens and enquirers, attached to the church but not yet members of it . . . The dining room of the house (*triclinium*) which usually opened off the *atrium* could be used for the Christian "love-feast."[8]

An obvious disadvantage in the adaptation of the household model by the early Christians was that the Christian script itself had to be tailored

---

6. Becker, "Paul and His Churches," 165.
7. Cf. Richard Ascough: "Christians were able to look to the various groups around them as models for group formation, while at the same time adding their own variations to the group structure chosen" (*What Are They Saying About the Formation of Pauline Churches?* [New York: Paulist, 1998], 98).
8. Dom G. Dix, *The Shape of the Liturgy* (Norfolk: Biddles, 1945; repr. New York: Continuum, 2007), 23.

to fit the patriarchal structures of the Graeco-Roman household. Early on there was a clear dichotomy between the more egalitarian vision for Christian community (Gal 3:28) and the one which sanctified the existing status quo (Eph 5:22, 6:5-8). As is evidenced from the letter of James (2:1-7), at least some of the early Christian communities struggled to overcome an almost natural preference for the rich and powerful within the congregation. In other words, the household setting made it clear who was in charge of the fellowship.

Another possible shortcoming of the Christian appropriation of the household model was that the members of the household in most cases had to follow the decision of the *paterfamilias*. Along with an almost instantaneous numerical growth the early Christian community accumulated adherents who joined the church for reasons other than their devotion to Christ. As N. Taylor indicates, incorporation into the Christian community was often "a consequence of social relationships rather than personal conviction."[9] In a culture in which religion was part and parcel of political and family life, the subordinates (wives, children, slaves) often did not have a choice but to join their superiors in worshiping their gods. As a result of this lack of personal conviction, the early adherents of Christianity displayed "varying degrees of commitment, and . . . were incorporated to varying degrees in the life of the Christian communities." What is also important is that "the abandonment of previous beliefs, practices and social relationships varied accordingly."[10] It is our contention that "varying degrees of commitment" might have been a factor which led to the formation of a deviant Christian group at Philippi.

In our previous discussion (see ch. 2) we already pointed to the significant overlap between the household and voluntary association. Both formed a type of small group setting whose goal was to provide the means for socialization and upward social mobility. Both utilized private houses

---

9. Nicholas H. Taylor, "The Social Nature of Conversion in the Early Christian World" in *Modelling Early Christianity. Social-Scientific Studies of the New Testament in its Context* (ed. Philip F. Esler; London: Routledge, 1995), 132. Cf. Bruce Malina's assessment of conversion in Mediterranean culture as being a "collectivist" rather than an "individual" phenomenon (*The New Testament World: Insights from Cultural Anthropology* [rev. ed.; Louisville, Ky.: Westminster John Knox, 1993], 85).

10. Taylor, "Social Nature," 136.

for their meetings. Activities in both were accompanied with a devotion to a certain deity. The function of both depended on influential patrons, which is why in both the system of patronage was fostered and encouraged.

There are reasons to believe that along with the household, early Christianity evolved within the context of professional *collegia*. Relevant to this point are Luke's references to Paul's own professional activity as a tentmaker (Acts 18:3); he worked with his own hands to support himself (20:34-45).[11] Luke's testimony seems to be corroborated by Paul himself in statements such as one finds in 1 Thes 2:9: "You remember our labor and toil, brothers and sisters, that working (ἐργαζόμενοι) night and day, so that we might not burden any of you, we proclaimed (ἐκηρύξαμεν) to you the gospel of God (cf. 1 Cor 4:12)." The present participle (ἐργαζόμενοι) designates the circumstances under which the preaching was accomplished: "their working night and day was done simultaneously with their preaching of the gospel."[12] By adopting a missionary strategy that necessitated his working for his own sustenance (cf. 1 Cor 9:6), Paul "had little choice but to use the workshop as a place for communicating the gospel since so much of their time was spent there."[13] In fact, as several scholars have pointed out, Paul's preaching activity along with his engagement in the tentmaking

---

11. It is generally asserted that Paul's occupation as σκηνοποιός is a fairly reliable part of the tradition related by Luke. Cf. Lüdemann, *Early Christianity*, 198. As Ronald Hock further indicates, in view of the fact that making leather out of skin (tanning) was an unclean trade for a Jew, Paul was most probably a leather worker, rather than a tanner (*The Social Context of Paul's Ministry: Tentmaking and Apostleship* [Philadelphia: Fortress, 1980], 21).

12. Charles A. Wanamaker, *The Epistles to the Thessalonians: A Commentary on the Greek Text* (NIGTC; Grand Rapids: Eerdmans, 1990), 104. It seems that some modern translations have a misplaced emphasis in translating 1 Thess 2:9: "we worked...*while* we proclaimed" (NRSV) or "preached" (NIV). As James Frame argued, "ἐργαζόμενοι marks the circumstances attending the preaching" (*A Critical and Exegetical Commentary on the Epistles of St. Paul to the Thessalonians* [ICC; New York: C. Scribner's Sons, 1912], 103). Cf. also Abraham J. Malherbe, *The Letters to the Thessalonians: A New Translation with Introduction and Commentary* (AB; New Haven: Yale University Press, 2008), 149. Daniel Wallace likewise reminds us that "the *present* participle is normally *contemporaneous* in time to the action of the main verb" (*GGBB*, 625). So, Paul was preaching *while* working, not the other way around (as suggested in the above translations).

13. Wanamaker, *Thessalonians*, 104.

business (as in Acts 18:3) could have easily created an impression of his setting up a kind of professional association.[14]

> The household groups organized by Paul under the patronage of Stephanas, Gaius, Prisca, Chloe, and others, all together gathering occasionally at Gaius's place as the "civic assembly of God in Corinth," was like an association of, as it were, artificial immigrants – made aliens by their conversion to the God of Israel and baptism into Messiah Jesus.[15]

Richard Ascough's analysis of 1 Thessalonians suggests a strong resemblance between the Christian community at Thessalonica and a professional voluntary association.[16] Paul's own characterization of his work as accompanied with κόπος and μόχνος[17] (2:9) and his admonition to the Thessalonians to "work with their own hands" (4:11) points to physically challenging manual labor which was usually the case in professional associations. Once again, Paul's phrase "preaching while working" (2:9) most naturally suggests that "the most likely candidates for proselytizing"[18] were his fellow workers and customers. Especially interesting is Ascough's take on the phenomenon of the Thessalonians' conversion in 1:9b.[19] The second person plural of the verb ὑποστρέφω might be an indication of a collective rather than an individual experience within the existing voluntary association, especially because of the mention of their previous involvement in idol worship (an essential part of the activity in voluntary associations). Moreover, some of the terminology used by Paul is reminiscent of the setting in voluntary associations This is related primarily to Paul's characterization of the believers' behavior as ἄτακτοι (5:14). Contrary to the conventional

---

14. Clarke, *Serve the Community of the Church*, 65; Kloppenborg, "Collegia and *Thiasoi*, 24; Malherbe, "Social Aspects," 90-91; Meeks, *First Urban*, 32.
15. Meeks, "Artificial Aliens," 137.
16. See Ascough, "The Thessalonian Christian Community as a Professional Voluntary Association," *JBL* 119 (2000): 311-28.
17. The two words form a part of a proverbial expression in the antiquity indicating "labor, exertion, hardship" (*BDAG*, 528, 660).
18. Ascough, "Thessalonian Christian Community," 315.
19. Ascough, "Thessalonian Christian Community," 322-24.

rendering of the word ἄτακτος, which is usually taken as referring to personal laziness or idleness, Ascough argues that the word should be understood in the context of inter-personal rivalry which was a commonplace in voluntary associations.[20] In our consideration of the voluntary associations in chapter 2 we already cited the regulation of the Iobacchoi association against "anyone [who] is found disorderly (ἀκοσμέω),[21] sits in someone's seat, or is insulting or abusing someone else."[22] The signs of the interpersonal rivalry among the Philippian Christians will be considered later in our discussion.

There are similar observations made by other scholars. J. Kloppenborg, for example, argues that reference to ἡ κατ' οἶκον ἐκκλησία (Rom 16:5; cf. Col 4:15) is possibly a technical phrase which is paralleled to the terminology used of the household *collegium*.[23] A. Malherbe likewise suggests that a significant number of the Corinthian Christians would have been handworkers familiar with the structures and function of the professional associations.[24] As we are going to argue further, there are some indications that the Christian community at Philippi likewise was structured and functioned as a type of voluntary association.

5.2 Philippian Christian Community

In this second section we are going to take a closer look at the Philippian Christian community. In doing so we will rely on the information supplied for us from the letter to the Philippians and the book of Acts. We are going to argue that from the point of view of the social and ethnic prosopography, the role of women, and organizational structure, the Christian *ekklēsia* at Philippi bore a striking resemblance to a voluntary association.

---

20. See the argument in Ascough, "Thessalonian Christian Community," 318-21.
21. That ἀκοσμέω is synonymous with ἀτακτέω is clearly attested in Plutarch, *De def. orac* 424a and Philo, *Praem.* 20.
22. *IG* 2.2 1368, line 60.
23. Cf. *CIL* 6. 9148: "collegium quod est in domo Sergiae L(uci) f(iliae) Paullinae" (cited in Kloppenborg, "Collegia and *Thiasoi*," 23).
24. Malherbe, *Social Aspects*, 75.

5.2.1 The Social and Ethnic Prosopography

Both the book of Acts and the letter to the Philippians provide us with a limited number of clues which give us some idea about the community's ethnic and social outlook. Among the first converts were a certain "God-fearing" woman by the name of Lydia and a Roman jailor along with their households (Acts 16:14-15, 30-34). The letter to the Philippians supplies several other names: Ἐπαφρόδιτος[25] (2:25), Εὐοδία[26] (4:2), Συντύχη[27] (4:2), and Κλήμης[28] (4:3). Even from this limited evidence we can deduce the following. In view of the fact that Clement was a well-known plebeian's *cognomen*,[29] there are good reasons for considering Clement of Philippians 4:3 a Roman citizen.[30] Reumann suggests that perhaps he was "an army veteran, retired in the Roman *colōnia*."[31] Unless he is part of some unknown later veteran influx, this is quite unlikely. He definitely could have been a veteran's descendant. Other names are of Greek, and mostly servile, origin, which suggests that they were *liberti* and belonged to the class of

---

25. Quite a popular name during the Roman period (it corresponds to the Latin "Venustus" [Reumann, *Philippians*, 424]); cf. the two references to Venustus in the inscriptions from Philippi: P. Herennius Venustus (*CIL* 3.633.2; Appendix 2 [col. 1, line 17]); also Lucius Accius Venustus (Pilhofer, Philippi, 2:186 [169/L007]). Ἐπαφρόδιτος is found both in literary sources (Plutarch, *Sull.* 34; Appian, *Civ.* 1:97; Dio Cassius, 51:11, 13; Tacitus, *Ann.* 15:55; Josephus, *Ap.* 1.1 etc.) as well as in inscriptions (*OGIS* 441; P Oxy IV. 743[25]; *IGCB* 1.66). Also cf. the Agrippinilla inscription which contains three references to Ἐπαφρόδιτος (4.7; 4.28; 6.23) and one to the shortened form Ἐπαφρᾶς (8.38).

26. A possible meaning of the name Εὐοδία is "Success" (Reumann, *Philippians*, 607) or "Prosperous Journey" (Fee, *Philippians*, 390). For the inscriptional evidence see MM 263; *NewDocs* 4:178–79; Lightfoot, *Philippians*, 158.

27. From the Gk. τύχη = "Lucky" (Reumann, *Philippians*, 607). It is attested in inscriptions *CIG* 2.2326[2], 3098[3-10]; *CIL* 12. 4703 (MM 615). The popularity of the derivatives from Συντύχη can be demonstrated by a quite noticeable variation of both male and female names in the Agrippinilla inscription: Εὐτυχίς (2.17; 9.60); Εὐτύχης (2.45; 5.10; 6.30; 7.37), Τυχικός (2.48), Εὐτυχία (3.18; 9.57) Εὐτυχᾶς (4.3; 6.7), Εὐτυχόνς (6.22), Εὐτυχίδης (7.4, 15) 4.3), Τύχη (9.50). Cf. Acts 20:4, 9; 1 Cor 16:17; Col 4:7.

28. Gk. form of a fairly common Latin name, Clement (Clemens). The name is attested on both the members' list of the Agrippinilla inscription (Κλήμηνς; *IAgrip.* col.4, line 35), and of the Silvanus association at Philippi (Valerius Clemens; *CIL* 3.633.2 [col. 4 line 72]). D. Peterlin mistakenly lists Valerius Clemens as a member of the Dionysus cult. The reference to *CIL* 3.733 is also misleading (*Disunity in the Church*, 167, n. 182).

29. See our previous discussion in ch. 2.

30. Cf. Peterlin, *Disunity in the Church*, 168.

31. Reumann, *Philippians*, 610.

artisans or craftspeople.³² The unnamed jailor was not necessarily a Roman officer, but rather may have been a Greek citizen.³³ Peterlin argues³⁴ from Pliny (*Ep.*10.9) that people of this occupation were usually public slaves, yet Oakes rightly remarks³⁵ that the mention of the jailor's οἰκία in Acts 16:33 speaks in favor of his being a *libertus*.

Lydia, the first convert to Christianity in Philippi (according to Acts 16:15) is of special interest for us. While it is possible to translate the phrase γυνὴ ὀνόματι Λυδία (16:15) as "a woman from Lydia"³⁶ (where Lydia is a region in the Roman province of Asia), there is a clear epigraphic evidence for its being a proper name.³⁷ Several factors point to her being a woman of means and status.³⁸ Of no small importance is the fact that she is called by her first name, which was quite unusual, unless the woman was of notable or notorious character (we will say more on this in the coming discussion on Euodia and Syntyche). References to her house and household, and her being a πορφυρόπωλις,³⁹ suggest "that she should not be seen as someone of servile status."⁴⁰ Even if she was a *liberta*, her well-to-do status should

---

32. De Vos, *Church and Community Conflicts*, 252; Abrahamsen, *Women and Worship*, 84; Peterlin, *Disunity in the Church*, 167–69. The two names, Ἐπαφρόδιτος and Εὐοδία, are found in the list of slave names compiled by Linda C. Reilly in *Slaves in Ancient Greece: Slaves from Greek Manumission Inscriptions* (Chicago: Ares, 1978), 45.

33. See Tellbe, *Between Synagogue and State*, 224.

34. Peterlin, *Disunity in the Church*, 144.

35. Oakes, *Philippians*, 65.

36. Cf. Dahl: "As she may have been called the "Lydian," it is conceivable that she might be identical with either Euodia or Syntyche, but that is a conjecture without any proof" ("Euodia and Syntyche and Paul's Letter to the Philippians," in *The Social World of the First Christians: Essays in Honor of Wayne A. Meeks* [ed. L. Michael White and O. Larry Yarbrough; Minneapolis: Fortress, 1995], 12).

37. *New Docs* 4:54.

38. One of the dissenting voices which contest the view that Lydia was a well-to-do woman is that of Ivoni Reimer (*Women in the Acts of the Apostles: A Feminist Liberation Perspective* [trans. Linda M. Maloney; Minneapolis: Fortress Press, 1995], 109-17). She reminds us that Lydia as a foreigner from the East "carried on a despised trade" and was "required at all times to work with [her] hands to earn [her] income and livelihood" (p. 112). Although we cannot exclude the supposition that Lydia herself worked with her hands, some of features in the story (her mobility, her house big enough to host strangers) point into a different direction.

39. The term πορφυρόπωλις refers to a seller of purple cloth (*CIG* 2519). The purple-dyeing was an imperial monopoly so that people involved in this trade were considered as members of "Caesar's household" (*New Docs* 2:26, 28).

40. Ben Witherington III, *The Acts of the Apostles: A Socio-Rhetorical Commentary* (Grand

not be a surprise, for, as Meeks contends, there were many liberated slaves with high income and low social status.[41] A clear example of that is the case of Publius Hostilius Philadelphus who, although a *libertus,* was one of the patrons of the Silvanus association and an elected official (*aedile*) at Philippi (see ch. 4).

Lydia's role as the head of the household was also something of an exceptional case: a woman could usually assume that role in case of the male *paterfamilias*' death.[42] Her house should have been big enough to accommodate strangers; otherwise it would have been socially inappropriate for a single woman to share the house with four men.[43] Possibly her house consisted also of the workshop which would have been shared by the members of the household.

It looks like the first Christian gatherings in Philippi took place also in Lydia's house (Acts 16:40). Lydia's role as the head of the household and a businesswoman is of special importance. Being the head of the household speaks in favor of her being in charge of the business. It is reasonable to suppose that Lydia's household consisted of those involved in business and, in this sense, her household shared the function of a professional association.[44] Her house possibly was the place of work and socializing for the members of the household. Being the head of the household, Lydia most naturally assumed the role of a social network facilitator. The well being of her employees depended on her benevolence, and the success of the business depended in turn on their loyalty. This mutual bond is evidenced in the fact that Lydia's decision to embrace Christianity meant that the members of her

---

Rapids: Eerdmans, 1998), 491.

41. Meeks, *Urban Christians*, 73.

42. Garnsey and Saller, *The Roman Empire*, 130-36. Women who married without *manus* formally remained a part of their fathers' *familia* (James Jeffers, "Jewish and Christian Families in First-Century Rome," in *Judaism and Christianity in First-Century Rome* [ed. K. Donfried and P. Richardson. Grand Rapids: Eerdmans, 1998], 135).

43. Paul, Silas, Timothy and Luke.

44. Cf. Reimer: "*Purpurarii* were mainly freed persons who settled in other cities to do their work, normally in small groups; in such groups women were frequently in the majority. This association and shared work was a form of organization practiced by common people who were attempting, together, to earn a subsistence income and at the same time to shape their social and religious lives in common. Slaves and freed persons were almost entirely organized in 'collegia' and 'houses', and it was not exceptional for one of them to be found at the head of the group," (*Women in the Acts*, 111-12).

household would follow in her steps. If Luke indeed relates a historically accurate account, then we have a clear example of an instrumental role that the household, with the features of a professional association, played in the formation of the Christian community at Philippi. Lydia's leading role as the head of the household will be further substantiated by reference to the leading role of women in the Philippian church. If indeed, as we shall argue, women played the role of patrons in the church, then the disagreement between them – namely, between Euodia and Syntyche – would inevitably result in rivalry between the members of their respective households.

Another noticeable feature of the Philippian church is the meager Jewish representation, which seems to correspond to the conspicuous absence of evidence (besides the book of Acts) for the Jewish presence in the city at large (see the discussion in ch. 3). The very fact that Paul spoke to some Jewish women who came together on the Sabbath for prayer outside the city gates (Acts 16:13), indicates that there were not enough Jewish men to establish a proper synagogue at Philippi.[45] Lydia is the only person mentioned who was in some ways sympathetic to the Jewish faith.[46] Paul's argument against Judaizers (3:1-3) implies that (male) believers in the congregation were mostly uncircumcised. An additional indicator for the absence of strong Jewish influence in the church is the active role of women (as we shall argue).[47]

The general scholarly consensus tends to conclude that the Philippian congregation consisted primarily of freeborn *plebeians*, *liberti*, and some slaves, almost all of whom belonged to the lower socio-economic strata of society. Some indirect evidence, like Paul's reference to the poverty of the Macedonian churches (2 Cor 8:1-2), as well as his mentioning of the "lack of opportunity" in Philippians 4:10, seems to corroborate this latter supposition. Several features suggest that a significant number of members of the Christian community were Roman citizens: most of the listed members

---

45. W. Derek Thomas, "The Place of Women in the Church at Philippi," *ExpT* 83 (1972): 117.

46. For some reason Ben Witherington calls Lydia "a devout Jew from Thyatira" ("Lydia," *ABD* 4:442), whereas her status as a "God-fearer" (Acts 16:14) clearly points to her non-Jewish origin.

47. Marshall, *Philippians*, 110.

were probably *liberti*; Paul's specific form of address, Φιλιππήσιοι⁴⁸ (4:15); his intentional choice of the politically and militarily⁴⁹ charged terminology (πολιτεύεσθε, 1:27; πολίτευμα, 3:20), and allusions to the emperor (see following discussion), strongly suggest that at least some members of the Christian community were indeed Roman citizens.⁵⁰

The study of the social prosopography of the Philippian Christian community undoubtedly points to similar features with the social prosopography of voluntary associations. We can concur with B. McLean that, in terms of membership, "the inclusion of women, slaves and freedmen in early churches was by no means greater than their inclusion in association."⁵¹

5.2.2 Elevated Status of Women

The second feature that brings together the Christian *ekklēsia* and voluntary associations is a similar egalitarian stance with regard to the role of women. It follows from Luke's account in Acts 16 and from the letter to the Philippians that women seemed to have played an important role in the life of the Christian community.⁵² This seems to reflect the general trend

---

48. On the use of Φιλιππήσιοι D. Peterlin gives the following comment: "Paul had in mind the earliest Philippian Christians of ethnic Roman extraction for whom precisely the Latin form of their city carried particular significance" (*Disunity in the Church*, 167).

49. Edgar Krentz, "Military Language and Metaphors in Philippians," in *Origins and Method: Towards a New Understanding of Judaism and Christianity: Essays in Honour of John C. Hurd* (ed. Bradley H. McLean; Sheffield: JSOT Press, 1993), 105-27.

50. Bockmuehl's remark is relevant here: "It is worth noting, however, that Paul neither highlights his own Roman citizenship nor in any way presupposes that of his readers; indeed by writing in Greek he is clearly appealing to a wider audience than that of the Latin-speaking highest echelons of Philippian society. The rhetorical force of Paul's language is to play on the perceived desirability of citizenship in Roman society at Philippi, and to contrast against this the *Christian* vision of enfranchisement and belonging" (*Philippians*, 98).

51. McLean, "Agrippinilla Inscription," 270.

52. On the role of women especially in the church of Philippi, see Valerie Abrahamsen, "Women at Philippi: The Pagan and Christian Evidence," *JFSR* 3 (1987): 17-30; S. Agouridis, "The Role of Women in the Church at Philippi," *BBS* 1 (1980): 77-85; Dahl, "Euodia and Syntyche," 3-15; George Gilbert, "Women in Public Worship in the Pauline Churches," *BW* 2 (1893): 38-47; Ronald Graham, "Women in the Pauline Churches: A Review Article," *LTQ* 11 (1976): 25-33; A. Boyd Luter, "Partnership in the Gospel: The Role of Women in the Church at Philippi," *JETS* 39 (1996): 411-420; Francis Malinowski, "The Brave Women of Philippi," *BTB* 15 (1985): 60-64; Carolyn Osiek et al., *A Woman's Place: House Churches in Earliest Christianity* (Minneapolis: Fortress, 2006); W. Thomas, "The Place of Women," 117-20.

of women's active participation in the social, religious, and political life in the colonies of Macedonia.[53] Paul's appeal to Euodia and Syntyche in 4:2 is a remarkable testimony in itself and requires our additional attention. The very fact that he directly addresses[54] them by their first names,[55] along with mentioning that they "struggled along," points to their place of prominence and importance in the community. The letter to the Philippians abounds with admonitions to be "of the same mind" (1:27; 2:2-5, 14). If the same admonition remains applicable to Euodia and Syntyche, "why are the two women singled out since more Philippian Christians were guilty of the same shortcomings and the same misdemeanor?"[56] In other words, if these women were on a par with other members of the community, "why name names?"[57] As we are going to argue shortly, the quarrel between Euodia and Syntyche epitomizes Paul's concern for unity. It is precisely because of their roles of leadership that the continual disagreement between them causes the whole congregation to be "adversely affected."[58]

The important status of the two women is corroborated by Paul's testimony whereby he characterizes them as those who "struggled (συνήθλησαν) beside [him] in the work of the gospel, together with Clement and the rest of [his] co-workers (συνεργῶν)" (Phil 4:3). Euodia and Syntyche are Paul's συνεργοί,[59] the term which Paul uses for the designation of "a specific group

---

53. W. Tarn and G. Griffith give in this regard an outspoken testimony: "They [women] played a large part in affairs, received envoys, and obtained concessions from them for their husbands, built temples, founded cities, engaged mercenaries, commanded armies, held fortresses, and acted on occasion as regents or even co-rulers" (*Hellenistic Civilization* [London: E. Arnold, 1952], 98).

54. Cf. Silva: "The apostle's directness confirms how close he felt to this church; one does not take risks of this sort unless one can depend on thick cushions of love and trust to absorb the impact of a rebuke" (*Philippians*, 192). The repeated admonition Εὐοδίαν παρακαλῶ καὶ Συντύχην παρακαλῶ possibly points to the fact that Paul "refuses to take sides but makes the same appeal to both" (O'Brien, *Philippians*, 478).

55. D. Schaps reminds us that Roman women were usually called in public by their *cognomen* not by their first names. Also in Greek and Roman oratory women's names were not mentioned unless they were of notable or notorious character ("The Woman Least Mentioned: Etiquette and Women's Names," *CQ* 27 (1977): 323–30).

56. Peterlin, *Disunity in the Church*, 103.

57. Garland, "The Composition and Unity of Philippians," 172.

58. Thomas, "The Place of Women," 118.

59. The term συνεργός is attested in the terminology used of members of professional associations. See *ISmyrna* 218, 715, 721; *IEph* 444, 454, 2078, 2079, 2080, 2976;

or class [of Christians] and [thus] not used of believers generally."[60] Usually it is applied to people of prominence who made some significant contribution to the cause of the gospel. Epaphroditus is called συνεργός (Phil 2:25) because he was willing to "risk his own life" for "the work of Christ" (2:30). Philemon, probably a man of substance, who allotted his own house for the needs of ministry, is also called συνεργός (Phlm 1). Priscilla and Aquila likewise are called συνεργοί (Rom 16:3-4).[61] This is an especially instructive case, for Paul is referring to a self-supporting married couple who together were involved in a teaching and preaching ministry (cf. Acts 18:24-28) to the point of "risking their lives" (Rom 16:4). This same kind of commitment is seen in Paul's characterization of Euodia and Syntyche who "struggled along" with Paul and other men in ministry. As E. Krentz reminds us, the verb συναθλέω, "occurs in athletic, gladiatorial and military contexts" and in the context of Philippians "stresses the need for joint action."[62] The same verb is used earlier in the epistle in the admonition to the whole congregation to "stand firm in one spirit, striving side by side (συναθλοῦντες) with one mind for the faith of the gospel" (1:27). The admonition, overburdened by military or athletic terminology, begs the comparison of Paul with "a commanding officer or a coach who is determined to inspire his troops, or to encourage his contestants."[63] The phrase στήκετε ἐν ἑνὶ πνεύματι, μιᾷ ψυχῇ συναθλοῦντες ςdescribes the attitude of the soldiers drawn up in line"[64] whose task was to keep the line unbreakable at all costs. Obviously in view of mounting social ostracism (1:28), Paul is concerned that the continuing disagreements, especially among the leadership ranks, can make the Christian community easy prey for competing groups.

IGRR 907.
60. Earle Ellis, "Paul and his coworkers," in *DPL*, 183.
61. Paul uses συνεργός also of himself (1 Cor 3:9, "co-worker of God"), Urbanus (Rom 16:9), Timothy (Rom 16:21; 1 Thess 3:2), and Titus (2 Cor 8:23).
62. Krentz, "Military Language," 122-23.
63. Hawthorne, *Philippians*, 54.
64. Krentz, "Military Language," 120. Cf. Vegetius 1.26: "There is nothing which has proved to be of greater service in action than for the men . . . keep their allotted positions in the line. . . . [I]f they are scattered and there is too much daylight between them they give the enemy an opportunity of breaking through. Inevitably, if the line is cut through and the enemy attacks the fighting troops from behind, there is immediate panic and universal disorder" (cited in G. Watson, *The Roman Soldier*, 70-71).

> In the face of external opposition to the Gospel Paul exhorts the Philippians *sunathleo*, to stand together in resistance, . . . to be like athletes in deadly combat who, aware of each other and looking for each other, not only in unison ward off the blows of their opponents but go forward toward the foes, bravely exerting themselves in teammate fashion to achieve victory.[65]

The references to συνήθλησαν in 1:27 (along with mentioning of the "same kind of struggle" in 1:30) and in 4:3 suggest that Euodia and Syntyche took a stand with Paul during his initial mistreatment at Philippi (1 Thess 2:2; Acts 16:20-24).[66] If that is the case, then the two women "represent a steady connection and link with the earliest times of the church as foundation members."[67] The time factor is of importance. They have been Christians for a considerable period of time and were able to sustain themselves throughout.[68] Only "women of status, . . . and perhaps single women or more well-to-do women with considerable power in their families who could count on their servants to take care of the domestic responsibilities"[69] could afford the leisure of the continual commitment to ministry. F. Malinowski seems to be missing the point when he argues that Euodia and Syntyche were "fellow-Christians" but not "fellow-ministers" of Paul.[70] He allots these women a role of passive cheerleaders who agreed to suffer humiliation along with Paul.[71] But the fact that Paul puts them alongside other "co-workers" who struggled *for the sake of the gospel* puts them into an active role, meaning "that these women were involved in the evangelization of nonbelievers."[72]

---

65. Malinowski, "Brave Women," 62.
66. Malinowski, "Brave Women," 62.
67. Peterlin, *Disunity in the Church*, 126.
68. The very fact that their names are written in "the book of life" (4:3) confirms their active Christian status.
69. Witherington, *Friendship and Finances*, 108.
70. Malinowski, "Brave Women," 62.
71. "The most we can say is fellow-Christians standing bravely together, fearless, in the face of common and fierce enemies" (Malinowski, "Brave Women," 62).
72. Osiek, *Woman's Place*, 227.

The elevated role of women in the Philippian Christian community may have been due to the fact that women in other cults of the time played similarly elevated roles. We have seen earlier (see ch. 2) that it was almost natural for women of high status and means to assume the role of priestesses and/or patrons in different Graeco-Roman cults. This is one example which testifies to the attempts of the early Christian community to break out from the grid of the patriarchal household structure. Ironically though, it seems that the trend may have been sponsored by the church's pagan counterparts.

5.2.3 Organizational Structure

In the letter to the Philippians there are some clear indications of the presence of some organizational structure inside the Christian community. Evidence is found, first of all, in Paul's address to the ἐπίσκοποι and διάκονοι (1:1) who obviously were officers in some capacity. We argued earlier that Paul's singling out the two women (Euodia and Syntyche) underlines their role as leaders of the community. To this circle belonged also Clement and other unnamed workers who "struggled along" (4:3) with Paul "from the first day" (1:5) of his ministry at Philippi. Paul's other references in the letter to the believers' participation in the gospel (1:5), to their sending messengers (like Epaphroditus), and their financial support, all imply organized communal effort. It follows from the tenor of the letter that Paul still considers himself as one of their leaders. His authority seems to be hovering over the Philippian Christians. Paul speaks of believers being obedient to him in his presence (2:12) and of his concern that in his absence they might be acting differently (1:27; 2:12). He sets himself as an "example" for them to follow (3:17), and deems his presence with them as vital for their well being (1:25). He weeps over the fact that not everyone follows his example (3:18). In other words, Paul still believes and acts as if he has an important position of authority in the congregation of Philippi.

One of the important indicators of how the church of Philippi was structured is the terminology used by Paul for the designation of the community itself and for the leaders of the community. In addressing Christian communities in his letters, Paul consistently uses the word ἐκκλησία.[73] The

---

73. Paul uses ἐκκλησία to refer to local congregations (Rom 16:1, 5; 1 Cor 1:2; 11:8) as

term is used twice in Philippians. The first time it is used in a generic sense: "Out of jealousy I persecuted τὴν ἐκκλησίαν (3·6). The second time it is used in reference to the Philippian church: "When I left Macedonia, not one ἐκκλησία showed me hospitality and support, except for you" (4:15). In view of the fact that ἐκκλησία is widely attested in the LXX,[74] it is most natural to suppose that its use of the term lies in the background of Paul's use of the term. Yet, as Ascough points out, there are reasons to believe that it was not just the LXX which influenced Paul's decision in using ἐκκλησία.[75] Had the LXX been the predominant influence on Paul, one might have expected him to choose συναγωγή, a term used even more frequently in the LXX for Israel's gatherings. The epigraphic evidence shows that the term ἐκκλησία was used for the designation of voluntary associations (admittedly not as widely as other designations).[76] Whether Paul's choice of ἐκκλησία was influenced by the LXX is not the point here. Most importantly, "in the environment of Greek cities, the term [ἐκκλησία] would almost certainly be understood as one of the names for a voluntary association."[77]

The usage of ἐπίσκοποι and διάκονοι points in the same direction.[78] In trying to ascertain the meaning of these terms scholars have often sought to read them within the context of the later NT books (Acts, Pastoral epistles), or post-apostolic writers (Ignatius). In all probability the Philippian text (1:1) is the first reference in the NT to ἐπίσκοποι and διάκονοι.[79] The

---

well as in a more generic (universal?) sense (1 Cor 10:32; 15:9; Gal 1:13). He also uses the term in the plural in reference to local Christian groups (Rom 16:6; 1 Cor 7:17; 11:16; 16:19; 2 Cor 8:1; 11:28; Gal 1:22).

74. In the LXX ἐκκλησία most often stands for the assembly of the Israelites (translating the Hebrew קהל).

75. Ascough, "Voluntary Associations,"158.

76. *OGIS* 488; *IGLAM* 1381; 1382; *IDelos* 1519.

77. Kloppenborg, "Churches and *Collegia*," 231.

78. On the subject I find especially helpful the discussion in the two articles by John Reumann: "Church Office in Paul, Especially in Philippians," in *Origins and Method: Towards a New Understanding of Judaism and Christianity: Essays in Honour of J.C. Hurd* (JSNTSup 86; ed. B. McLean; Sheffield: JSOT Press, 1993), 82-91; and "Contributions of the Philippian Community to Paul and to Earliest Christianity," *NTS* 39 (1993): 446-50. See also Ascough, "Voluntary Associations," 162-69; idem, *Macedonian Associations*, 79-83; 129-38; Cotter, "Our *Politeuma*," 102-3; Kloppenborg, "Churches and *Collegia*," 231-34.

79. This is the only place where the pair is found in Paul (although ἐπίσκοπος is found separately in Acts 20:28; 1 Pet 2:25; 1 Tim 3:2; Tit 1:7; διάκονος in Rom 13:4; 15:8; 16:1;

plurality of leadership in a relatively small congregation at Philippi is an additional indicator that we are dealing with an incipient stage of church development not overburdened with complicated hierarchical structure. The surest sign of this is the noticeable variety of different terms used in the Pauline churches, a variety "which can scarcely be homogenized into a pattern."[80] The time of writing the letter to the Philippians is still the stage when "each congregation seems to develop *ad hoc* and on its own, with what Collins calls in Philippi "local idiosyncrasy."[81]

The attempts to understand ἐπίσκοποι and διάκονοι within the context of the Jewish world[82] seem to be quite precarious, given the predominantly Gentile context of Philippi. In our previous discussion (see ch. 2) we mentioned a noticeable terminological overlap between Christian groups and voluntary associations. The practice of modeling clubs and associations along civic lines was "the rule rather than the exception in Graeco-Roman antiquity."[83] It is thus more natural to suppose that "the Philippians chose their terms for leaders from a world they know, of government, guilds, societies and *oikos*."[84] This assertion undoubtedly follows that by E. Hatch who, as early as 1881, argued "with probably no single exception, the names of Christian institutions and Christian officers [were] shared by them in common with institutions and officers outside Christianity."[85] Hatch's publication provoked an array of opposing voices not least because for many "it was simply intolerable that the Church should have owed its structure to paganism."[86] In reality, as J. Kloppenborg showed, Hatch's claims were "in some ways more modest, and his method considerably more sophisticated,

---

1 Cor 3:5; 2 Cor 3:6; 6:4; 11:25, 23; Gal 2:17; 1 Thess 3:2; Eph 3:7; 6:21; Col 1:7, 23, 25; 1 Tim 3:8, 12; 4:6), and as far as we can tell nowhere else in the epigraphic materials (cf. Reumann, *Philippians*, 64).

80. Reumann, "Church Office," 89. Cf. 1 Thess 5:12; 1 Cor 12:28; Rom 12:6-8; Gal 6:6.

81. Reumann, "Church Office," 90, quoting John N. Collins, *Diakonia: Re-interpreting the Ancient Sources* (New York: Oxford University Press, 1990), 234.

82. See references in Reumann, "Church Office," 88-89.

83. Cotter, "Our Politeuma," 102.

84. Reumann, "Church office," 90.

85. Hatch, *Organization*, 16. See in particular his second lecture on bishops and deacons (pp. 26-55).

86. Kloppenborg, "Churches and *Collegia*," 224.

than his opponents recognized."[87] Comparison of Christian assemblies with non-Christian ones was taken by his opponents as intimation of the alleged borrowings from paganism. For Hatch, however, the comparison was not a matter of discovering genealogical dependence but rather of studying similar phenomena analogically. "[Hatch] assumed what was evident from ancient sources – that associations proliferated in the Imperial period and that Christian groups would *look* like just another association."[88]

The word ἐπίσκοπος was a well-known term for a "supervisory office in the state, in various societies, and other groups of the Graeco-Roman world, often with the financial responsibilities."[89] For example, two inscriptions from Rhodes contain references to five ἐπίσκοποι, members of a council, and to ἐπίσκοπος, an official of the Apollo temple.[90] Most importantly there is inscriptional evidence for the use of the term within voluntary associations. Edwin Hatch was the first to point to an inscription from Thera (Aegean islands; 2nd century BCE) which refers to the financial officers of an association (κοινόν) as ἐπίσκοποι.[91] A similar function of ἐπίσκοπος as a financial officer of a temple is found on the inscription from Salkhat (Nabataea).[92] It led Hatch somewhat hastily to conclude that ἐπίσκοπος was an exclusively financial office.[93] Other evidence, however, does not support such a claim. For example, an inscription from Delos (2nd century CE) refers to an ἐπίσκοπος as the head of a Dionysiac association.[94] Similar references to ἐπίσκοπος as a different cult functionary are found in inscriptions from Thracia,[95] Bostra,[96] and Kanata.[97] We can concur with R.

---

87. Kloppenborg, "Churches and *Collegia*," 228-29.
88. Kloppenborg, "Churches and *Collegia*," 229.
89. Reumann, "Church office," 88. For the references in classical literature, see MM, 244; Lightfoot, *Philippians*, 91.
90. *IMAe* 49.43; 731.8; cited in MM, 244.
91. *IG* 12.3 329: "It is resolved that the ἐπίσκοποι Dion and Meleippus shall accept the offer and invest the money" (cited with translation in Hatch, *Organization*, 37, n. 26)
92. *IGL*1990, also mentioned by Hatch, *Organization*, 37, n. 26.
93. Cf. Kloppenborg, "Churches and *Collegia*," 232.
94. *IDelos* 1522.
95. Poland, *Geshichte*, 375.
96. *OGIS* 2. 614.
97. *OGIS* 2. 611; cf. *IGBulg* 4.2214.

Ascough that, "overall, the evidence for the use of the ἐπίσκοπος in associations is clear, but the specific function attached to it is ambiguous."[98] The lack of context in Phil 1:1 makes it "impossible to determine the identity and role of the ἐπίσκοποι,"[99] other than to ascribe to them some general leadership function. It is not improbable that given the prominent role that women at Philippi played in the life of the church that some of them, like Euodia and Syntyche, were also among the ἐπίσκοποι.[100]

The *oikos* structure in Greek society must not be forgotten for the house churches. The *oikodespotēs* would, as patron and *pater familias*, exercise great influence and so there is a good chance that *episkopoi* first appeared as house church supervisors (hence the plural at Phil 1:1). In Paul's day women were likely to be included among them.[101]

The second word, διάκονος, is an even more widely attested term in the antiquity.[102] All of the attempts to locate the term within the Jewish background "pale for the Philippian use in the face of references to *diakonoi* in Greek guilds and societies."[103] Moulton and Milligan likewise concur that "there is now abundant evidence that the way had been prepared for the Christian usage of this word by its technical application to the holders of various offices."[104] Of particular interest are two inscriptions: the first one comes from Ambrakia and tells us of nine διάκονοι, one of whom presided as a ἱερεύς in the service of Serapis, Isis, and other Egyptian gods;[105] the second inscription comes from Metropolis (Lydia) and contains references to two male διάκονοι and a female διάκονος who together with the priest

---

98. Ascough, "Voluntary Associations," 164-65.
99. Kloppenborg, "Churches and *Collegia*," 232.
100. Peterlin, in view of the lack of evidence in biblical and extra-biblical sources ascribing to women the role of ἐπίσκοποι, "cautiously and tentatively" argues for Euodia and Syntyche to have been the deacons of the church (*Disunity in the Church*, 107). He thus disregards the possibility that this was a uniquely Philippian practice, a part of what earlier was deemed as "local idiosyncrasy."
101. Reumann, "Church Office," 88.
102. The generally accepted meaning "servant" is contested by John Collins, who places the meaning of διάκονος in between messengers, agents, and attendants (*Diakonia*).
103. Reumann, "Philippian Community," 448.
104. MM 149.
105. *CIG* 2. 1800.

and priestess were the ministers of τῶν δώδεκα θεῶν.[106] An inscription from Kyzikos (Smyrna) likewise lists a female διάκων and the five male διάκονοι of a religious association.[107] The scarcity of information in the letter to the Philippians precludes any elaboration on the function of the διάκονοι in the Philippian community. Possibly, as Reumann suggests, they helped the ἐπίσκοποι with "fund-gathering and distribution for Paul, and for Jerusalem, missionary advance, . . . maintaining unity and discipline in and among house churches."[108]

Concluding our assessment of the organizational structure of the Philippian community we may state that the first Gentile Christians in that city most naturally assumed the patterns and terminology which made sense within the socio-religious practices of the time, so at least to "the non-Jew [the Christian *ekklēsia*] would appear as a 'confraternity'."[109]

5.2.4 Community of Friends

In the letter to the Philippians friendship is considered to be one of the prominent themes.[110] Although Paul did not use the word "friendship" or

---

106. *CIG* 3037.
107. *Mouseon*, 93.
108. Reumann, "Church Office," 88.
109. Lightfoot, *Philippians*, 194.
110. On the issue of friendship at Philippi see four illuminating articles published in *Friendship, Flattery, and Frankness of Speech: Studies on Friendship in the New Testament World* (ed. John T. Fitzgerald; Leiden: Brill, 1996): John Reumann, "Philippians, Especially Chapter 4, as a 'Letter of Friendship': Observations on a Checkered History of Scholarship," 83-106; Ken L. Berry, "The Function of Friendship Language in Philippians 4:10-20," 107-24; Abraham J. Malherbe, "Paul's Self-Sufficiency (Philippians 4:11)," 125-40; John T. Fitzgerald, "Philippians in the Light of Some Ancient Discussions of Friendship," 141-60. Also see idem, "Christian Friendship: John, Paul, and the Philippians," *Int* 61 (2007): 284-96; Joseph A. Marchal, "With Friends Like These . . .: A Feminist Rhetorical Reconsideration of Scholarship and the Letter to the Philippians," *JSNT* 29 (2006): 77-106; Pheme Perkins, "Christology, Friendship and Status: The Rhetoric of Philippians," in *Society of Biblical Literature 1987 Seminar Papers* (ed. Kent H. Richards; Atlanta, Ga.: Society of Biblical Literature, 1987), 509-20; John Reumann, "Philippians and the Culture of Friendship," *TrinSR* 19 (1997): 69-83; Stanley K. Stowers, "Friends and Enemies in the Politics of Heaven: Reading Theology in Philippians," in *Pauline Theology*, vol.1: *Thessalonians, Philippians, Galatians, Philemon* (ed. Jouette M. Bassler; Minneapolis: Fortress, 1991), 89-104; L. Michael White, "Morality between Two Worlds: A Paradigm of Friendship in Philippians," in *Greeks, Romans, and Christians. Essays in Honor of Abraham J. Malherbe* (ed. David Balch et al.; Minneapolis: Fortress, 1990), 210-15; Witherington, *Friendship and Finances in Philippi*.

the word "friend,"[111] the concept of friendship nevertheless is present in the letter throughout. For example, the letter abounds with Paul's words of affection for the Philippians: they are his "beloved" brothers and sisters (1:12; 2:12; 3:13; 4:1 [2], 8), his crowning jewel (4:1) whom he has "in his heart" (1:7) and whom "he loves with the affection of Jesus Christ" (1:8). For Cicero, love is the essence of true friendship: "For it is love (*amor*), from which the word 'friendship' (*amicitia*) is derived, that leads to the establishing of goodwill."[112] Seneca joins Cicero in describing friendship in overtly idealized terms: "Pure love, careless of all other things, kindles the soul with desire for the beautiful object, not without the hope of a return of the affection."[113] A friend is like one's *alter ego*: "he who looks upon a true friend, looks, as it were, upon a sort of image of himself."[114] Related to this is the understanding of friends as being "one soul" (μιᾷ ψυχῇ),[115] exactly the same expression which is situated by Paul in the context of his admonition to "stand firm" (Phil 1:27). For Cicero likewise, *stabilitatis* = "firmness, stability" is that "which we look for in friendship."[116] Friendship is what holds the universe together.[117] It evokes the best there is in humans

---

111. As J. Fitzgerald reminds us, "it is extremely problematic to use the presence of a specific Greek term . . . as the exclusive criterion for detecting the presence of a concept or for observing a phenomenon" ("Christian Friendship, 286).

112. Cicero, *Amic.* 26. Also Cicero: "For friendship is nothing else than an accord in all things, human and divine, conjoined with mutual goodwill and affection" (*Amic.* 20).

113. *Ep.* 9. Cf. Cicero: ". . . all believe that without friendship life is no life at all, or at least they so believe if they have any desire whatever to live the life of free men" (*Amic.* 86). Both Cicero and Seneca are critical of any attempts by Epicurus and other Greek philosophers to mar this "pure love" concept with the explanation of friendship as necessitated by a need or want. Cf. Seneca: "He who begins to be your friend because it pays will also cease because it pays. A man will be attracted by some reward offered in exchange for his friendship, if he be attracted by aught in friendship other than friendship itself" (*Ep.* 9). Also Cicero: "For it is not so much the material gain procured through a friend, as it is his love, and his love alone, that gives us delight" (*Amic.* 51).

114. Cicero, *Amic.* 23. His further comment is reminiscent of 2 Cor 6:8-10: "Wherefore friends, though absent, are at hand; though in need, yet abound; though weak, are strong; and—harder saying still— though dead, are yet alive; so great is the esteem on the part of their friends, the tender recollection and the deep longing that still attends them" (*Amic.* 23).

115. Aristotle, *Eud. Eth.* 9.8.2.Cf. also Cicero: ". . . the effect of friendship is to make, as it were, one soul out of many" (*Amic.* 92).

116. *Amic.* 74.

117. "But if you should take the bond of goodwill out of the universe no house or city could stand, nor would even the tillage of the fields abide" (*Amic.* 23).

and inspires a person for self-sacrificial acts.[118] Friendship opens the doors for an egalitarian type of relationship: "it is of the utmost importance in friendship that superior and inferior should stand on equality."[119] Cicero's language of submission[120] and of selfless attitude[121] is remarkably similar to Paul's admonition in Philippians 2:3-4: "Do nothing from selfish ambition or conceit, but in humility regard others as better than yourselves. Let each of you look not to your own interests."

Another important element of friendship is reciprocity, for "nothing gives more pleasure than the return of goodwill and the interchange of zealous service."[122] This reciprocal relationship entangles friends into the exchange of giving and receiving gifts, not because they were obliged to do so,[123] but because it is the duty of a "grateful mind."[124] Giving and receiving gifts was a sign of friendship (that is what friends do), and thus was essential for the ongoing relationship.[125] This virtually unstoppable circle of exchange transformed the ties of friendship into a partnership (κοινωνία), an extremely important term in the Graeco-Roman political vocabulary.[126] For Greeks κοινωνία was essentially that which procured the stability and

---

118. Both in Cicero and Seneca, the willingness to die for a friend (cf. Rom 5:7) epitomizes the relationship. Cf. Seneca: "For what purpose, then, do I make a man my friend? In order to have someone for whom I may die, whom I may follow into exile." (*Ep.* 9). Cicero refers to a play in which one of the main characters "wished to be put to death instead of his friend" (*Amic.* 24).

119. Cicero, *Amic.* 69; cf. *Amic.* 71.

120. "In friendship, those who are superior should lower (*submittere*) themselves, so, in a measure, should they lift up their inferiors" *Amic.* 72. To be sure for Cicero the submission to an inferior excludes going down as low as "nurses and slaves" (*Amic.* 72).

121. "Let not a sort of ungoverned goodwill . . . hinder your friends' advantage in important matters" *Amic.* 75. Cf. Seneca: "though the sage may love his friends dearly, often comparing them with himself, and putting them ahead of himself" (*Ep.* 9).

122. Cicero, *Amic.* 50.

123. Seneca stays faithful to his idealistic notion of friendship, when a giver "does not wish anything to be given to him in return, or else it becomes an exchange of commodities, not a bestowal of benefits" (*Ben.* 2.31.4). What matters "is not . . . the thing which is done or given, but the spirit in which it is done or given" (*Ben.* 1.6.1).

124. Seneca, *Ben.* 4.40.1.

125. Cf. Seneca, *Ben.* 6.16.1-5.

126. Cf. Plato ". . . gods and men are held together by communion and friendship (τὴν κοινωνίαν καὶ φιλίαν);" (*Grg.*, 508a).

good life within the *polis*.[127] For Aristotle φίλια (friendship) and κοινωνία (fellowship) are intrinsically interconnected: while the primary objective of the *polis* is the good life of its citizens, φίλια, being the "motive of social life," is the means for achieving that objective.[128] An intrinsic link between partnership and friendship is sustained by Cicero:

> Virtue cannot attain her highest aims unattended, but only in union and fellowship (*societas*) with another. Such a partnership (*societas*) as this should be considered the best and happiest comradeship along the road to nature's highest good. In such a partnership, I say, abide all things that men deem worthy of pursuit—honor and fame and delightful tranquility of mind.[129]

The letter to the Philippians discloses Paul's fondness for the concept of κοινωνία,[130] which seems to be a key term for the description of his relationship to the Philippians. The fact that this partnership is being sustained through the Spirit (2:1) ensures their continual "participation in the gospel from the first day until now" (1:5) and gives them the privilege to be "partners in Christ's sufferings" (3:10; cf. 1:28). Their partnership is of a reciprocal nature: Paul is the founder and spiritual nurturer of the community who, on their behalf, is involved in the "defense and confirmation of the gospel" (1:7). The Philippians, on their part, sustain Paul through the "ministry of giving and receiving"[131] (4:15) as well as by their prayers

---

127. Cf. Aristotle: "The state (πόλις) is partnership (κοινωνία) of clans and villages living a full and independent life, that is happy and noble life" (*Pol.* 3.1280b).
128. *Pol.* 3.1280b.
129. *Amic.* 83-84.
130. In this relatively short letter Paul uses the word κοινωνία three times (1:5; 2:1; 3:10), also its cognates: συγκοινωνός, 1:7; συγκοινωνέω, 4:14; and κοινωνέω, 4:15.
131. The puzzling absence of a "thank you" note for the financial gift can be explained by the cultural conventions of the time. A friend is one who is in reciprocal, but nevertheless independent, relationship with others. He is like a self-sufficient "wise man" (cf. Seneca: "The wise man needs hands, eyes, and many things that are necessary for his daily use; but he is in want of nothing. For want implies a necessity and nothing is necessary to the wise man" [*Ep.* 9]). But so is Paul: "Not that I am in need; for I have learned to be content with whatever I have" (Phil 4:11; cf. v.17). An author of a private letter to a physician friend confirms receiving the letter with joy and adds: "but I can disregard writing you with

(1:19) and participation in the proclamation of the gospel through word and worthy living (1:5, 27).

The bond of friendship should not be taken for granted. For if the goodwill is taken out of friendship, "no house or city could stand . . . For what house is so strong, or what state so enduring that it cannot be utterly overthrown by animosities and division?"[132] Nothing can have more disastrous repercussions for friendship than the presence of disagreements and discord: "the struggle for honor . . . the lust for money . . . the strife for preferment and glory [are] the deadliest enmities between the dearest friends."[133] Paul's references in Philippians to "selfish ambition or conceit" (2:3), "seeking one's own interests" (2:4), and "murmuring and arguing" (2:14), seem to be clear indicators that the fellowship among believers is under the threat of discord.

This discussion of friendship has relevance also from the point of view of voluntary associations, for in it some of the members called each other friends (φίλοι). Such is the case with an association from the region of Piraeus (Attica; 3d – early 2nd century BCE)[134]:

καὶ ἄν τις ἀδικῆται, βοηθεῖν καὶ αὐτοὺς καὶ τοὺς φίλους ἅπαντας, ὅπως ἂν πάντες εἰδῶσιν ὅτι καὶ εἰς τοὺς θεοὺς εὐσεβοῦμεν καὶ τοὺς φίλους ταῦτα δὲ ποιοῦσιν αὐτοῖς πολλὰ κἀγαθά

---

lavish thanks, for it is required that one say thanks in words (only) with those who are not friends" (*PMerton* 1.12; CE 58; cited in John Reumann, "Culture of Friendship," 77). In other words, friends do not have to say thank you. And obviously Paul wants to keep it this way. His relationship with the Philippians is based on equality and reciprocity. To have it otherwise would have meant his dependent, subservient position on the benevolence of the Philippians. And that is definitely wrong for Paul, for he does his ministry depending solely on God's grace and, for that reason, it is God alone who deserves to be thanked (cf. Phil 1:3).

132. Cicero, *Amic.* 23.

133. Cicero, *Amic.* 34; cf. *Amic.* 78: "Wherefore, in the first place, pains must be taken that, if possible, no discord should arise between friends, but in case it does, then our care should be that the friendships appear to have burned out rather than to have been stamped out."

134. *IG* 2.2. 1275 (lines 8-11).

If somebody would be treated unfairly, [the members of the association] and all the friends shall come to his defense, so that everyone would know that we revere the gods and that we treat our friends with much respect.

Another inscription spells out the decision of an Athenian association (2nd century CE) to establish the ordinances of friendship:[135]

ἔρανον σύναγον φίλοι ἄνδρες καὶ κοινῇ βουλῇ θεσμὸν φιλίης ὑπέγραψαν.

The fellow men having convened the association, by common consent of the council established the ordinances of friendship.

In our discussion of the voluntary associations at Philippi we came across the term φιλοκυνηγοί, which was used of members of the gladiator's association (see ch. 4). There are numerous funerary inscriptions from Asia Minor which testify to the existence of associations of "friends."[136] It is of no surprise, then, that voluntary associations were often equated with the notion of κοινωνία: "Some fellowships (κοινωνίαι) seem to exist for the sake of enjoyment, such as the cultic associations (θιασωτῶν) and the dining clubs (ἐρανιστῶν)."[137] The very fact that the term τὸ κοινόν was used as a generic title of many associations[138] points to "communality"[139] as an essential constitutive element of the social interaction within such groups.[140]

---

135. *IG* 2.2. 1369 (lines 25-29)
136. *TAM* 5.79-93. For other examples of the φίλοι terminology in voluntary associations, see *IG* 3. 1081; 1089; 1102; *IGUR* 1169; *SEG* 29.1188, 1195; *IGLAM* 798.
137. Aristotle, *Eth. Nic.* 8.9.5.
138. *IG* 9.1. 670; 12.3. 330; *IG* 2.2. 1291; 1297; 1327; 1368.
139. The word κοινόν pertaining to things "of mutual interest or shared collectively" (BDAG 551) is an important Greek term from which κοινωνία is formed. It was widely used in many different contexts, also "of persons, connected by common origin or kindred" LSJ, 969.
140. Cf. Aristotle: "For these [associations] exist to celebrate the sacrifices and to spend time together" (*Eth. Nic.* 8.9.5).

Concluding this part of our discussion, we may say that our analysis of the φίλια- related terminology in Philippians betrays Paul's familiarity with the friendship *topos* of Graeco-Roman culture. The usage of such terminology in voluntary associations enhances the probability that the Christian community at Philippi was considered just such an association. The language of friendship in Philippians coexists with the language of rivalry and enmity. This seems to correspond to an antithetical relationship between friendship and enmity found in the ancient literature (see the discussion in ch. 6). To bring back Cicero's just-cited dictum: the pursuit of honor and glory makes the dearest friends into enemies. The Philippians, by exhibiting signs of interpersonal rivalry, are at risk of departing from the company of friends. We are going to argue in the next chapter that this is what most probably happened to those of whom Paul now writes "even with tears" (3:18).

5.2.5 Seeking Honor and Creating Rivalry

It is generally agreed that love for honor, prestige, and status were dominant features of Greaco-Roman culture: "In the literature of the period, the love of honor and praise (*philotimia*) is the primary motive for benefactions."[141] Membership in the Christian community, like membership in a voluntary association, provided an opportunity for marginalized groups to participate in a kind of *cursus honorum*,[142] to which otherwise they would not have access.[143] As J. Kloppenborg suggests, "The language of the Pauline churches is replete with allusions to the structures of honor, and, in a markedly intensified way, to the structures of belonging."[144] Particularly instructive is the case of Epaphroditus, whom Paul dignifies with five honorific titles: brother, co-worker, fellow-soldier, messenger, and minister (Phil 2:25). This listing might not be accidental in the letter to the Philippians, given

---

141. Osiek, "*Diakonos* and *Prostasis*," 360.
142. The term *cursus honorum* (Lat. "course of honors") was applied to a successive service of the highly ranking officials in different military or administrative capacities.
143. Cf. MacMullen: "[Professional] associations [were] focusing. . . their energies on the pursuit of honor rather than [on] economic advantage. They cared a lot more about prestige, which the members as individuals could not ordinarily hope to gain" (*Social Relations*, 76).
144. Kloppenborg, "Churches and *Collegia*," 238.

their general preoccupation with titles and honors, which is evidenced from various inscriptions.[145] As a spiritual leader of the community, Paul admonishes the believers to "honor such people" (2:29). Paul undoubtedly capitalizes on the Philippians' love of honor, introducing, however, a significantly revised version of the *cursus honorum*. For whereas in the conventions of Graeco-Roman culture the way to honor lay through self-aggrandizement and self-assertion, in Christianity it lay through humility and self-denial. For the one who is hailed now by Christians as Lord and Savior (Phil 3:20) gained this honor through radical humiliation and the shameful death of a criminal on the cross. In this way Epaphroditus is worthy of honor because in imitation of Christ he risked his life "for the work of Christ" (2:30).

In Philippians 4:1 Paul addresses the members of the community as στέφανός μου, another term "particularly common in the honorific language of the civic cults."[146] Below I would like to supply three inscriptions which illustrate the prominence of the φιλοτιμία motif in the life of voluntary associations:

Inscription #1 (c. 100 BCE; Sardis)[147]:

οἱ τοῦ Διὸς θεραπευταὶ τῶν εἰ[ς] τὸ ἄδυτον εἰσπορευμένων καθιερώσαντες ἐστεφάνωσαν Σωκράτην Πολεμαίου Παρδαλαν τόν

πρῶτον τῆν πόλεως, διακείμενον ἐκ προγόνων πρὸς τὸ θεῖον εὐσεβῶς.

---

145. An overwhelming majority of almost seven hundred inscriptions compiled in Pilhofer's second volume on Philippi (*Philippi*) testifies to a particular fondness of the Philippians for honor and titles. In our previous discussion of voluntary associations at Philippi (ch. 4) we came across a number of such inscriptions in which private individuals and officials were praised for their deeds of benefaction. To cite just one example, an inscription sponsored by the devotees of Serapis and Isis honored Valerius Voltinia Priscus for his role in organizing the gladiatorial games. We noticed earlier that the inscription meticulously lists all the titles of the honoree: "decorated with the decurions' honor, a decurion, an eiranarch, a magistrate." A number of other examples pertinent to our case is supplied in an article by Hellerman, "Brothers and Friends in Philippi," 15-25, esp. 16-20.
146. Kloppenborg, "Churches and *Collegia*," 238.
147. *Sardis* 7.1 22.

[The members] of Zeus association who entered the shrine set up a crown on Socrates Pardalas, son of Polemaios, an outstanding citizen, who inherited the reverence toward the deity from his ancestors.

Inscription #2 (237 CE, Athens)[148]:

. . . ἐπειδὴ Σώφρων καλῶς καὶ φ[ιλ]οτίμως συνγήγαγε τὸν θίασον, ἐπέδωκεν δὲ καὶ στήλην ὥστε ἀνατεθῆναι εἰς τὸ ἱερὸν βουλόμενος αὔξειν τὸ κοινὸν ἐκ τῶν ἰδίων ὅπως ἂν οὖν ἐφάμιλλον εἶ τοῖς βουλομένοις εὐεργετεῖν τὸ κοινὸν εἰδόσιν ὅτι κομιοῦνται τὰς χάριτας... ἀγαθεῖ τύχει, δεδόχθ[α]ι τοῖς θιασώντας στεφανῶσαι τὸν ἀρχερα[ν]ιστὴν Σώφρονα θαλλοῦ στεφάνωι καὶ λημ[ν]ίσκωι...

. . . after Sofron out of his goodness and love for honor organized the association, and wishing to enhance the *koinon*, he, out of his own expense, erected the stele in the temple so that [his deed] will stir rivalry (ἐφάμιλλον) in those who would wish to patronize (εὐεργετεῖν) the *koinon* realizing that they will receive back gratitude (χάριτας) . . . for good fortune. It has been resolved by the members of association to crown the president Sofron with the wreath of palm leaves and ribbon . . .

Inscription #3 (178 CE, Athens)[149]:

ἀγαθεῖ τύχει. δεδόχθαι τοῖς ὀγρεῶσιν, ἐπαινέσαι Ἑρμαῖον Ἑρμογένου Παιονίδην καὶ στεφανῶσαι ἀρετῆς ἕνεκεν καὶ εὐσεβείας τῆς πρὸς τοὺς θοὺς καὶ κοινεῖ πρὸς τοὺς ὀργεῶνας, ὅπως ἂν ἐφάμιλλον εἶ καὶ τοῖς βουλομένοις φιλοτιμεῖσθαι εἰδότας ὅτι χάριτας ἀξίας κομιοῦνται.

---

148. *IG* 2.2 1297; cf. 1261, 1326; 1368; 2936.
149. *IG* 2.2 1327.

To good fortune. It has been decided by the members [of the association] to commend Hermaion Paionides, the son of Hermogenus and crown [him with crown] of excellence for his reverence to the gods and for retaining fellowship with the members [of the association], so that to stir rivalry in others who are after love of honor knowing that they will receive back gratitude [and] dignity.

All three inscriptions praise prominent members/patrons of the associations for their deeds of benefactions. Of particular interest is that in inscriptions #2 and #3 the benefactions are intentionally mentioned to stir jealousy (lit. to "produce rivalry"[150]) in other potential benefactors or in those who wanted to enhance their social status. Paul seems to combat the same tendency among the Philippians to act out "of selfish ambition or conceit" (Phil 2:3). On the contrary, in imitation of Christ he admonishes the believers "in humility [to] regard others as better than yourselves" (2:3). While the earthly benefactors were honored with crowns of olive and palm trees, the heavenly benefactor Jesus was honored with a crown of thorns. This thought might be in the background of Paul's usage of the στέφανός in 4:1, as he uses it of those who were willing to partake with him in Christ's sufferings (3:10).

In a kind of paradoxical fashion the zeal for honor produces the spirit of rivalry and competition, so that often "the dearest friends become the deadliest enemies."[151] As was stated in the previous section, internal rivalry and disunity threatened to disrupt the fellowship among believers at Philippi. Paul's language of doing something "out of selfish ambition and conceit" and of "seeking one's own interests" fits well with the context of interpersonal rivalry and disorderly behavior in voluntary associations. We may recall from our discussion in chapter 2 the "horses"[152] needed to restrain the disorderly in the Iobacchoi association from Athens, as well as the restrictions of the Lanuvium association against anyone who "speaks abusively of

---

150. Both inscriptions contain a reference to ἐφάμιλλος which indicates "an object of rivalry or contention" (LSJ 740).
151. The paraphrase of Cicero's dictum in *Amic.* 34.
152. *IG* 2.2 1368, line 145.

another or causes an uproar ... [or] uses any abusive or insolent language,"[153] and the similar regulation of the Zeus Hypsistos association from Egypt against anyone who "makes factions or leaves the brotherhood."[154]

It is my contention that the interpersonal rivalry among the Philippian Christians was not a matter of sporadic misbehavior by some eccentric individuals, but rather was fueled by the disagreement between the leading women of the church, namely by Euodia and Syntyche.[155] With the growing tendency to read the Corinthian internal conflict in terms of the competition between the wealthier members for the "privilege to patronize the church,"[156] the study of the Philippian patrons and their role in Paul's argument with the "enemies" should be given a new impetus. Previously we indicated that Paul's singling out the names of the two women in Philippians 4:2 does not make much sense unless they occupied some prominent place in the community.[157] In the Philippian context it is women of relative wealth and independence, like Euodia and Syntyche, who should be considered as the most likely candidates for being the patrons of the church.[158] Such patrons provided "not only a meeting place but also validity with authorities, a core group of family and slaves, hospitality for visitors and skills

---

153. *CIL* 14.2112, page 2, lines 25-28.

154. *PLond* 2193, lines 13-14.

155. Cf. David Black, "The bulk of the letter is directed toward solving the issue of disunity arising from the exigence reflected most clearly in 4:2-3" ("The Discourse Structure of Philippians: A Study in Textlinguistics," *NovT* 37 [1995]: 16). Cf. Luter: "The verses focusing on Euodia and Syntyche ... are the key to the disunity that had begun to trouble the church" ("Partnership in the Gospel," 413-14).

156. De Vos, *Church and Community Conflicts*, 221. Cf. also McLean: "The structured social relationships in a church such as Corinth, with its fictive kinship, probably facilitated opportunities for patronage, clientellism, employment and social and political mobility" ("Agrippinilla Inscription," 269).

157. As O'Brien contends, unless these women were of importance, "it is difficult to explain why their names were mentioned in a letter to be read publicly in church" (*Philippians*, 478).

158. Cf. Peterlin: "The two women were prosperous local Christian patronesses who opened their houses for local Christians and hosted the gatherings of house-congregations" (*Disunity in the Church*, 124). The supposition that Euodia and Syntyche were among the patrons of the church squares well with the practice within the religious association of the time (see our previous discussion in ch. 2), also with the evidence from other Pauline churches (Phoebe of Cenchrea being the most noticeable example), and with the fact that women at Philippi seem to have played a prominent role from the very beginning of the Christian community there (Acts 16).

in leadership."¹⁵⁹ The multiplicity of the Philippian leadership (ἐπισκόποις καὶ διακόνοις; Phil 1:1) might be an indication of the existence of several house-churches,¹⁶⁰ with Euodia and Syntyche hosting Christians at their homes for worship.¹⁶¹ The formation of Christianity under the umbrella of different households seems to have contributed to the complexity of the inter-group relationships and explains the intrinsic "proneness to division" within such groups.

"Separation from Christians of somewhat different background, views, and interests must have operated to prevent the growth of mutual understanding. Each group had its feelings of pride and prestige. Such a physically divided church tended almost inevitably to become a mentally divided church."¹⁶²

Although the context of Philippians 4:2-3 is quite terse, most scholars agree that "what we have here is not a personal quarrel between cantankerous old ladies, but rather a substantive division within the church leadership,"¹⁶³ in which case the disagreement between them might have had "disastrous repercussions for the unity of the church."¹⁶⁴ As we are going to argue in the next chapter this disagreement is directly related to the unresolved issue of the "enemies of the cross" (Phil 3:18). Paul's language of

---

159. Reumann, "Church Office," 87.
160. Peterlin, *Disunity in the Church*, 125.
161. Hawthorne, *Philippians*, 241. Actually it was Albert Klöpper who, as early as 1893, argued that Euodia and Syntyche represented two women in each of whose houses a separate congregation gathered for worship (*Der Brief des Apostel Paulus an die Philipper* [Berlin: G. Reimer, 1893]).
162. Filson, "Early House Churches," 110.
163. Silva, *Philippians*, 192. Cf. also Dahl, "Euodia and Syntyche," 7; Thomas, "The Place of Women," 118.
164. Garland, "The Composition and Unity," 173. The internal rivalry related to the disagreement between the leading women of the church is reminiscent of the rivalry among voluntary associations in trying to win the continuing support of a benefactor. Harland provides a number of relevant examples in his discussion of the Lepidus family, members of which were an object of rivalry between different associations in Sardis (*Associations*, 140-47). As we also noticed before, many of the honorary dedications had an implied pragmatic objective of stirring the rivalry among the potential benefactors or honor-loving members. A somewhat neutral statement about Socrates Pardalas from Sardis who "inherited the reverence toward the deity from his ancestors" (*Sardis* 7.1. 22) in fact fixes in stone the loyalty of this particular family to the association and expresses an implicit hope that that will be the case in the future.

enmity is an indication of the inter-group rivalry between Paul and his opponents which entices the Philippian believers into taking sides either with Paul or with his opponents. The reiterated character of Paul's admonition (3:18) signals that the issue remains an unresolved matter.

Conclusion

We have concluded our study of a possible role that voluntary associations played in the formation of the Christian community at Philippi. There is enough evidence to concur with J. Becker that Christian community in that city resembled "a private religious association in the form of the house church."[165]

In our analysis of the social context of Paul's ministry we came to the conclusion that it was in the context of the small group setting that his ministry took place. Both the Graeco-Roman household, as is illustrated by the conversion of Lydia's and the jailor's households, and the voluntary association, as can be seen in Paul's own practice of preaching while working as tentmaker, played its role in the early Christians' structuring of their communities. By assuming these models for their development Christians inherited their in-built "blessings" and "curses." On the one hand, the *oikos* immediately provided the stage for worship and instruction and, on the other, it clearly delineated the place and role of each member. As was indicated in our discussion, Christianity's struggle to overcome the patriarchal structures of the household never really succeeded. Our analysis of the social prosopography, elevated status of women, organizational structure, and other features pointed to a close resemblance between the Christian community and voluntary associations. We have noticed a significant role of women, especially in leadership at the church at Philippi, a feature which is consistent with the general trend within the civic cults of the time. In terms of organizational structure, the Philippian ἐπίσκοποι and διάκονοι are examples of the "local idiosyncrasy" of a church in its incipient stage of development. We argued that in the predominantly Gentile context of

---

165. Becker, "Paul and His Churches," 163.

Philippi, both terms most naturally were adopted from the terminology used in voluntary associations. Paul's terminology of friendship, honor and rivalry fits well within the context of voluntary associations of the time. The Philippians are his beloved friends who contrary to the conventions of the day are to seek honor through humility and self-denial. Paul's warnings against acting from "selfish ambition or conceit" or "seeking one's own interests" seem to strongly indicate that the bond of friendship is under the threat of being dissolved. As we are going to argue in the next chapter, one of the major reasons for the interpersonal rivalry was an unresolved issue of the "enemies of the cross."

CHAPTER 6

The Earthly *Politeuma* of the Enemies of the Cross and Paul's Vision of the *Politeuma* in Heaven (Phil 3:18-20)

This final chapter will consist of two major parts. In the first part we will argue that lexical and inscriptional studies of the word πολίτευμα allow us to locate Paul's opponents within the context of voluntary associations. This supposition will be further substantiated by references to the language of enmity and the polemical description of the opponents, both of which fit best the context of voluntary associations. In the second part we will consider Paul's counter-arguments against his opponents. Paul intentionally borrows the Hellenistic term πολίτευμα to argue his alternative vision of the πολίτευμα understood as a heavenly governing body. Certain features in the letter to the Philippians point to his opponents' involvement in emperor worship, which is for Paul a clear sign of the compromising of their loyalty to the κύριος and σωτήρ, Jesus. Paul insists that only the path of humility and self-denial will lead to the ultimate vindication of believers.

6.1 The Earthly Πολίτευμα of the Enemies of the Cross (Phil 3:18-20)

Philippians 3:18-20 is one of those peculiar Pauline texts which contains harsh criticism and a somewhat nasty characterization of his opponents:

For many (πολλοί) of whom I often told you, and even now am writing with tears, walk (περιπατοῦσιν) as the enemies of the cross of Christ: they walk to their final destruction, their god is the belly and their glory is in shameful things, their minds are earthly-bound. But our πολίτευμα is in heaven from where we expect the Lord Jesus Christ, who is our Savior.

In this part of the discussion we are going to argue that Paul's opponents in Philippians 3:18-20 are, in his eyes, a deviant group who, by, their membership in a πολίτευμα, understood as a local voluntary association, enjoyed a legitimate status within Graeco-Roman society and presented a tempting alternative to Paul's way of discipleship. We are going to build our argument on three factors:

a) First, lexical study of the word πολίτευμα (3:20) will show that it was one of the terms used for voluntary associations;

b) Second, structural analysis of Paul's argument in Philippians 1:27-4:3 will lead us to the conclusion that the "different thinking" (3:15) among the leaders of the church was related to the different "walk" of the opponents (3:18). Paul's language of enmity (3:18) fits well with Graeco-Roman conventions and the context of inter-group rivalry which existed between voluntary associations; and

c) Third, study of Paul's intentionally exaggerated portrayal of the opponents' socializing activities (3:18-19) will show that it best fits the description of the social activities within voluntary associations. Intrinsically connected with such activities were the issues of the religious devotion and political loyalty.

6.1.1 What is the Πολίτευμα of Phil 3:20?
In Philippians 3:20 we encounter the word πολίτευμα: "But our πολίτευμα is in heaven from where we expect the Lord Jesus Christ, who is our Savior." As was already suggested in the Introduction, the emphatic position of the pronoun ἡμῶν in 3:20 (ἡμῶν γὰρ τὸ πολίτευμα ἐν οὐρανοῖς ὑπάρχει) "shows that those described are emphatically contrasted with the opponents

of the preceding verse."¹ In his analysis of the phrase Paul Böttger pioneered a proposal that πολίτευμα came from the opponents' vocabulary, which Paul appropriated for his own use.² In Paul's statement, "but *our* πολίτευμα is in heaven," he implicitly but clearly juxtaposes "our πολίτευμα" to "their πολίτευμα." Being one of Paul's *hapax legomenon*, the definition of πολίτευμα is destined to remain a scholarly riddle, as is well expressed in a modern commentary: "[Πολίτευμα] is a technical term of some sort."³ So what is a πολίτευμα?

6.1.1.1 Lexical and Inscriptional Study

Πολίτευμα is an important word with multiple meanings which could be viewed as derived from the verb πολιτεύειν, "to be a citizen," or πολιτεύεσθαι, "to fulfill duties of a citizen, to practice politics" (cf. Phil 1:27). Thus, πολίτευμα implies the idea of "political action."⁴ Gert Lüderitz thus summarizes the meaning of the word: "Πολίτευμα as a technical term for an institution within a *polis* stands for the ruling class as a sovereign body with specific rights, voting procedures, etc."⁵ Πολίτευμα was applied to a) the governing body within a Greek *polis*; and b) other social groups within a *polis*, including voluntary associations.⁶

---

1. O'Brien, *Philippians*, 459. Cf. Fee, *Philippians*, 378, n.14: "'Our' stands in the emphatic first position, intending the strongest kind of contrast to 'them.'" The emphatic ἡμῶν "is intended to provide a contrast with "the enemies'" frame of mind," (Silva, *Philippians*, 183).
2. Böttger, "Eschatologische Existenz," 259. That Paul borrows at times his opponents' terminology to argue his case is a well established fact. In this same chapter of Philippians, for example, he uses a derogative Jewish word κύνας to argue against the Judaizers' attempts to subvert the Philippian Christians. See also an important contribution on the πολίτευμα terminology in Andrew T. Lincoln, *Paradise Now and Not Yet: Studies in the Role of the Heavenly Dimension in Paul's Thought with Special Reference to His Eschatology* (Cambridge: Cambridge University Press, 1981), 97-100.
3. Thurston et al., *Philippians*, 133.
4. Thus Böttger, "Eschatologische Existenz," 245. This is the meaning πολίτευμα has in Isocr. 7.78 and in Dem. 18.122; 18.109; 18.110; 22.47. Demosthenes also uses the word with a slightly different meaning: "political measures" (8.72; 18.108), "rule" (17.7), "public affairs" (18.257), "public performance" (26.16), and "decree" (18.302). For the citations see Appendix 3.
5. Lüderitz, "What is Politeuma?" 187-88.
6. Lüderitz, "What is Politeuma?" 185-89.

The concept of πολίτευμα as a governing body within a *polis* is found in Aristotle's tractate on *Politics*, where it is applied, first of all, to the wielders of power, e.g., the government or administration of a *polis*.[7] Πολίτευμα also can refer to the power invested in a written document, e.g., a constitution. In one of his central dictums Aristotle equates the government and the constitution: "for the government (τὸ πολίτευμα) is . . . supreme over the state (τῆς πόλεως) and the constitution is the government (πολίτευμα δ' ἐστὶν ἡ πολιτεία)."[8] Thus both, the constitution and the government operate on the basis of delegated authority and have the power to influence the life of the community at large. In a similar way, Aristotle uses πολίτευμα as a reference to "governing class, assembly,"[9] which utilizes the right to vote and thus determine the politics of the city.

Josephus also manifests the Aristotelian usage of πολίτευμα as "government." A clear case of this usage is found in *Against Apion* where he elaborates on different forms of governments: "Some legislators have permitted their governments (τῶν πολιτευμάτων) to be under monarchies, others put them under oligarchies, and others under a republican form . . . But our legislator had no regard to any of these forms, but he ordained our government (τὸ πολίτευμα) to be . . . a theocracy."[10] Josephus also uses πολίτευμα as an equivalent of the Jewish commonwealth or community (e.g., *Ant.* 1.5). What is peculiar for Josephus is the way he interweaves the law and the life of the community. As a constitution for Greeks predisposed the inner dynamics of the life of the *polis*, so for Josephus it was the law which defined the life of the Jewish πολίτευμα. In *Against Apion* he is confident that nothing can supersede the Jewish law which was the expression of the will of God. Any alteration of this law would lead to a change in the Jewish πολίτευμα (*C. Ap.* 2.184).

---

7. Arist. *Pol.* 3.1278b (2); 1279a (2); 3.1283b (2); 3.1293a (2); 5.1302b; 5.1305b; 5.1306a; 5.1308a; 6.1321a; 7.1332b. For the citations see Appendix 3.
8. Arist. *Pol.* 3.1278b.
9. Arist. *Pol.* 4.1297; 5.1308a; 6.1321a. Cf. his use of the word with the meaning "political power" (*Pol.* 5.1301b) and "state" (*Pol.* 3.1283b; 5.1303b). See Appendix 3.
10. Jos. *C. Ap.* 2.164-165, cf. *Ant.* 1.13. See Appendix 3.

Philo likewise uses the word πολίτευμα at least three times in his tractates.[11] Although, as Böttger remarks, Philo transfers the meaning of πολίτευμα to the metaphysical level and thus "geht der konkret politische Sinn des Wortes verloren,"[12] he does it in full compliance with the Hellenic philosophical heritage. In spite of Philo's attempts to spiritualize the concept, the notion of πολίτευμα as some powerful entity (state, commonwealth, community) which affects and influences the lives of the individuals remains intact.

Most importantly for our present discussion is that πολίτευμα was used for the designation of voluntary associations. Gert Lüderitz argues that πολίτευμα "can also be applied to festival associations of women, a cult society, a club of soldiers, association of citizens from the same city living abroad, and ethnic communities."[13] Thus, there is an inscription found on a stele in Philadelphia (dated 93 CE) which contains the dedication to the emperor Domitian on behalf of the πολίτευμα of the supreme goddess of Sachypsis:

Ὑπὲρ Αὐτοκράτορος Καίσαρος [Δομιτιανοῦ] Σεβαστοῦ Γερμανικοῦ τόπος πολιτεύματος Ἀρθώτου μεγάλου μακαρίτου θεᾶς μεγίστης Σαχύψεως ἀνοικοδομήθη ἐπὶ Πετρωνίου Σεκούνδου ἐπάρχου Αἰγύπτου διὰ Ἄβδωνος προστάτου Πρώταρχος ἔγραψεν ἐπ' ἀγαθῶΙ |L| ιβ ν, Φαρμοῦθι ιβ ν.

For the Imperator Caesar Domitianus Augustus Germanicus, the area of the *politeuma* of the blessed Harthotes the Great of the supreme goddess Sachypsis has been rebuilt in the time of the praefectus Aegypti Petronius Secundus by Abdon, chairman. Written by Protarchos. Fortune year 12, 12ᵗʰ Pharmuthi.[14]

---

11. Cf. *Opif.* 143-44; *Ios.* 69; *Agr.* 81. See Appendix 3.
12. Böttger, "Eschatologische Existenz," 252.
13. Gerd Lüderitz, „What Is Politeuma?" in *Studies in Early Jewish Epigraphy* (ed J. W. van Henten and Pieter Willem van der Horst; Leiden: Brill, 1994), 189. Cf. Ascough, "Voluntary Associations," 14.
14. *SIG* 3.1107, cited with translation in Lüderitz, "What Is Politeuma?" 190-91.

This seems to be a clear example of πολίτευμα being used of a cult association in Egypt. It was presided over by a προστάτης Abdon, a common title for the leading officer of guilds and clubs. The association was named after Harthotes the Great, possibly its founder or benefactor. Because of its location in the temple of Sachypsis/Isis, the πολίτευμα also bore the name of this goddess. The dedication of the inscription to Caesar Domitianus illustrates the combination of religious devotion to Sachypsis with political loyalty to the emperor.

A dedicatory inscription (dated 112/11 or 76/5 BCE) mentions a πολίτευμα of soldiers stationed in Alexandria:

> Διὶ Σωτῆρι καὶ Ἥραι Τέλειαι τὸ πολίτευμα τῶν ἐν Ἀλεξανδρείαι φερομένων στρατιωτῶν, ὧν προστάτης Διονύσιος Κάλλωνος γραμματεὺς δὲ Φίλιππος Φιλίππου κτίσται, εὐχὴν. L σ v.

> To Zeus Soter and Hera Teleia, the *politeuma* of the soldiers brought to Alexandria, their chairman Dionysios of Callon and secretary Philippos of Philippos, the founders, ex voto, year 6.[15]

This case of the πολίτευμα used of the association of soldiers is of interest because it enhances the chances of a voluntary association in Philippi using the same designation. Although there were no troops in active service deployed in Philippi, the word πολίτευμα undoubtedly had currency among former servicemen. Notice also the reference to Zeus as σώτηρ (cf. Jesus as σώτηρ in Phil 3:20), a feature which will be the subject of future discussion.

Among the 400 inscriptions (dated from 200 BCE to 300 CE) found at the sight of the Zeus Panamaros temple complex near Stratomicaea, three texts mention the πολίτευμα of the women:

---

15. *SEG* 20.499, cited with translation in Lüderitz, "What Is Politeuma?" 192-93.

Inscription #1[16]:

Ἱερεὺς ἐν Ἡρ[αίοις] Μένιππος Λέοντος [καθ' ὑ]οθεσίαν δὲ Εἰροκλέο[υς (Κωραζεὺς)] Ἱέρηα Παπιαινὰ Μενεσθεώς [...] ἐκάλεσεν δὲ καὶ τὸ πολ[εί]τευμα τῶν γυνα[ι]κῶν.

The priest in the [year] of the Hera festival Menippos Leontos for the adoption of Heirokleus Korazeus [and] the priestess Papiaina Menestheos [...] invited also the *politeuma* of women.

Inscription #2[17]:

ὑπ[εισ]δεξάμενος δὲ καὶ τὸ πολείτευμα τῶν γυναικῶν ἐν τοῖς Ἡραίοις....

Having invited also the *politeuma* of women [to take part] in the Hera festival.

Inscription #3[18]:

[. . .] [τὸ Ἥ]ραιον πολυ[τελῶς κ]αλέσας τὸ πολεί[τευ]μα τῶν γυναικῶν, [δοὺς δὲ] ἑκάστῃ μετὰ τῶν λ[οιπ]ῶν τῶν ἐξ ἔθους [ἀ]νὰ (δηναρίους) α ν, ὁμοίως καὶ τ[αῖς] σὺν ἀνδράσιν ἀν[αβᾶσιν εἰς τὴ]ν π[όλ]ιν ἐν τοπίο[ις.

The generous organizers of the Hera festival having invited the *politeuma* of women, gave to the rest of the women each one denarius, as well to those who came to the city with their husbands.

---

16. Gaston Deschamps and Georges Cousin, "Inscriptions du temple de Zeus Panamaros," *BCH* 15 (1891): 169-209 (181 [#123], 204-6 [#145]); G. Cousin, "Inscriptions du sanctuaire de Zeus Panamaros," *BCH* 28 (1904): 20-53 (40 [#23]). Cited in Lüderitz, "What Is Politeuma?" 189-90.
17. Deschamps and Cousin, "Inscriptions," 204-6 [#145]). Cited in Lüderitz, "What Is Politeuma?" 190.
18. Cited in Lüderitz, "What Is Politeuma?" 190.

As Lüderitz explains, τὸ πολείτευμα τῶν γυναικῶν in these three inscriptions refers to a temporary association of women which functioned every second year during the Hera festival.[19] Used of an association of women, πολίτευμα possibly was a familiar term in Philippi given the active role that women played in the religious life of the city.

Concluding this part of the discussion I would like to submit that both meanings of πολίτευμα as a "governing body" and "voluntary association" are relevant for our understanding of Philippians 3:20. By borrowing the word from his opponents who pride themselves on belonging to a local πολίτευμα (voluntary association), Paul argues for the existence of the heavenly πολίτευμα (governing body) in allegiance to which Christians live on earth. An extended paraphrase of Philippians 3:20 would sound something like this:

> While *they* [the "enemies of the cross of Christ"] pride themselves on belonging to a local πολίτευμα (voluntary association), *our* πολίτευμα is of a different sort; it is our governing body in heaven in allegiance to which we, as Christians, live on Earth.

We are going to further elaborate on this in the coming discussion.

6.1.1.2 English Translations of Πολίτευμα

With the results of our lexical and inscriptional studies in mind, I would like to offer some critical remarks on some of the contemporary translations of the word πολίτευμα.

a) πολίτευμα as "citizenship"

Almost all of the English sources studied, after supplying the list of possible meanings of πολίτευμα, prefer "citizenship" as the most appropriate translation.[20] Gordon Fee, for example, prefers this translation, stating at the same time that: "The concept of 'citizenship' itself is poorly attested

---

19. Lüderitz, "What Is Politeuma?" 189–90.
20. See NRSV, NIV, NASB, NAB, WBC.

[for πολίτευμα]."²¹ My own study of about 150 cases of πολίτευμα in the Graeco-Roman and Jewish literary sources basically confirms this conclusion.²² "Citizenship" is indeed poorly attested – if attested at all – as the meaning of πολίτευμα in ancient literature. A probable explanation for the frequently cited meaning "citizenship" is found in the commentary by Thurston and Ryan: "Paul has apparently chosen it [πολίτευμα] here [3:20] to recall 1:27 and the high status of Philippi as governed by the Roman law."²³ In other words, they seem to be saying that "citizenship" is the most appropriate translation of πολίτευμα in view of Paul's previous admonition "to be good citizens" (1:27), and also in view of Philippi having been a Roman colony where citizenship was a coveted dream for many. The translation of πολίτευμα as "citizenship," in my opinion, takes the contrast between "their" and "our" πολίτευμα down a false route. As we are going to argue further, if Paul indeed borrows the term from those who prided themselves in belonging to a local guild (πολίτευμα), it is unlikely that citizenship was that which constituted the essence of their pride. Paul's disagreement with the "enemies" is not about citizenship but rather about belonging to a different πολίτευμα.

b) πολίτευμα as "homeland"
The meaning of πολίτευμα as "homeland" or "dwelling place" is poorly attested in English translations.²⁴ Yet this way of defining it fits with the theme of Christians as sojourners on their way to the heavenly country, attested elsewhere in the NT. For example:

> All of these died in faith without having received the promises, but from a distance they saw and greeted them. They confessed that they were strangers and foreigners on the earth, for people who speak in this way make it clear that they are seeking a homeland. If they had been thinking of the land that they had

---

21. Fee, *Philippians*, 378, n.17.
22. See Appendix 3.
23. Thurston et al., *Philippians*, 133.
24. But see, e.g., NJB, RST.

left behind, they would have had opportunity to return. But as it is, they desire a better country, that is, a heavenly one. Therefore God is not ashamed to be called their God; indeed, he has prepared a city for them. (Heb 11:13-16; NRSV)

There is indeed the tempting possibility of reading Philippians 3:20 in light of this passage, touched by Platonic philosophy, in Hebrews.[25] We find a modern example of this understanding in the Russian Synodal translation, which reads: "Наше же жительство - на небесах (our dwelling place is in heaven)" – which clearly points to "heaven" as the place of believers' habitation.[26] There is in Paul, however, no dichotomy between the "foreign land" (meaning "earth") and the "native land" (meaning "heaven") to which the Christian longs to return. In Philippians 3:20 Paul reminds the believers of the heavenly πολίτευμα *from where* they are to expect their Lord and Savior; i.e., the idea is of the leader *coming down from*, and not the believers' *going up to*, heaven.[27] It is not escape from the current evil order but the transformation of the corrupted creation which is in Paul's agenda.

c) πολίτευμα as "colony"

A. Klijn and others argue that πολίτευμα means "colony," understood as "a group of foreigners living abroad, but privileged to form a separate

---

[25]. Cf. the remarkable thematic parallels in Philo: "For this reason all the wise men mentioned in the books of Moses are represented as sojourners, for their souls are sent down from heaven upon earth as to a colony (ἀποικία); and on account of their fondness for contemplation, and their love of learning, they are accustomed to migrate to behold all the mortal objects of the outward senses by their means, they then subsequently return back from thence to the place from which they set out at first, looking upon the heavenly country (πατρίς) in which they have the rights of citizens (πολιτεύω) as their native land (μητρόπολις), and as the earthly abode in which they dwell for a while as in a foreign land" (*Conf.* 4.77-78).

[26]. It is even more important to realize the crucial role that this verse continues to play in the Russian evangelical (Protestant) eschatology. For the community which from the very beginning was a marginalized and often persecuted minority this verse laid a solid foundation for the escapist type of theology which is well reflected especially in worship songs. "This world is not my mother country," is still occasionally sung in many Russian churches. For many it is based on a "solid scriptural foundation" whereas in a more careful examination Philo's handwriting can be discerned.

[27]. Cf. the vision of the heavenly city coming down to earth in Rev 21:2.

community with its own leaders and laws."[28] This is indeed another tempting solution because of the suggestive parallel between Philippi as a colony of Rome and the Christian community as a heavenly colony. The Philippian believers then would constitute a πολίτευμα, a community of resident aliens living in subjection to a different authority. This reading, however, is problematic on two counts. First of all, the long-lived scholarly assumption that πολίτευμα was used of "a recognized, formally constituted corporation of aliens enjoying the right of domicile in a foreign city and forming a separate, semiautonomous civic body, a city within the city"[29] is now critically undermined.[30] An instrumental role here belongs to G. Lüderitz, whose study of the papyrological and epigraphic materials led him to the conclusion that there was no "fundamental difference between *politeumata* and other associations."[31] By that he means that ethnic πολιτεύματα did exist but functioned no differently than any other type of voluntary association of the time.

Second, in Philippians 3:20 Paul does not say, "We are a πολίτευμα of heaven," but rather "Our πολίτευμα is in heaven." As we are going to argue further, Paul, by borrowing the term from his opponents, uses it in the sense of a governing body, and this governing body is in heaven. The analogy with the colony is appropriate only if we do not equate πολίτευμα with "colony." As the city of Philippi was the colony of Rome and thus Rome was the Philippians' governing body (πολίτευμα)[32] so the Christian community

---

28. A. Klijn, "Paul's Opponents in Philippians iii," *NovT* 7 (1964): 283. Cf. Philo, *Conf.* 4.77.

29. M. Smallwood, *The Jews under Roman Rule: From Pompey to Diocletian* (Leiden: Brill, 1976), 225.

30. Meeks, "Artificial Aliens," 137. See also the discussion in John Barclay, *Jews in the Mediterranean Diaspora: From Alexander to Trajan (323 BCE–117 CE)* (Edinburgh: T&T Clark, 1996), 63-65; and M. Zetterholm, *The Formation of Christianity in Antioch: A Social-Scientific Approach to the Separation between Judaism and Christianity* (London: Routledge, 2003), 36-37.

31. Lüderitz, "What Is Politeuma?" 203.

32. See Beare, *Philippians*, 136: "'[Philippi was] an outpost governed by the laws of the homeland [Rome] and attached to it by the deepest sentiments of loyalty." Unfortunately Cotter misses this point, arguing that Paul "is not contrasting heaven with Rome, because the home city of the Philippians is Philippi itself" ("Our Politeuma," 104). In this rendering the "Roman connection" which is further suggested in Paul's implied contrast between the emperor and Christ is lost.

in a sense is a "colony" which is governed by the heavenly πολίτευμα. If we take the heavenly πολίτευμα to be contrasted to that of the "enemies," the meaning "colony" does not make sense. Paul is not saying that Christians do not consider themselves part of the Roman colony (while the "enemies" do). Instead, they have a different governing authority over them.

d) πολίτευμα as a colony of the Jews

This case is actually a variation on the meaning of πολίτευμα just discussed, yet this time understood specifically as a Jewish πολίτευμα. M. Tellbe and others argue that Christians in Philippi, in view of the coming persecution (1:29-30), allegedly were seeking to hide under the protective umbrella of the Jewish πολιτεύμα, a well-known phenomenon in diaspora Judaism.[33] In view of G. Lüderitz' analysis, an understanding of a Jewish (or any other ethnic) πολίτευμα as a separate, semiautonomous civic body is no longer viable.[34] Also, in a city which exhibits clear signs of anti-Jewish bias,[35] it is highly unlikely that a group of (uncircumcised!) Gentiles would have claimed the protection of the Jewish πολίτευμα.

---

33. Mikael Tellbe, "The Sociological Factors behind Philippians 3:1-11 and the Conflict at Philippi," *JSNT* 55 (1994): 97-121, esp. 116-19. Cf. Pilhofer, *Philippi*, 1:132-34; Demetrius Williams, *Enemies of the Cross of Christ: The Terminology of the Cross and Conflict in Philippians* (JSNTSS 223; London: Sheffield Academic Press, 2002), 230.

34. Lüderitz suggests that the idea of the πολιτεύμα as a formally recognized body of alien residents belonged to a French scholar Perdrizet who considered πολίτευμα to have been a public institution as opposed to a privately constituted κοινόν. It was also "co-sponsored" by a reference to πρεσβύτεροι τῶν ἀπὸ τοῦ πολιτεύματος in the letter to Aristeas (1.310) which was understood as referring to the Jewish πολιτεύμα in Alexandria. Lüderitz argues, however, that if πολίτευμα "designates the sovereign body of a city or a state or government, there is usually no further determiner; if on the other hand it stands for a group of aliens or some other association, it is normally explicitly said which association is meant . . . otherwise the wording would not have been understandable, also in his [Aristeas'] time" ("What Is Politeuma?" 207, 208). So what is most probably meant in the letter is the reference to the elders of Alexandria's *polis* (πολίτευμα τῶν Ἀλεξανδρείων is attested in *CPJ* 2.150) who were present among others at the time of reading the Septuagint.

35. One of the possible signs of anti-Jewish sentiment is heard in the charge against Paul: "These men *being Jews* advocate customs which are inappropriate for us *Romans* to accept or observe" (Acts 16:20-21; emphasis added).

e) πολίτευμα as "veteran association"

In view of the fact that πολίτευμα was used of associations of soldiers the hypothesis that veteran associations might have been known in Philippi under that name deserves our consideration.[36] As Lawrence Keppie testifies, "veterans preserved some form of association after settlement, which commemorated their common origin and past successes."[37] Although the earliest inscriptions commemorating *collegia veteranorum* are attested in the 2nd–3d century CE, the origins of these associations go back to the Augustan age.[38] Whereas Rome was quite suspicious of the proliferation of thousands of voluntary associations in fear of sedition, at the same time it was keenly interested in "associations of privileged groups such as officers and the personnel assigned to special duties."[39] If, as we are going to argue, the main issue between Paul and the "enemies" was their allegiance to Rome, where could better candidates be found than among the veterans of war? Such veteran associations undoubtedly did exist in Philippi for the simple reason that they were "patterned after the regular burial societies [which] ensured their members an honorable interment."[40] In other words, somebody had to take care of the deceased veterans.

The question is not whether such associations were present at Philippi, but rather whether πολίτευμα understood as veteran association fits the Philippian context. If our previous reconstruction of the social outlook is correct, then it is doubtful whether there were many converts to Christianity among the settled veterans at Philippi. Even if there were some Roman citizens with a military past, it would be quite unrealistic to expect a significant number of them.

---

36. Cf. Jerry L. Sumney: "Such [veteran] associations were present and well-known in Philippi" (*Philippians: A Greek Student's Intermediate Reader* [Peabody, Ma.: Hendrickson Publishers, 2007], 94). Unfortunately, the author does not provide any relevant references.
37. Keppie, *Veteran Settlement*, 110. Cf. Michael Ginsburg: "Upon the completion of his service a veteran had the right to join one of the many *collegia veteranorum*" ("Roman Military Clubs and Their Social Functions," *TAPA* 71 [1940]: 150); also George Stevenson H. and Andrew W. Lintott: "Many clubs of *iuvenes* existed mainly for sport, and associations were formed among ex-service men (*veterani*)" in "Clubs, Roman," in *OCD*, 352. See also John B. Campbell, "Veterans," in *OCD*, 1592.
38. Keppie, *Veteran Settlement*, 110.
39. Ginsburg, "Roman Military Clubs," 150.
40. Ginsburg, "Roman Military Clubs," 150.

f) πολίτευμα as "voluntary association"

It is our contention that in the context of Philippians 3:18-20 πολίτευμα best fits the definition of "voluntary association." In favor of this supposition one should include, first of all, the presence of such associations at Philippi (ch. 4) and their influence on the formation of the Christian community in that city. We have argued (ch. 5) that several features, like social prosopography, organizational structure, and inner group dynamics (as seen in the terminology of friendship and rivalry), point to striking similarities between the Christian *ekklēsia* and voluntary associations.

Second, the supposition will be further substantiated by the analysis of Paul's description of the opponents in Philippians 3:18-19. We are going to argue that Paul's polemical description of the opponents best fits the socializing practices within voluntary associations. As was argued previously, the appropriation of Christianity at Philippi and other cities took place within the context of a small-group setting (household and/or artisan's workshop). Lydia's household/workshop may serve as an example of this. We have also argued that conversion to Christianity within the Graeco-Roman context often involved reasons other than ideological commitment to Christ. Following N. Taylor we pointed out that in conversion to Christianity "the abandonment of previous beliefs, practices and social relationships varied."[41] In the pervasive syncretistic atmosphere of the Graeco-Roman world, appropriation of Christ as a cultic deity was not a problem, but an exclusive religious commitment was. There are reasons to believe that at Philippi we are dealing with a deviant group of believers who compromised their commitment to Christ by their continual commitment to Caesar. As we are going to argue, Paul's characterization of Christ as κύριος and σωτήρ brings Christian and imperial discourses into polemical confrontation, for the same titles were also used in Nero's characterization. As the epigraphic evidence from Philippi (ch. 4) shows, the imperial cult took firm root within the religious practices of various associations. In this clearly pro-Roman city, veneration of Caesar was considered an appropriate means of expressing gratitude for the benefits of the *Pax Romana*. Membership within local πολιτεύματα would have granted an obvious advantage to their adherents,

---

41. Taylor, "Social Nature," 136.

for such membership would have legitimized their existence within the Graeco-Roman political universe and exempted them from the prospects of social ostracism.

Taking on the opponents' terminology Paul capitalizes on the metaphorical meaning of the πολίτευμα as the "governing authority" within a *polis*. In effect he is saying to the opponents: "While you structure your life in accordance to the earthly πολίτευμα, we have a governing body of a different sort, and it is the πολίτευμα in heaven!"

6.1.2 The Alluring Walk of the "Enemies" (Phil 3:18)

Philippians 3:18 introduces the theme of the "enemies of the cross" who, precisely because they are enemies of the cross, are Paul's opponents: "For many (πολλοί) of whom I often told you, and even now am writing with tears, walk (περιπατοῦσιν) as the enemies of the cross of Christ." The difficulty in the identification of these opponents proceeds from the fact that indeed "nothing in the letter has quite prepared us"[42] for this task. Quite obviously vv. 18-20 are set in contrast to the preceding verse 17 where Paul admonishes the believers to "join in imitating [him]... and [others] who "walk" (περιπατοῦντας) according to the example you have in us." Paul admonishes the Philippians to follow his positive example because, as he regretfully states, there are those who by their mischievous behavior exert a negative influence.

In Graeco-Roman literature the language of enmity to which Paul resorts in Philippians 3:18 was often used in the context of competitive social relations.[43] Following Plato, "benefiting friends and harming enemies" was considered one of the virtues of a leading man.[44] With regard to personal enemies, Isocrates gives prudent advice: ignore them, they are not worthy

---

42. Fee, *Philippians*, 367.
43. David E. Fredrickson, "Envious Enemies of the Cross of Christ (Philippians 3:18)," *WW* 28 (2008): 22-28; Vasiliki Limberis, "The Eyes Infected by Evil: Basil of Caesarea's Homily on Envy," *HTR* 84 (1991): 163-84.
44. Plato, *Menex.* 71. From his own words Plato inherited the maxim from Socrates: "Finally, Socrates, I put these questions to you yourself also, and you told me that it belonged to justice to injure one's enemies and to do well to one's friends "(Plat. *Cleit.* 410). Cf. also Xen. *Cyr.* 1.4.13.

of your attention.[45] Aristotle likewise concurs that the "great-souled man" should not speak evil "even of his enemies" except "when he deliberately intends to give offence."[46] It looks like that was just the case with Paul: in Philippians 3:18-20 he is on the offensive against his opponents.

Another noticeable feature of Graeco-Roman conventions is that the language of enmity was often connected or contrasted with the language of friendship. In fact, there is a close connection between the two: would-be friends could become enemies and vice versa. A fifth century BCE historian Andocides suggests that, "if [friends] do not identify their interests as individuals with yours as a community, they can only be public enemies."[47] People who do not take care of their community take sides with the real enemies of the city: "It is impossible to defeat the enemies of our city until you have chastised those who within our very walls make themselves their servants."[48] The *topos* of the antithetical relationship between "enemy" and "friend" is corroborated by an ancient grammarian, Ammonius Grammaticus (1st – 2nd century CE), who suggests "ἐχθρός is one who has been φίλος, but is now alienated."[49] Moreover, it was known as early as the 8th century BCE that enmity and envy were often provoked by the competitive relationships between people of the same trade or craftsmanship.[50] An important point here is that rivalry is often sparked between two or more parties that are keenly interested in triumphing over another.

The inter-group competition, although rarely expressed in explicit terms, was a well-known phenomenon among voluntary associations. It was not uncommon for members of associations to claim their superiority over others, as suggested, for example, in the by-laws of the Iobacchoi association

---

45. "Should I turn upon my enemies and denounce those who are accustomed always to speak falsely of me and do not scruple to say things which are repugnant to my nature? But if I showed that I took them seriously and wasted many words on men whom no one conceives to be worthy of notice I should justly be regarded as a simpleton" (Isoc. 12. 22).
46. Aristotle, *Nic. Eth.* 4.3.31.
47. Andocides, 2.3.
48. Demosthenes, 9.53.
49. LSJ, 748.
50. Cf. Hesiod: ". . . potter is angry with potter, and craftsman with craftsman, and beggar is jealous of beggar, and minstrel of minstrel" (*Op.*25-26). Similarly Dio Chrysostom contends that it is not right "for a craftsman to be jealous or angry because of his craft, whether it was blacksmith against blacksmith or joiner against joiner" (*Or.* 77/78. 13).

from Athens: "Now we are the best (πρῶτοι) of all Bacchic societies!"[51] Or sometimes a similar claim was made with regard to the superiority of the worshiped deity: "Mankind exceptionally makes this god [Serapis] alone a full partner in their sacrifices . . . so that while different gods contribute to different banquets, he is the universal contributor to all banquets."[52]

Another effective way for the members of associations to ensure their superiority was to pride themselves in having an influential official as their benevolent patron. We may recall (see ch. 4) the two honorary inscriptions by the Serapis worshipers at Philippi addressed to Quintius Flavius Hermadion and to his son for their benefaction. As was indicated earlier, honorary inscriptions were a shrewd way to secure the benevolence of several generations of donors. Sometimes the beneficiaries were not shy in stating explicitly their objective to "stir rivalry"[53] among the potential patrons or prospective members. Membership in more than one association also "stirred" rivalry between different groups for the right to be lawful guardians of the bequest.[54] Still other associations, like the guild of Zeus Hypsistos from Egypt, intentionally guarded themselves from those who "make factions or leave the brotherhood."[55]

The language of enmity in Philippians 3:18-20 fits well the Graeco-Roman conventions of inter-group rivalry. There are good reasons to believe that Paul's opponents are former friends now turned enemies. Paul's words "of whom I *often* told you now am writing *even* with tears" (3:18) suggest that he knows at least some of them personally; otherwise it would be difficult to explain his emotional state. The reiterated character of Paul's

---

51. *IG* 2.2 1368, lines 26-27.
52. Aristotle, *Or.* 45. 27.
53. *IG* 2.2 1297; 1327 (cited in ch. 5).
54. This was evidenced in the case of Aurelius Zipuron and his wife Valeria Montana from Philippi, who stipulated in their bequest that "if they [members of the association of the god Souregethes] do not light [an offering] they should give double of the amount written above to the members of Heros association" (Pilhofer, *Philippi*, 2:134-35 [134/G441]).
55. *PLond* 2193, lines 13-14.

admonition speaks in favor of the opponents' proximity[56] to the congregation and their ability to exert influence on the believers in Philippi.[57]

Likewise, it is doubtful whether Paul would have wept over the fate of non-believers.[58] The "enemies" here are not "enemies of Christ," but rather "enemies of the cross." For Paul, the cross seems to have been the central, defining symbol in reference to which everything stands or falls. Thus in 1 Corinthians he combats the "wise," the "powerful," and those of "noble birth" with the message of the "foolishness of the cross" (1 Cor 1:17-31). Likewise, in Galatians he confronts those who make circumcision a matter of boasting (Gal 6:12-13), whereas for Paul the only thing worthy of boasting in is the "cross of our Lord Jesus Christ, by which the world has been crucified to me, and I to the world" (Gal 6:14). In the Philippian context, with its central example of Christ's humility and subsequent death on the cross (2:6-11), an "enemy of the cross" by implication would be considered anyone who rejects this example of humility. To be sure, such humility led to Christ' death and suffering. But for Paul, suffering with Christ is part and parcel of discipleship, not a matter of choice (1:29).

I submit that the polemics in Philippians 3:18-20 testifies to a competitive kind of relationship between Paul and his opponents.[59] That Paul's success could provoke rivalry is clear from Philippians 1:15-17. The situation described in Philippians 3:18-20 seems to be different, for the rhetoric of the passage does not put Paul on the winning side. Paul's words ("of whom

---

56. Cf. Bockmuehl: "...they are too close to the church for Paul to adopt a detached frame of mind" (*Philippians*, 230); also Sandnes: "Paul is not talking about a distant or remote challenge, but something visible to his addressees. Their presence has caused Paul's weeping, which suggests that they are insiders" (*Belly and Body*, 144). The limited information in Philippians, in my view, does not warrant the assumption that "their field activity is not limited to Philippi and they are to be found at work in one guise or another in several churches founded by the apostle" (Collange, *Philippians*, 136-37). This assumption could be sustained only by reading the opponents' identity from other contexts into the Philippian situation.

57. Cf. Jewett: "[A] portion of the congregation was apparently unwilling to view them as heretics, or Paul's warnings would have been unnecessary" ("Conflicting Movements," 377).

58. Cf. Fowl: "These are people who bear the name "Christian" yet are the enemies of the cross of Christ" (*Philippians*, 170); also Kennedy: "Plainly they were persons inside the Christian Church" (*Philippians*, 461).

59. Cf. Fredrickson: "From the ancient perspective, . . . Paul could only call enemies those who share in his kind of work" ("Envious Enemies," 27).

I *often* told you," 3:18) suggest that the opponents' position persisted for some time and in time became entangled in inter-church politics.[60] The lack of response to Paul's previous warning – apparent from the fact that he has to come back to this issue – suggests that at least some believers at Philippi remained unpersuaded by Paul. What makes it especially a serious matter is that the opponents' position had a negative impact on the leadership ranks of the church.

6.1.2.1 Paul's Line of Reasoning in Phil 1:27-4:3

There are reasons to believe that the internal rivalry – which, in my view, is epitomized in the conflict between Euodia and Syntyche – is directly related to the unresolved issue of the "enemies of the cross." Paul's admonition to Euodia and Syntyche "to be of the same mind" (4:2-3) is preceded by an inferential conjunction ὥστε in 4:1 which, according to P. O'Brien, "spells out the consequences of the preceding paragraph, i.e., vv. 17–21" (*Philippians*, 474).

In my view, however, the conjunction ties together Paul's argument, which starts in 1:27. The noticeable lexical repetitions point to a sustained train of thought from 1:27 to 4:3. Paul's appeal to "stay firm" (στήκετε; 1:27) and to "struggle together" (συναθλοῦντες; 1:27) is repeated in 4:1 (στήκετε), with special reference to Euodia and Syntyche who "struggled together" (συνήθλησάν; 4:3) with Paul. The success of the Philippians' advance is, however, at risk of being thwarted by the lack of "same-mindedness" (τὸ αὐτὸ φρονῆτε; 2:2) which results in "murmuring and arguing" (2:14). Paul admonishes the Philippians to adopt the mindset which was in Christ Jesus (τοῦτο φρονεῖτε; 2:5) who, contrary to the Philippians (cf. 2:4; 21), did not seek his own interest, but in humility chose the path of sacrificial service to God (2:6-9). This same mindset is being exemplified in the lives and ministry of Timothy (2:19-14), Epaphroditus (2:25-30), and of Paul himself (3:1-14). All three men, in imitation of Christ's pattern, chose to deny their own interests and privileges. The Philippians should not be intimidated at the prospect of suffering (πάσχειν; 1:29) for Christ

---

60. So Collange: "But now the situation has deteriorated and the apostle's supplication is 'with tears'" (*Philippians*, 137).

himself willingly embraced suffering on the cross (2:6-9) and thus opened for believers an opportunity to "participate in his sufferings" (κοινωνία τῶν παθημάτων; 3:10). After spelling out what in effect can be deemed as his personal credo (3:7-14), Paul asserts that the same kind of thinking (τοῦτο φρονῶμεν; 3:15) should distinguish those who are mature (τέλειοι; 3:15).

Yet there are signs of "different thinking" (ἑτέρως φρονεῖτε; 3:15) precisely among the leadership ranks; otherwise the admonition to Euodia and Syntyche (τὸ αὐτὸ φρονεῖν; 4:2) would be simply unfathomable. In view of the fact that in the verses immediately following (3:17-18) Paul deliberately contrasts his own "walk" (περιπατοῦντας; 3:17) with that of his opponents (περιπατοῦσιν; 3:18), it is reasonable to suppose that that is exactly what the "different thinking" is related to. In other words, Paul seems to be saying that if the Philippians join in imitating him and others "who walk according to the example" (3:17) ultimately set by Jesus (2:6-9), then it would restore the state of unanimity (τοῦτο φρονῶμεν; 3:15). If, on the contrary, they allow "different thinking" to take over, it will lead them to the dangerous walk with the "enemies" toward their destruction (3:18-19).

As we basically accept the veracity of Luke's account of the conversions of Lydia and the jailor, with their households following them in embracing Christianity, it seems plausible that nurturing in Christian faith took place through the existing household structures. As we have argued previously, the multiplicity of leadership (ἐπίσκοποι and διάκονοι; 1:1) and the prominent role of Euodia and Syntyche suggest the existence of several house churches at Philippi. The incipient period of Christian development was no doubt characterized by much improvisation when, in the absence of any overseeing ecclesiastical authority, many issues were "defined by individual Christians . . . as members of non-Christian households, professionals, citizens of a city, participants at social functions, and taxpayers."[61] Paul himself seems to suggest that his own presence is a factor in the way the Philippians behave (1:27; 2:12). It is thus plausible that the opponents of Philippians 3:18-19 are a group of believers who, in the eyes of Paul, have strayed and so have walked over the line which demarcates friends from enemies. Paul speaks of the "many" (πολλοί; 3:18) who walk this different path and even

---

61. Becker, "Paul and His Churches," 204.

if the word "many" has mostly a rhetorical force,[62] it is of significance that Paul is not talking of two or three isolated deviant members. What is also important is that the danger proceeds from their *unified* "walk,"[63] for which membership in a local πολίτευμα would have been the most likely setting. For such membership would have provided an organizational structure and ideological rationale for pursuing an alternative path. In a culture which professed "many gods, many lords" (1 Cor 8:5), becoming a Christian, at least for some, meant adding another deity to others.[64] We indicated previously that an exclusive commitment to a particular deity was not a prerequisite for membership in a voluntary association. Behind much of what Paul might have considered as deviant behavior[65] lay rather complex and critical issues of social standing, prestige, and economic well-being.

---

62. Cf. Sandnes, *Belly and Body*, 144.

63. Several scholars have pointed out that Paul, in using the verb περιπατέω, puts the emphasis on the opponents' wrong *walking*, not their wrong *teaching*. Cf. O'Brien's statement: "The presence of περιπατοῦσιν in the first clause indicates that it was the *behavior* of these people that made them 'the enemies of the cross of Christ'" (*Philippians*, 453). Also, Fee: "Paul does not in fact refer to their teaching as such, but to their 'walk,' to the way they live" (*Philippians*, 367-68); and Cotter: "There is no 'teaching' of theirs that needs to be contested but it is their περιπατεῖν that Paul denounces" ("Our Politeuma Is in Heaven," 101). In view of this, the designation of the opponents as "false teachers" (Martin, *Philippians*, 143) is unwarranted. Gnilka likewise designates the opponents as "those who are teaching a false doctrine at Philippi" (*Philippians*, 60). In general I agree with this assessment which, by the way, serves as an additional reason why Paul might have found it difficult to rebut the opponents: formally there were no developed doctrinal disagreements with Paul. And yet something made them walk a different path of life.

64. Strictly speaking, the issue of syncretistic worship was a purely Jewish-Christian dilemma. As R. MacMullen points out, the very absence of such a category as "orthodoxy" within Graeco-Roman religious tradition suggests that while "it was possible to be right or wrong in Judaism and Christianity . . . it was *not* possible in any other ancient religion" ("Conversion: A Historian's View," *SecCent* 5 [1985]: 71). He further illustrates his point: "There was no way of telling whether a person was an Isiac except by asking him if he believed in Isis. If he said "Yes," whatever he added further, he had sufficiently established his right to the title" ("Conversion," 72).

65. As we introduce the category of deviancy, one note of clarification is necessary. Deviancy is not "a particular quality inherent in certain acts or persons" (John Barclay, "Deviance and Apostasy: Some Applications of Deviance Theory to First-Century Judaism and Christianity," in *Modeling Early Christianity: Social-Scientific Studies of the New Testament in Its Context* [ed. Philip F. Esler; London: Routledge, 1995], 115). As Barclay further explains, "what makes an act socially significant as deviant is not so much that it is *performed*, as that it is *reacted to* as deviant" ("Deviance and Apostasy," 116). For this reason we should be cautious in taking some of Paul's negative valuations (like the "enemies of the cross" in Phil 3:18) at face value. For many of his contemporaries Paul himself exemplified deviant behavior *par excellence*.

Whereas for Paul becoming a Christian was a matter of radical resocialization, for other members of the Christian community, it was not. By retaining their fellowship within a πολίτευμα these "Christians" were able to keep (to play on Meeks' designation) a status of consistency – a recognized place within the overall system of societal relationship which, among other things, would exempt them from the prospect of social ostracism. Of course that would have been possible only at the cost of compromising their exclusive loyalty to the κύριος and σωτήρ Jesus (3:20). We will return to this issue in the next section of this chapter.

6.1.3 Paul's Polemical Characterization of the Opponents (Phil 3:19)

We will currently concentrate our attention on Paul's polemical characterization of the opponents: "They walk to their final destruction, their god is the belly and their glory is in shameful things, their minds are earthly-bound" (3:19). There are three basic descriptions given of them: a) their end is destruction; b) their god is the belly and their glory is in shame;[66] and c) their minds are set on earthly things.

The first and third characteristics are deliberately set in contrast by Paul with his own life's agenda. Whereas Paul is Christ-minded (τοῦτο φρονεῖτε ἐν ὑμῖν ὃ καὶ ἐν Χριστῷ Ἰησοῦ, 2:5; τὸ αὐτὸ φροενῖν ἐν κυρίῳ, 4:2) his opponents' minds are set on earthly things (οἱ τὰ ἐπίγεια φρονοῦντες). Whereas Paul is in pursuit of gaining the prize of his "upward calling" (ἄνω κλήσεως, 3:14; cf. 3:20), his opponents are bound by earthly things. Whereas Paul sets his τέλος as the glorious resurrection with Christ (3:11-12), ironically his opponents' τέλος is destruction (3:19). This is indeed a very harsh statement which we are going to keep in mind when we try to decide exactly what kind of people deserve this kind of an end from Paul's point of view.

For our present study, of particular interest are Paul's phrases: "their god is the belly (ἡ κοιλία)" and "their glory is in their shame (αἰσχύνη)." What are κοιλία and αἰσχύνη referring to?[67] In ancient literature, κοιλία was com-

---

66. Sandnes (*Belly and Body*, 145), as well as others, points out that both phrases are governed by the same relative pronoun (ὧς), and therefore "must be seen together."
67. A number of scholars argue in favor of taking both κοιλία and αἰσχύνη as references to the Jewish dietary laws and circumcision. See Hawthorne, *Philippians*, 224; Klijn,

monly used for the designation of the stomach as the seat of hunger and desire. Quite often expressions like the Pauline ὁ θεὸς ἡ κοιλία were used to describe promiscuous and decadent behavior. In Athenaeus we find an insulting phrase "you glutton, whose god is your belly" (κοιλιόδαιμον).[68] Also in Euripides one of the characters sacrifices to the "greatest of gods, his stomach" (τῇ μεγίστῃ γαστρί///. . . δαιμόνων).[69] In his tractate *On Drunkenness*, Philo specifically refers to a disobedient son who chose not to imitate the virtue of his brothers, but rather went to "an additional length in his transgressions, so as to make a god of the body" (θεοπλαστεῖν μὲν τὸ σῶμα).[70] Philo further writes of Aaron who succumbed to the request of the people and "made them a god of Typhus, who is especially honored among the Egyptians, the emblem of whom was the figure of a golden bull."[71]

"Paul's Opponents," 282-83; Koester, "Pauline Fragment," 324-31; Lincoln, *Paradise*, 95; Melick, *Philippians,* 143. Taking the phrases in this way, however, can be done only at the expense of total disregard of the usual meaning these words acquired in ancient literature. Sandnes, in his analysis of the word κοιλία, came to a similar conclusion that "nowhere in Graeco-Roman or Jewish sources is the belly a reference to people who are devoted to Jewish customs in general and dietary laws in particular" (*Belly and Body*, 145); cf. Tellbe, *Between Synagogue and the State*, 270. Contrary to Mearns' insistence ("Paul's Opponents," 198), neither κοιλία nor αἰσχύνη can be considered as references to genitals or nakedness exposed during circumcision (cf. Fee, *Philippians*, 373, n. 46; De Vos, *Church and Community Conflicts*, 271). Moreover, Paul never considered circumcision to be a shameful act, rather it was simply irrelevant (cf. Gal 5:6). The belly *topos* was applied by Jews to those who, under the demands of pagan rulers, stopped living like Jews (3 Macc 7:10-11; 4 Macc 13:1-5). There is one more line of argumentation which, following R. Jewett, can be labeled the "resultant inappropriateness of Paul's polemic" ("Conflicting Movements," 379). Even taking into account the rhetorical force of the phraseology "the polemic would have been far too gross to be effective" ("Conflicting Movements," 379). Cotter similarly remarks: "It is unlikely that Paul, who was so aware that he was writing to a Gentile community, would have used two insults so loaded with sexual connotations if he meant to refer to religious fanaticism over the observance of dietary laws" ("Our Politeuma," 93). Sandnes likewise concurs that for the text to be fully understandable "within a perspective which Paul has in common with his contemporary sources… [he] would hardly coin a new meaning for a maxim with whose meaning his readers must have been familiar" (*Belly and Body*, 146). In the end, it is doubtful that Paul would use the ἀπώλεια terminology with regard to his Jewish compatriots (cf. Tellbe: "ἀπώλεια is never explicitly used [by Paul] in referring to non-Christian Jews; it seems to be too strong a term for their destiny" ["Sociological Factors," 105, n. 40]).

68. Athenaeus, *Deipn.* 97.
69. Euripides, *Cycl.* 335.
70. Philo, *Ebr.* 95.
71. Philo, *Ebr.* 95.

In a similar way the word αἰσχύνη ("shame") was often associated with licentiousness and illicit sexual behavior. Thus, Philo considers the wages of a harlot as a "shameful gain."[72] He further associates a "woman who has lived as a concubine" with "shame, . . . drunkenness, and gluttony."[73] In Proverbs 26:11a (LXX) αἰσχύνη is used of a person who willfully returns to his sin (ἔστιν αἰσχύνη ἐπάγουσα ἁμαρτίαν). Elsewhere in LXX αἰσχύνη is used also as a euphemism for idols (Jer. 3:34-25; Hos. 9:10).[74] Peter O'Brien, among others, seems to be going this direction: "Paul is thus condemning the opponents who surrendered to gluttony and licentiousness, that is, who worshiped their sensual nature."[75]

Paul's language of "belly" and "shame," referring to gluttony and illicit sexual behavior in Philippians 3:19, best fits the context of the socializing practices within a voluntary association. As was previously shown (see ch. 2) the socializing functions of voluntary associations quite naturally included festivities and banqueting. As many such events took place in local taverns, the voluntary associations acquired a notorious reputation for outrageous drinking parties and debauchery, which often carried along a form of political protest.[76] W. Cotter finds that Paul's negative labeling of the opponents in Philippians 3:18-19 resonates with Philo's similarly negative portrayal of the gatherings of pagan associations. In Philo's valuation these gatherings were nothing other than the gatherings of "revelers, which from drunkenness and intoxication proceeded to violence, so as to disturb the peaceful condition of the country."[77] Philo further reports that Flaccus, the governor of Egypt under the emperor Tiberius "prohibited all associations and meetings which were continually feasting together under pretence of sacrifices, making a drunken mockery of public business."[78] A similar denunciation

---

72. Philo, *Spec.* 1.280.
73. Philo, *Spec.* 1.281.
74. See also examples in Aristotle, *Rhet.*1383b.2-4a.14; Dio Cassius, 38.25.5; Diodorus Siculus, 23.15.4.
75. O'Brien, *Philippians*, 456.
76. Cotter, "Our Politeuma," 96-97. Cf. De Vos' comment that members of Roman *collegia* were often criticized "for this sort of indulgent behavior" (*Church and Community Conflicts*, 273).
77. Philo, *Legat.* 311-312.
78. Philo, *Flacc.*136-137.

of the voluntary associations is found in Varro: "[There are] organizations in the city in whose fellowship you could find no sound elements but only liquor, tippling, drunkenness and the outrageous conduct they lead to, associations and 'couches' as they are called locally [in Alexandria]."[79]

My contention is that, although Paul does care about moral behavior (cf. 2:14-15), it is not his primary concern in 3:18-19; there is something more significant than that.[80] Here I concur with Koester (and many others) who argue that Paul's words in 3:19 should not be taken "at face-value, as though they were a direct and accurate description of the people Paul had in mind."[81] The extremely harsh wording in Philippians 3:18-19 is an example of Paul's intentionally exaggerated rhetoric[82] to make his point: these are dangerous people, do not follow their path! So what made them so dangerous from Paul's point of view?

Philip Harland reminds us of the "inseparable nature of the social and religious dimensions of feasting" when he writes, "banqueting activities [were] infused with varying degrees of religious significance for the participants, being viewed as a means of honoring or communing with gods."[83] Virtually in all associations the banquet festivities were preceded or accompanied with prayers, sacrifices, or libations in honor of the gods. Thus, for

---

79. Varro, *Rust.* 3.2.16.

80. Cf. Hawthorne, who states that Paul's statement in 3:18-19 "is not necessarily a comment on their [opponents'] moral performance" (*Philippians*, 222).

81. Koester, "Pauline Fragment," 324.

82. Harland makes a valid point in stating that "we must refrain from accepting descriptions of wild 'impious' meetings and associations, whether Jewish, Christian, or other, at face value, as though they realistically describe actual practices among a significant number of the groups in question" (*Associations*, 75). He also reminds us that "stories of secretive nocturnal, and uncontrolled banquets involving drunkenness and, at times, somewhat extreme rituals – incestuous sex, ritual murder, and cannibalism among them – were the mainstay of mudslinging and a source of novelistic shock value among upper-class authors in antiquity" (*Associations*, 74). There is a certain irony in that Paul's critical assessment of the opponents comes back full circle in the criticism of Christians by pagans (see Stephen Benko, "Pagan Criticism of Christianity during the First Two Centuries AD," *ANRW* II. 23.2 1055-1118). It is not that we deny the fact the festivities took place, or that they occasionally could be viewed by some as being out of proportion. The main point is that we always have to keep in mind the difference between the reality and the rhetorical portrayal of that reality.

83. Harland, *Associations*, 77. Cf. Plutarch, *Mor.* 1102A: "It is not the abundance of wine or the roasting of meat that makes the joy of festivals, but the good hope and the belief that the god is present in his kindness and graciously accepts what is offered."

example, in the guild of Zeus Hypsistos a monthly banquet in the sanctuary of Zeus was to be accompanied with "pouring [of] libations, pray[er], and perform[ance of] the other customary rites on behalf of god and lord (κύριος),[84] the king."[85] The Lanuvium's by-laws specify that "on the festive days . . . each *quinquennalis* is to conduct worship with incense and wine and is to perform his other functions clothed in white."[86] The ample consumption of wine in the Dionysus cult was one of the means "to be possessed [by a greater power], and by that infusion . . . to gain powerful revelations."[87] R. MacMullen adds: "Much more often, however – indeed almost everywhere in the Greco-Roman world – we find ceremonial drinking . . . for plain pleasure was shared with the deity."[88]

In this regard Paul's designation of Jesus as σωτήρ (Phil 3:20) is of special importance, for in Graeco-Roman culture the term was often applied to gods. In the inscription studied earlier (see ch. 2) of a religious cult of Zeus from Philadelphia there is a reference to Ζεῦ Σωτήρ.[89] Also in the study of the voluntary associations (ch. 4) at Philippi we already mentioned that some of the gods and goddesses worshiped at Philippi (Isis, Serapis, Thracian Horseman) were invoked as savior gods. Furthermore, as we shall see, in the context of the imperial ideology where σωτήρ was applied to the Roman emperor, Paul's designation of Jesus in Philippians 3:20 acquires an additional significance. We have seen the tendency, as in the associations of Isis and Serapis (*dedrophorus Augustales*), for other cult societies to embrace the imperial cult. Religious devotion, especially in Philippi, a city with a clearly pro-Roman stance, is intrinsically connected with the issues of polit-

---

84. The association of the king with θεός and κύριος betrays the longstanding Eastern tradition of equating the earthly rulers with the gods. This case is of importance, for as we are going to see, during the Nero's rule the title κύριος became increasingly popular with the emperor.
85. *PLond* 2193: line 9.
86. *CIL* 14.2112: page 2, lines 29-30.
87. R. MacMullen, "Conversion," 79.
88. MacMullen, "Conversion," 79. Cf. Aristides, *Or.* 8.54.1: "In sacrificing to this god [Serapis] men keenly share a vivid feeling of oneness, while summoning him to their hearth and setting him at the head as guest and diner. . . . . He is the fulfilling participant in all cult association."
89. *SIG* 3.985; line 60. Zeus as σωτήρ is attested also in *IG* 4.840; 841; 2.2.1291; 10.2 67.

ical loyalty. That is why we are going to argue further that it was not just the issue of religious pluralism that angers Paul but the continual veneration of Caesar that provoked Paul's indignation in Philippians 3:18-20.

6.2 Paul's Counter-Argument Against the "Enemies of the Cross"

In the second part of the chapter we are going to spell out Paul's counter-arguments against his opponents. These are related primarily to two different visions of the πολίτευμα, two different objects of the believers' ultimate devotion, and two different patterns of discipleship. Against those who found safe haven under the umbrella of a local πολίτευμα, Paul sets his own vision of the πολίτευμα in heaven. Paul's anti-imperial polemics in Philippians, in my view, are aimed primarily at those who, under the umbrella of the πολίτευμα, continue in their devotion to the emperor as the κύριος and σωτήρ of the nations. Finally, by hiding under the protective umbrella of the earthly πολίτευμα, the opponents miss an opportunity to "participate in Christ's sufferings," an essential attribute of discipleship for Paul.

6.2.1 Paul's Vision of the Heavenly Πολίτευμα

Paul was a great thinker, and in so far as his thinking related to the life of a community, he was a political thinker.[90] Paul, on his own admission, considered himself to be σοφὸς ἀρχιτέκτων (1 Cor 3:4), and as a "wise architect" he saw his role in defining the place and mission of the newly founded Christian ἐκκλησία within Graeco-Roman society. In order that this could be intelligible for the Hellenistic audience of his time he often had to put his Jewish apocalyptic heritage within the framework of political terminology of his day. Paul pioneered in verbalizing what in effect could be deemed as the first "political theory for Christianity."[91]

---

90. Blumenfeld appropriately reminds us of this important dimension in Paul's theology (*Political Paul*, 88).
91. Blumenfeld, *Political Paul*, 88.

Alongside the two dominant *loci* of the Hellenistic socio-political system (πόλις and βασιλεία)[92] he constructs an alternative "two layered society."[93] The one layer reflected the reality of the newly founded Christian community (*ekklēsia*), and the other (in no small way prompted by his Jewish-Christian heritage) the reality of the not yet revealed kingdom of God, the heavenly city.

The letter to the Philippians basically confirms Paul's preoccupation with the two layers of his alternative societal model. In this sense, a Hellenistic term, πολίτευμα, perfectly fits Paul's agenda in that it becomes (at least in this letter) a catchword for the designation of the not yet revealed heavenly reality. The fact that it is not yet visible does not make it for Paul less than real. In fact, as Blumenfeld argues, for Paul the first (earthly) layer is "not only incomplete, it is not even a state, for it is not legally constituted unless joined to the second layer." Paul's theologizing "explodes the distinction between human and divine affairs" with the result that "human government is no longer just imitation of God's rule." For Paul "the Divine validates and governs"[94] the earthly community to the effect that it should reflect here and now the character of its heavenly ruler, Jesus Christ.

It is my contention that behind the borrowed Hellenistic term of πολίτευμα there lurks the anticipated ἄνω Ἰερουσαλήμ of which Paul writes in Galatians 4:26. Is there any reason to believe that the ἄνω Ἰερουσαλήμ in Galatians has anything to do with the πολίτευμα in Philippians? There is indeed a good reason to suppose that Paul's ideas in Philippians and Galatians are inspired by the same OT reference. In Philippians 4:3 there is an interesting reference to a "book of life" in which the names of Paul's Gentile (!) co-workers are written down. The idea of the Gentiles' inclusion into a heavenly "registry" and the designation of the ἄνω Ἰερουσαλήμ

---

92. The Hellenistic period was characterized by a quite unnatural coexistence of monarchic power structures with democratic traditions of the Greek *polis*. The king was the final authority and arbiter, the savior and benefactor who sought to be revered and obeyed. At the same time, the cities continued to be governed through the assemblies, councils and magistrates. The cities were expected to sponsor the king's military campaigns by housing the garrisons and making financial contributions. In turn, the kings lavished the cities with monumental buildings and other gifts; see Blumenfeld, *Political Paul*, 88.

93. Blumenfeld, *Political Paul*, 267.

94. Blumenfeld, *Political Paul*, 267.

as our μήτηρ (Gal 4:26) are found in only one common OT reference, namely, Psalm 87:4-6. Before we turn our attention to Psalm 87 I would like to briefly comment on Paul's indebtedness to the "restoration of Zion" tradition.

6.2.1.1 Paul's Hope for the Heavenly Μητρόπολις

The city of Jerusalem with the temple in its midst was one of the defining symbols of the Jewish nation. Besides being a marvelous city, Jerusalem is an important theological symbol: it symbolizes Zion,[95] the city of Yahweh who founded it (Isa 14:32) and chose for his name to dwell in it (Deut 12:11). The presence of God in "the midst of the city" was always a sure guarantee that "it shall not be moved" (Ps 46:5; cf. Isa 37:35). However, the historical realities often put this assurance to a severe test. The events of the temple's destruction in 586 BCE and the following period of the Babylonian captivity certainly intensified the expectations for the restoration of the temple and the city: "The Lord will inherit Judah as his portion in the holy land, and will again choose Jerusalem" (Zech 2:12).[96] The fact that the actual restoration during the Persian period was for many more like a disappointment gave rise to two major stands of the tradition: some expected that Jerusalem would be supernaturally transformed;[97] others suggested a scenario whereby the original (heavenly Jerusalem) would finally altogether replace an imperfect copy.[98] The same contrast between the present and the "heavenly Jerusalem" could be traced in later rabbinic

---

95. Zion is another name for Jerusalem usually preferred by the prophets. Cf. the synonymous parallelism between Zion and Jerusalem in Amos 1:2: "The Lord roars from Zion, and utters his voice from Jerusalem."
96. Cf. also Isa 2:1-5; 49:14-18; 54, 60-62; 65: 17-25; Jer 31: 38-40; Mic 4:1-4; Ezek 40-48.
97. Cf. Tob 13:8–18; *T. Dan.* 5:12–13; *Sib. Or.* 5.420–27; *1 En.* 90:28–29.
98. Cf. 2 Esdr 7:26; 10:25–28; 13:36; *2 Bar.* 4; 32:1–4. The idea of two Jerusalems, one of which is an imperfect copy of the other, may have its origin in the story of Moses building an ark from a heavenly original (Exod 25:40). This idea is further developed 1 Chr 28:19 and finalized in Wis 9:8: "You have given command to build a temple on your holy mountain, and an altar in the city of your habitation, a copy of the holy tent that you prepared from the beginning." The *Apocalypses of Baruch*, a document written in the wake of the destruction of the temple and the city in 70 CE, confirms that the earthly copy was a fake after all, but the original is still being "preserved with [God]" (*2 Bar* 4:2-6).

literature as well.[99] It is quite certain that the first followers of Jesus likewise fully embraced the hope for the "new" or "heavenly" Jerusalem (cf. Heb 11:10, 14–16; 12:22; 13:14; Rev 3:12) the revelation of which will epitomize God's ultimate plan for human history.

It is in the letter to the Galatians that Paul likewise utilizes the theme of the ἄνω Ἰερουσαλήμ, "the Jerusalem above" (Gal 4:26).[100] The direct quotation in Galatians 4:27 of Isaiah 54:1 betrays Paul's general indebtedness to the "restoration of Zion" theme in Deutero-Isaiah (Isa 51-54; 60-62; 66).[101] It is one of the foundational texts for Paul with regard to understanding the heavenly Jerusalem and its function as μητρόπολις:

> Sing, o barren one who did not bear;
> Burst into song and shout, you who have not been in labor!
> For the children of the desolate woman will be more
> Than the children of her that is married, says the Lord
> (Isa 54:1; NRSV).

---

99. See e.g. *b. Ta'an.* 5a; *b.Hag.* 12b; *Gen. Rab.* 55.7; 69.7; *Num. Rab.* 4.13; *Midr. Pss.* 30.1; 122.4; *Cant. Rab.* 3.10; 4.4; *Pesiq. R.* 40.6.

100. See on the subject: F. F. Bruce, *The Epistle to the Galatians: A Commentary on the Greek Text* (NIGTC; Grand Rapids: Eerdmans, 1982): 220; Timothy George, *Galatians* (NAC 30; Nashville: Broadman & Holman, 2001, c.1994), 342; Richard N. Longenecker, *Galatians* (WBC 41; Dallas: Word, 2002), 213; Charles H. Cosgrove, "The Law Has Given Sarah No Children," *NovT* 29 (1987): 219-35; Karen H. Jobes, "Jerusalem, Our Mother: Metapepsis and Intertextuality in Galatians 4:21-31," *WTJ* 55 (1993): 299-320; Anna M. Schwemer, "Himmlische Stadt und Himlisches Bürgerrecht bei Paulus (Gal 4,26 und Phil 3,20)," in *La Cité de Dieu = Die Stadt Gottes : 3. Symposium Strasbourg, Tübingen, Uppsala, 19.-23. September 1998 in Tübingen* (ed. M. Hengel et. al.; WUNT 129; Tübingen: Mohr Siebeck, 2000), 195–243; Duane F. Watson, "New Jerusalem" in *ABD*, 4:1095.

101. A slightly different but similar development of Deutero-Isaiah's imagery is found in *4 Esdras*. The author of this early second century CE pseudepigraphon also utilizes the theme of a barren woman who personifies Zion (10:44). This woman finally (after three thousand years) bore a son (10:46), yet because of misfortune, the "son entering into his marriage-chamber died" (10:48; the destruction of Jerusalem in AD 70 is implied). God comforts the woman with the promise that his "Son, the Messiah" (7:26) will be revealed and that would mean a turn of fortune: "For you is opened paradise, planted the tree of life; the future age prepared, plenteousness made ready; a city builded, a rest appointed" (8:52). Philo (*Praem.* 158–160) likewise treats Is 54:1 within the canons of his allegorical method of interpretation. For him the image of the "barren one" is an ethical allegory of the history of the soul: the children of the married woman being vices and those of the barren woman (the virgin impregnated by divine seed) virtues (cf. *Mig.* 224-25).

The "barren one" in this passage personifies the desolate, ruined Jerusalem of the post-exilic period. In Isaiah 54:11 the city is characterized as "afflicted," "storm-tossed, and not comforted." God, however, promises to return to Zion and to restore the glory of Jerusalem (Isa 52:7-9). In this context sounds the encouraging admonition: "Rouse yourself, rouse yourself! Stand up, o Jerusalem, you who have drunk at the hand of the Lord the cup of his wrath" (Isa 51:17; cf. Isa 52:1-3). Although Isaiah 54:1 does not contain an anticipated connection between the "barren one" and Sarah, since Isaiah's emphasis is on Zion, not on Sarah, the missing link is found in Isaiah 51:3: "Look to Abraham your father and to Sarah who bore you." It is this metaphorical linkage of Abraham and Sarah with the eschatologically restored Jerusalem that helps Paul to establish a clear connection between the "barren" city of Isaiah 54:1 (צקרה, LXX στεῖρα) and the "barren Sarah" of Gen 11:30 ("now Sarah was barren (צקרה, LXX στεῖρα); she had no child").[102] Yet as the barren Sarah bore children by God's creative power, so the barren Zion will be transformed into the "garden of the Lord" (Isa 51:3) and bear many children. As the barren Sarah "broke into hilarious laughter and shouts of joy at the birth of Isaac,"[103] so the believers at Galatia have all the reasons to rejoice because they are the true children of Abraham.

From the time of Exile, prophets consistently identified Jerusalem as "daughter Zion,"[104] or as "virgin Israel."[105] Likewise, the cities of the other nations are described in similar terms.[106] This usage reflects a long standing Semitic tradition of personifying a city as a woman.[107] Most naturally the feminine image of a city serves as a useful metaphor for expressing a com-

---

102. Longenecker suggests that most probably Paul follows here the seventh *middôt* of rabbinical interpretation (the so-called *gezera shawa*, or interpretation by verbal analogy). When the same word (στεῖρα) occurs in two separate passages (Gen 11:30 and Is 54:1), then the considerations of the one can be applied to the other (*Galatians*, 215).

103. George, *Galatians*, 344.

104. Cf. Isa 1:8; 37:22 (2); 52:2; 62:11; Jer 4:31; 6:2, 23; Lam 1:6; 2:1, 4, 8, 10, 13(2), 18; 4:22 (2); Mic 1:3; 4: 8 (2), 10, 13; Zeph 3: 14 (2); Zech 2: 7, 10; 9: 9 (2).

105. Cf. Amos 5:2; Isa 37:22; Jer 18:13; 38: 4, 21; Lam 2:13.

106. Cf. Isa 23:12; 47:1, 5; Ps 136:8.

107. See Aloysius Fitzgerald, "The Mythological Background for the Presentation of Jerusalem as Queen and False Worship as Adultery in the OT," *CBQ* 34 (1972): 403-16. Cf. Christl Maier, "Psalm 87 as a Reappraisal of the Zion Tradition and Its Reception in Galatians 4:26," *CBQ* 69 (2007): 479; Schwemer, "Himmlische Stadt," 203.

plex phenomenon of relationships within a city. Like almost any woman in the ancient world a city could be violated and ransacked by warring armies (the lot which befell Jerusalem). On the other hand, the city can be cherished and embraced as a beloved bride. Like a mother, the city provides nourishment and protection for its inhabitants (cf. Isa 66:11). Like a mother, the city "gives birth" to its children, and it is always a sure sign of rejuvenation and new life (cf. Isa 54:1).

6.2.1.2 Paul's Christological Rendering of Psalm 87 (LXX Psalm 86)

There are a few passages in the OT which could have inspired Paul to come up with the maternal image for the "Jerusalem above."[108] The very passage in Isaiah (54:1) implies that the "barren one" will fulfill its role as a mother for many children. Yet, as most scholars agree, no text is a better candidate than Psalm 87. It is a unique passage not because it contains one of the rare addresses to Zion as to "mother" but because the address is made by the God-fearing Gentile nations. Generally, Psalm 87 is a poem which praises Zion as the city of God and the center of life, eventually at least, for all peoples.[109] It is composed in the Zion tradition of Isaiah 66 and emphasizes the status of citizens of the city of God for the nations other than Israel.[110]

---

108. In 2 Samuel a city by the name of Abel of Beth-Maacah is called the "mother of Israel" (20:19). The image of mother for a New Jerusalem is implied in Isa 62:5. The Septuagint provides several more references to "mother-city" (μητρόπολις) in Josh 10:2; 14:15; 21:11; Isa 1:26. Philo used the same expression for one of the six cities of refuge: "the most excellent μητρόπολις" (*Fug.* 94; cf. *Som.* 1.41). In a first century Jewish romance *Joseph and Aseneth*, a daughter of a pagan priest by the name of Aseneth was transformed into a city and became the walled μητρόπολις for all who seek refuge (15:16; 16:16; 19:5, 8). Still another reference to Jerusalem as "mother" is found in *2 Baruch*: "And I said: O Lord, my Lord, have I come into the world for this purpose that I might see the evils of my mother?" (*2 Bar.* 3:1, cf. *4 Ezr.* 10:7).

109. On the structure and interpretation of the psalm, see Thijs Booij, "Some Observations on Psalm 87," *VT* 37, 1 (1987): 16–25; Johanna W.H. Bos, "Psalm 87," *Int* 47 (1993): 281–85; John A. Emerton, "The Problem of Psalm 87," *VT* 50 (2000): 183–99; Christl M. Maier, "Psalm 87 as a Reappraisal of the Zion Tradition and Its Reception in Galatians 4:26," *CBQ* 69 (2007): 473-86; Mark S. Smith, "The Structure of Psalm 87," *VT* 37 (1987): 16–25.

110. On the admission of one recent author, Ps 87 is "one of the more difficult poems in the Psalter" (Emerton, "Psalm 87," 183). Its peculiar style has led some scholars to conclude that a part of the psalm was lost and the lines were reorganized in a different order. However, as Johanna Bos points out, there are several structural markers which give

For our present study the Septuagint version of Psalm 87, Psalm 86:4-6, is of special interest:

μήτηρ Σιων, ἐρεῖ ἄνθρωπος,	A man shall say "mother Zion," –
καὶ ἄνθρωπος ἐγενήθη ἐν αὐτῇ	"for[113] 'Man'[114] was born in her,"
καὶ αὐτὸς ἐθεμελίωσεν αὐτὴν ὁ ὕψιστος	for the Most High himself has founded her [Zion].
κύριος διηγήσεται ἐν γραφῇ λαῶν	the Lord will tell in the registry of the nations.

Christl Maier argues that the Septuagint version emerges from a misreading of the Hebrew consonantal text.[113] Thus Psalm 86:5 (LXX) takes the Hebrew consonantal form יאמר as יֹאמַר = ἐρεῖ ("he will say") instead of the *niphal* form יֵאָמֵר ("he will be called") as did the *Masoretes*. As a result, the Hebrew distributive phrase "each man" (אִישׁ וְאִישׁ) is torn apart and its second half taken with the following clause.[114] This seemingly frivolous rendering of the Hebrew text, especially an introduction of Zion as μήτηρ, is in fact an example of the "deliberate interpretative interference,"[115] a creative reworking of the biblical text akin to the contemporary ways of thinking about Zion.[116]

---

us a reason to treat it as a complete literary work (Bos, "Psalm 87," 283). One of the most peculiar features of the psalm is the list of five Gentile nations who are described as "born in Zion." These are Rahab (Egypt, cf. Isa 30:7), Babel, Philistia, Tyre and Cush (perhaps Nubia or Ethiopia). Elsewhere in the Bible these nations are usually mentioned in a hostile context. The imagery moves from the large superpowers of the day (Egypt, Babylon) to smaller warring neighboring nations (Philistia and Tyre), to the far-away people of Namibia or Ethiopia. God's action in the Psalm is expressed through the mediation of three verbs: God *loves* Zion (v. 5), he *establishes* it (v. 5), and *records* the nations in the birth register (v. 6). The Most High (יהוה) loves Zion and thus he guarantees its existence as the birthplace of the nations in Zion. This is indeed very radical thought!

111. Following Maier and others who treat καί as epexegetical ("Psalm 87," 480).

112. Following Joachim Schaper's rendering of the word ἄνθρωπος (Eschatology in the Greek Psalter [WUNT 2.76; Tübin*gen: Mohr Siebeck*, 1995], 99).

113. Maier, "Psalm 87," 480.

114. Cf. Emerton, "Psalm 87," 195–96.

115. Schaper, *Greek Psalter*, 99.

116. Schaper (*Greek Psalter*, 99) refers specifically to one document approximately contemporaneous with the time of LXX translation of the Psalter: 11QPsª 154. In particular, column 22 of this psalm is an exuberant song to Zion ("I remember you, Zion, for blessing; with all my strength") in which Zion is portrayed as a mother (reminiscent of Isa 66: 7-11) who brings forth her children and feeds them at "[her] glorious breasts" (col.

In the same way, the rendering of the Hebrew phrase (אִישׁ וְאִישׁ) is not the result of the linguistic deficiency on the part of the translator[117] but yet another example of a creative reading of the original within the context of heightened Messianic expectations. The split of the Hebrew phrase "each man" into two ἄνθρωποι contributed to the text a "distinctively messianic connotation."[118]

There are thus good reasons to believe that the Septuagint version of Psalm 87 could have prompted Paul to read it in a similar (i.e., Christological) way. In emphasizing in Galatians the instrumental role of the "offspring" = Christ (3:16) in making God's promise to Abraham ("All the Gentiles shall be blessed in you," 3:8) a reality, Paul had at his disposal a biblical text to back up his argument. The κύριος promised to include the Gentile nations into the heavenly registry.[119] But how could that possibly be true? "Through the birth of the ἄνθρωπος in Zion!" answers Paul. "And this ἄνθρωπος is

---

22, 3) (*DDS* 2:1177).

117. *Contra* to Maier who supposes that "the translator did not recognize the Hebrew distributive expression" ("Psalm 87," 480).

118. Schaper, *Greek Psalter*, 100. On the significance of the ἄνθρωπος imagery in LXX, Qumran writings, and Targums, see Geza Vermes, *Scripture and Tradition in Judaism: Haggadic Studies* (Leiden: Brill, 1961), 56-66. As W. Horbury ("The Messianic Associations of the 'Son of Man'" *JTS* 36 (1985): 51) argues, the phrase καὶ ἄνθρωπος ἐγενήθη ἐν αὐτῇ indeed was understood messianically in the rabbinic sources. He refers to *Tg. Ket.* and *Midr. Teh.* 87:5 (admittedly later sources): "The nations of the world will bring gifts to king Messiah, as it is said, 'A man to a man is born in her' (Ps 87:5); these are the messiahs of the Lord, Messiah son of David and Messiah son of Ephraim."

119. The so called registry (γραφή) of Ps 86:6 provides an additional reason to believe that Paul in writing both the Galatians and Philippians drew on this particular OT passage. In Phil 4:3 Paul writes of "the rest of [his] co-workers, whose names are in the book of life" (ἐν βίβλῳ ζωῆς). For the Roman citizens of Philippi this reference to the "book of life" could have evoked the practice of registering the citizens of the empire by the local magistrates (Portefaix, *Sisters Rejoice*, 139). On the other hand, the notion of the "book of life/living" clearly belongs to a later Jewish apocalyptic heritage (cf. Exod 32:32; Ps 13:9; Isa 4:3; Dan 12:1; Mal 3:16; *1 En.* 47:3; 97:6; 104:1; 106:19; *2 Bar* 73:1). The expression "to be blotted out from the book of the living" (Exod 32:32) signified the prospect of an untimely end of life. The damnation of the "enemies of the cross" (Phil 3:19) and the record of the saved in the book of life (4:3) echoes the Danielic idea of the future deliverance of "everyone who is found written in the book" and the "resurrection to eternal shame" (Dan 12:1). The book of the living (of remembrance) is a metaphorical way of speaking of a birth record of the faithful Israelites whom God deemed worthy of eternal life. A reasonable question arises: what do Gentiles in Philippi have to do with Israel's record of the faithful? Psalm 86:6 provides the answer. Cf. Schwemer, "Himmlische Stadt," 230-35.

nobody else but God's Messiah! (Do you not read the Torah?)" (Gal 4:21). All these other people (Ps 87:4) were born in their respective locations, but after the Messiah was born in Zion they were "spiritually" born in Zion too, and thus their names are recorded in the city's register. Paul thus points his readers (and potential critics) to the scriptural foundation and to the instrumental role of the Messiah for the Gentiles' inclusion into the family of God. We should not lose, however, the metaphorical sense of the "Zion = Jerusalem" equation here. The point is not that Paul insists on the literal birth of the Messiah in the city of Jerusalem.[120] The point is that Sarah = Zion finally gave birth to the child of the promise, i.e., the Christ through whom Gentile believers both in Galatia and in Philippi become members of the motherly city, the city of God (πόλις τοῦ θεοῦ, v. 3).[121]

One final issue should be addressed here. What is the relationship between the πολίτευμα (ἄνω Ἰερουσαλήμ) and the local Christian ἐκκλησία both in Philippi and in Galatia? F.F. Bruce seems to equate the two: "In our present text, just as ἡ νῦν Ἰερουσαλήμ is not primarily the geographical site, so ἡ ἄνω Ἰερουσαλήμ is not spatially elevated but is the community of the new covenant."[122] Richard Longenecker, to the contrary, speaks of the "Jerusalem above" as a "reality that will exist in the future."[123] This statement is in direct contradiction with C. Maier's statement: "For Paul, 'the Jerusalem above' is not a future reality but a present entity that represents a people different from the one that actually lives in the city."[124] I believe it is here where πολίτευμα (Phil 3:20) can help us understand Paul's thought in Galatians. As a governing heavenly body, it is already in existence in heaven, and it exerts a direct influence upon the members of the local ἐκκλησία. But certainly to equate the πολίτευμα or, for that matter,

---

120. *Contra* Maier who insists that "no biblical text states that the Messiah will come from or even be born in Jerusalem" ("Psalm 87," 480, n.37).

121. Cf. Cosgrove "What Paul secures from Isaiah is the suggestion that Sarah remained barren throughout history until the coming of her child, Christ" ("The Law Has Given Sarah No Children," 231). This is indeed an astonishing thought in itself.

122. Bruce, *Galatians*, 221. Cf. also another Bruce's statement: "So by Paul the promises of Is 54 are understood as addressed to the church of the new age, Jerusalem above" (*Galatians*, 222).

123. Longenecker, *Galatians*, 213.

124. Maier, "Psalm 87," 485.

the ἄνω Ἰερουσαλήμ with the ἐκκλησία, would be a premature step. For Paul, the πολίτευμα is the reality in the process of being revealed. Here we have a classical Pauline "already" – "not yet" tension. The death and resurrection of Christ inaugurated the beginning of the *eschaton*, and that is why believers are already members of the πολίτευμα, and their names are already inscribed in the book of life (Phil 4:3).[125] Yet they are still in the process of waiting for the Lord and Savior of the future heavenly πολίτευμα to overcome the "not yet" dimension (Phil 3:20). In trying to relate his Jewish heritage to a Gentile audience, Paul in Philippians in essence is saying to the believers:

> The claim of the opponents of being followers of Christ is a false one, for in seeking the protective status of an earthly πολίτευμα they betray their ultimate allegiance to a different κύριος and σωτήρ, namely Caesar! We as Christians live our lives under a different governing authority. There is already set in heaven a new reality, or to use the term you would readily understand, there is a πολίτευμα in heaven from where we are expecting the arrival of our κύριος and σωτήρ Jesus!

6.2.2 Paul's Anti-Imperial Polemics

Whether the letter to Philippians contains elements of anti-imperial polemics is still a matter of lively debate.[126] If our conclusion that he is en-

---

125. Here is where Longenecker is correct in saying that "the believers had come into the eschatological situation of already participating in that future reality" (*Galatians*, 213).

126. Seyoon Kim in his recent publication (*Christ and Caesar: The Gospel and the Roman Empire in the Writings of Paul and Luke* [Grand Rapids: Eerdmans, 2008]) contests the anti-imperial character of Paul's proclamation. Particularly relevant for our discussion is his reference to Phil 1:19-26, on the basis of which he argues: "[Paul's] expectation for his acquittal clearly suggests that in his mind his gospel was not anti-imperial" (p. 44). First of all, the acquittal is not the only option in Paul's mind. He equally admits the prospect of his life's termination (1:20-21). Second, Paul's confidence in the possible acquittal proceeds from the fact that he *was not* a political prisoner of Rome. If we take Luke's account in Acts 22-25 as generally trustworthy (as does S. Kim), then it was Paul's disagreement with his fellow Jews, rather than with Rome, that made Paul basically to seek Roman protection from his Jewish compatriots.

S. Kim suggests quite a fanciful scenario whereby Paul "hoped to explain the gospel of Jesus Christ to Caesar himself (!) and obtain. . . an official recognition from the highest authority in the Roman empire that the gospel of Jesus Christ… posed no offense to the

gaged in such a polemic is correct, then what is the textual evidence to substantiate this conclusion?

We will currently consider some of the pertinent terms in Philippians which had currency both within the context of early Christianity and broader Graeco-Roman culture. The overlap of the terminology should not hasten the conclusion that one tradition necessarily borrowed or adapted the terminology from another. The "two plates"[127] of Graeco-Roman and

---

empire" (p. 49). Furthermore, S. Kim seems to be seriously considering that Paul "could explain to the court that his gospel did not mean this, that it was not treasonous, in spite of some language" (p. 44). All that Paul had to do was to explain "that the terms employed for his gospel, despite their superficial similarities, meant something quite different from those in the imperial ideology" (p. 44). Sure enough, "the judges at the court would also be intelligent enough to see this and would acquit him" (p. 45). I do not take this as a plausible scenario. First of all, Christianity at this time for the most part remained indistinguishable from Judaism. There were not yet clear criteria to delineate between the two. Except for a few Pauline letters in limited circulation, there were no written documents or creeds to convict Paul of any wrongdoing. Second, it is quite unlikely that Paul was preparing for a court hearing of his exposition of his Christian beliefs. He did not have to. Once again, at least in Luke's version, he was not imprisoned for preaching the gospel. Moreover, any attempts on the part of Paul to explain the Christian gospel in terms of the "fulfillment of Judaism" (p. 49) would make little sense to the judges, not to mention, to Caesar. It is equally doubtful that Paul's rhetorical skills in explaining "this in terms of that" would have been a success. What hermeneutical equilibristic would it take of Paul to explain to Caesar that a phrase like in Phil 2:10 ("at the name of Jesus every knee [including the emperor?] should bend") meant in reality quite a different thing than it stated? S. Kim's sound protest against some scholarly attempts to make out of Paul a first century revolutionary leads him, however, to a reductionist treatment of the gospel as purely religious, transcendental phenomenon. His repetitious insistence that Paul's gospel is "quite innocent of the anti-imperial charge, . . . politically quite harmless, . . . politically innocuous" (p. 45) point to a distinction, unknown to the Graeco-Roman mind, between the political and religious dimensions of social reality.

In all probability, as S. Kim concurs (pp. 50-52), Paul shared the hope for the imminent coming of the Messiah. For Kim, that imminence is an additional reason why Paul did not "actively [seek] to subvert the existing system of this world" (p. 52). To be sure, Paul did not see his role in bringing up an uprising *a la* the Jewish revolt of 66-70 CE. Yet, some of his terminology in Philippians loaded with the military overtones (στήκειν, συναθλοῦν, ἀγών, πάσχειν) testifies to anything but his passive expectation of Christ's return. Paul clearly sees the signs of the coming reversal: "the present form of this world is passing away" (1 Cor 7:31). He envisions the future in which Christ will "destroy every ruler [including the Roman emperor] and every authority and power" (1 Cor 15:24). The very fact of Paul's involvement in what S. Kim designates as "forming alternative communities" (p. 53) signified the challenge not only to the predominant social patterns of the time but to the imperial Roman ideology because the members of these communities pledged allegiance to a different κύριος and σωτήρ than the Roman emperor.

127. Cf. Crossan and Reed: "Deep down beneath an Augustus or a Jesus, a Paul or a Nero, two giant tectonic plates ground relentlessly against one another in that first century. Each was formed from a powerfully creative transmutation within prior tradition, one within

Jewish-Christian tradition were formed to some degree independently from each other. Yet the dominant linguistic tool of the time (Koine Greek) and the similarity of the aspirations within Graeco-Roman and early Christian eschatology brought these two traditions into a competitive relationship. It is within this competitive relationship that we can trace the signs of a "polemical parallelism between the cult of the emperor and the cult of Christ."[128] While drawing his words and ideas from the OT, Paul, by relating them to the predominantly Gentile audience in Philippi, inadvertently makes the recipients read and hear these words and ideas within the broader cultural context.

6.2.2.1 Equality with God

One of the clear indicators of Paul's critical engagement with the imperial cult is the peculiar characterization of Christ as ἴσα θεῷ (2:6), for, as Erik Heen points out, the same terminology had "a long history in the Greek ruler cult and in the first century CE was applied to the Roman emperor."[129] As was indicated earlier, the imperial cult was a natural outgrowth of the Greek honorific tradition which lavishly ascribed to rulers and kings the ἰσόθεοι τιμαί honors, i.e., honors equal to those paid to the gods.[130] What is important is that by the end of Augustus' reign the right to bestow divine honors (the ἰσόθεοι τιμαί) in the Eastern part of the empire was solely restricted to the emperor and his family.[131] Quite obviously by usurping the right to bestow divine honors Augustus underscored the uniqueness of his person. It is this impertinent self-elevation of the mortal human being

---

paganism, the other within Judaism. The tectonic plate of Hellenistic tradition mutated under the Roman challenge until, at least for many, Caesar's apotheosis meant not just the promise, but the start of the world's salvation, redemption, and justification" (*In Search of Paul*, 270–71).

128. Deissmann, *Light*, 342.

129. Heen, "Philippians 2:6-11," 125.

130. See Duncan Fishwick, *The Imperial Cult in the Latin West: Studies in the Ruler Cult of the Western Provinces of the Roman Empire* (EPaROdLR 108; Leiden: Brill, 1987), 21-31.

131. Price, *Rituals and Power*, 49-50. The reason why the regulation was applicable only in the East was in the difference with which the Greek and Roman mind perceived the divinity of the emperor. Whereas the Latin West clearly distinguished between *divus* and *deus* (with emperor becoming *deus* only after his death), in the Greek East the emperor was naturally worshiped as god (θ'εός) during his lifetime (see the discussion in Price, "Gods and Emperors," 79-95).

to grasp after equality with G/god[132] that finds an occasional critique in Jewish[133] and Graeco-Roman sources.[134] One particular Hellenistic ruler, Antiochus Epiphanes as portrayed in 2 Maccabees, readily comes to mind. When smitten by God's judgment, Antiochus allegedly confesses: "It is right to be subject to God; mortals should not think that they are equal to God (ὄντα ἰσόθεα φρονεῖν)" (2 Macc 9:12). Philo of Alexandria likewise offers an extensive discourse on the dangers of human arrogance and pride: "[E]very haughty arrogant man is full of vain groundless pride, looks upon himself as neither man nor demigod, but rather as an actual deity . . . thinking himself worthy to overstep all the boundaries of human nature."[135]

In two other treatises *On the Life of Moses* and *On the Embassy to Gaius*, Philo implicitly draws a contrast between the two leaders, Moses and the emperor Gaius. Both are said to be "like god," although they represent two diametrically opposed approaches toward gaining this status. On the one hand, there is a Roman emperor who "aspired to raise himself above [the

---

132. On the theme of the equality with G/god I profited much from the discussion in Samuel Vollenweider, "Der "Raub" Der Gottgleichheit: Ein Religionsgeschichtlicher Vorschlag zu Phil 2.6 (-11)," *NTS* 45 (1999): 413-33.

133. One of the peculiar features of the Hebrew Bible (nowhere found in the Ancient Near Eastern religions) is that a human being is presented as the one who dares to challenge the authority of God himself. A creature who was entrusted by God with the power to rule (Gen1:28) struggles with the temptation to be "like gods" (Gen 3:5). Most commonly in the OT it was an attitude of pride accompanied with wealth and the position of power which would bring an individual to the point of the arrogant denial of God (Ps 10:4b; Job 15; Zeph1:12). Particularly instructive is the passage in Isa 14 which portrays a blasphemous ruler who dared to grasp equality with God: "I will make myself like the Most High" (Isa 14:14). Another important pronouncement is found in Ezekiel against the ruler of Tyre:
> Because your heart is proud and you have said, "I am a god (θεός εἰμι ἐγώ);
> I sit in the seat of the gods, in the heart of the seas,"
> yet you are but a mortal, and no god,
> though you compare your mind with the mind of a god. (Ezek 28:2).

134. Cf., e.g., Herodotus: "Give a person this power, and straightway his manifold good things puff him up with pride, while envy is so natural to human kind that it cannot but arise in him. But pride and envy together include all wickedness – both of them leading on to deeds of savage violence" (Herod. 3.80.3). Similarly Isocrates: "When men look at their honors, their wealth, and their powers, they all think that those who are in the position of kings are the equals of the gods" (Isocr. 2.5). The following two maxims preserved in a second century CE Greek papyrus succinctly express popular perception of a ruler as being divine. "What is a god? Wielding of power (τὸ κρατοῦν). What is a king? Like a god (ἰσόθεος)" (cited in Price, *Rituals and Power*, 234).

135. *Virt.* 172; 174.

limits of human nature], and desired to be looked upon as a god"[136]; on the other hand, there is the leader of the Exodus, Moses, who in turn for his faithfulness was called "the god and king of the whole nation."[137]

In the Sybilline Oracles there are found two identical phrases which predict the return of the "destructive man" who, upon his return, will "make himself equal unto God" (ἰσαζῶν θεῷ).[138] As scholars generally agree, the prediction is a part of a legend, popular at the end of the first century CE, of the coming back to life of the emperor Nero (the so-called *Nero redivivus* myth). The claim to equality with God may have been a reflection on Nero's particular practice during his lifetime. For in 59 CE Nero established a corps of 5000 men (*Augustiani*) whose duty was to accompany the emperor in all public events and greet him with acclamations which betrayed his claim to divinity: "Our Apollo . . . by thyself we swear, O Caesar, none surpasses thee."[139]

So, what is the point of ἴσα θεῷ in Philippians 2:6 in the midst of such a negative valuation? It can be argued that in using ἴσα θεῷ terminology Paul applies it positively to Jesus who, although ἐν μορφῇ θεου,'[140] did not

---

136. *Leg.* 75; cf. 93.
137. *Mos.*1.156-158.
138. *Sib. Or.* 5.48-49; cf. 12.113-114.
139. Dio. 62.20.5. Dio further cites another, more elaborate acclamation: "Hail, Olympian Victor! Hail, Pythian Victor! Augustus! Augustus! Hail to Nero, our Hercules! Hail to Nero, our Apollo! The only victor of the Grand Tour, the only one from the beginning of time! August! Augustus! O Divine Voice! Blessed are they that hear you!" (62.20.5). See relevant discussion in D. Jones, "Roman Imperial Cult," 1030-31; also in Cuss, *Imperial Cult*, 77-81.
140. Whatever Jewish speculative thought is behind Paul's usage of the μορφὴ θεοῦ phraseology (see, e.g., Marcus Bockmuehl, "'The Form of God' (Phil. 2:6). Variations on a Theme of Jewish Mysticism," *JTS* 48 (1997): 1-23), within the context of Roman imperial ideology this term acquired an additional important meaning. With the rising aspirations of the Roman emperors to divinity the dissemination of the emperor's image throughout the empire becomes a matter of utmost importance. As G. Bowersock states, "Most persons in the empire of Rome could only have known their emperor from his bust or statue, and it was this which dominated the celebration of his cult" ("The Imperial Cult," 173). A particularly instructive case is the so-called Caligula crisis of 37-41 CE. Both Philo (*Legat.* 93-114) and Josephus (*Ant.*18.257-309) relate stories of Caligula's obsessive desire to present himself in divine appearance. He had a custom of dressing himself in elaborate costumes of various gods and goddesses, to which Philo sarcastically remarks: "...the form of God (θεοῦ μορφή) is not a thing which is capable of being imitated by an inferior one, as good money is imitated by bad" (*Legat.* 110). According to Suetonius Caligula ordered the removal of the heads of the most famous statues of the Greek gods in order to replace

consider grasping equality with God; negatively, then, Paul applies it to those who did grasp for such equality. As Heen rightly asserts, "it is not the status of *isotheos* that is being critiqued, but the grasping after it."[141] Indeed, Roman historical records abound with evidence of the emperors' usurping their positions of power at the cost of rivalry, intrigue, greed, and murder.[142] Contrary to these mighty rulers, like Antiochus, Gaius, and Nero, Jesus did not try to make himself equal to God;[143] he did not ascribe to himself the ἰσόθεοι τιμαί honors. God highly exalted him (2:9) for his humble submission.

That Christians, in total disregard of the imperial rule, claimed the ἴσα θεῷ status for "a nonenfranchised Jewish provincial of lower status, who had been executed by Rome"[144] must have been particularly outrageous. Such a claim could have been anything but politically innocuous for it set the figure of Jesus into competitive relationship with that of Caesar! In doing so the nascent Christian movement sailed on a course which in a short period of time led to an open confrontation with the prevailing imperial politics.

6.2.2.2 The Motif of Worship

The second indication of Paul's critical engagement with the imperial cult is the motif of worship found in Philippians 2:9-11.[145] Although, as A.

---

them with his own image. In the temple dedicated to his own divinity the golden statue of Caligula was daily dressed in the same clothes the emperor wore himself (*Caligula* 22,3-4). It is not necessary to suppose that Paul in writing Phil 2:6 was directly inspired by Caligula's blasphemous behavior, rather, given the general trend of the Roman emperors toward the usurpation of power, Paul might have prompted to utilize the μορφή-concept to set a contrast between Jesus and his earthly counterparts.

141. Heen, "Philippians," 148. Here we encounter in the term ἁρπαγμός one more of Paul's enigmatic terms. Vollenweider ("Raub," 415-27) critiques the attempts to render ἁρπαγμός as an idiomatic expression ("a useful gain;" cf. Roy W. Hoover, "The Harpagmos Enigma: A Philological Solution," *HTR* 64 [1971]: 95-119). He argues that such a meaning is not found until the fourth century CE. Instead the LXX supplies ample evidence for taking ἁρπαγμός in the negative sense of "booty" or "robbery" in an obvious allusion to kings and rulers who attained their position through usurpation.

142. Suetonius, *Calig.* 22; *Claud.* 26, 29, 34-37; *Ner.* 26-29; 33-39; 53; Tacitus, *Ann.* 14.59-65; 15.60.

143. Cf. Meeks, "Equal to God," 311.

144. Heen, "Philippians 2:6-11," 149.

145. The following two articles are especially relevant for the discussion: Richard J.

Collins argues, Philippians 2:6-11 strictly speaking is not a hymn or prayer addressed *to* Christ, she nevertheless concedes that the "last few lines [vv. 9-11] seem to advocate or expect the worship of Jesus Christ."[146] The idea implied behind the phrases ἐξομολογήσεται and γόνυ κάμψῃ is that of "veneration and political submission or obedience."[147]

Paul's primary source for this terminology is found in Isaiah 45:23. The passage in Isaiah is one of the most emphatically monotheistic in the whole of the HB. God is a sovereign ruler: "I am God, and there is no other" (v. 22). The useless idols cannot save (v. 20); God is alone the "righteous God and Savior" (v. 21) who pleads with his people to turn to him for salvation (v. 22). As a kind of special reassurance to those exiled in Babylon, the God who sits on the throne declares: "To me every knee shall bow (κάμψει πᾶν γόνυ), every tongue shall swear (ἐξομολογήσεται πᾶσα γλῶσσα)" (Isa 45:23, LXX). Paul sees this prophetic scene in Isaiah materialized in the mission of Jesus. In Paul's creative reworking of this passage it follows that the prophetic vision of "every knee's bowing" before God is being fulfilled through "every knee's bowing" before Christ: "God reigns and receives honor through Christ's reigning and receiving honor."[148]

No doubt, the intimations of worship of Jesus by the early Christians might have sounded like an encroachment on Jewish monotheism. Realizing the risk of being enticed into a prolonged discussion on this point, I will limit myself to some brief comments. Jewish thinking about God during the Second Temple period was characterized by interesting and at times provocative inner dynamics.[149] Two consistent tendencies can be

---

Bauckham, "The Worship of Jesus in Philippians 2: 9-11," in *Where Christology Began: Essays on Philippians 2, 5-11* (ed. Ralph P. Martin and Brian J. Dodd; Louisville, Ky.: Westminster John Knox, 1998), 128-39; Adela Yarbro Collins, "The Worship of Jesus and the Imperial Cult," in *The Jewish Roots of Christological Monotheism: Papers from the St. Andrews Conference on the Historical Origins of the Worship of Jesus* (ed. Carey C. Newman et al.; Leiden: Brill, 1999), 234-57.

146. Collins, "Worship of Jesus," 247. She further explains: "Although Phil 2:6-11 is not a prayer to Christ, the Aramaic prayer *maranatha*, discussed earlier, and Paul's report that he besought (παρεκάλεσα) the Lord three times about his "thorn in the flesh" (2 Cor 12:7-8) are evidence that communal prayers and private entreaties were directed to Jesus at an early date" ("Worship of Jesus," 247, n.56).

147. Collins, "Worship of Jesus," 247.

148. Oakes, *Philippians*, 169.

149. It should be noted that in the last thirty years the phenomenon of Jewish

delineated: a) fascination and experimentation with the world of intermediaries and exalted beings;[150] b) a strong hesitation toward worshiping any other exalted being, other than God.[151] Jewish experimentation with the

---

monotheistic belief has been increasingly a matter of a debate. It rages between those who continue to argue for the unique character of Jewish belief in one God (e.g., Richard Bauckham, *Jesus and the God of Israel: God Crucified and Other Studies on the New Testament's Christology of Divine Identity* [Grand Rapids: Eerdmans, 2008]; Larry W. Hurtado, *One God, One Lord: Early Christian Devotion and Ancient Jewish Monotheism* [Philadelphia: Fortress, 1988]; idem, "What Do We Mean by 'First-Century Jewish Monotheism?' in *SBL 1993 Seminar Papers* [ed. E.H. Lovering; Atlanta, Ga.: Scholars Press, 1993], 348–68; idem, "First-Century Jewish Monotheism," *JSNT* 71 [1998]: 3–26; idem, *Lord Jesus Christ: Devotion to Jesus in Earliest Christianity* [Grand Rapids: Eerdmans, 2003]; J. D.G. Dunn, "Was Christianity a Monotheistic Faith from the Beginning?" *SJT* 35 [1982]: 303–36; Alan F. Segal, "'Two Powers in Heaven' and Early Christian Trinitarian Thinking," in *The Trinity: An Interdisciplinary Symposium on the Trinity* [ed. D. Kendall et al.; Oxford: Oxford University Press, 1999], 73–95) and those who challenge this understanding (e.g., Margaret Barker, *The Great Angel: A Study of Israel's Second God* [Louisville, Ky.: Westminster John Knox, 1992]; Peter Hayman, "Monotheism – a Misused Word in Jewish Studies," *JJS* 42 [1991]: 1–15; Walter L. Moberly, "How Appropriate is 'Monotheism' as a Category for Biblical Interpretation?" in *Early Jewish and Christian Monotheism* [ed. Loren T. and Wendy E.S. North Stuckenbruck; London: T & T Clark, 2004], 216–34. In the views of the former, monotheism is the hallmark of the Jewish religious heritage; in the views of the latter, it is an anachronistic, misused category.

150. Cf. Andrew Chester, "Jewish Messianic Expectations and Mediatorial Figures and Pauline Christianity," in *Paulus und das Antike Judentum* (ed. Martin Hengel and Ulrich Heckel; Tübingen: Mohr Siebeck, 1991), 17–89. Some of the exalted beings were elevated so high as to bear the name of God (e.g., Yahoel in *Apoc. Abr.* 10:3, 8), or even the designation of the "second God" (Philo, *QG* 2.62). The developments within Merkabah mysticism stretched the limits of monotheism to an extent that rabbinic Judaism could not bear. There is a well-known exclamation of Elisha ben Abuya who, being overwhelmed by the majesty of the heavenly figure of Metatron, exclaimed: "Indeed, there are two divine powers in heaven!" (*3 En.* 16.3; cf. bHag. 15a). As a reaction to such unbridled speculation, as well as to the Christian and Gnostic teachings, the rabbis had to solidify the limits of monotheism and condemn those who teach that there are two powers in heaven (see the discussion in A.F. Segal, *Two Powers in Heaven: Early Rabbinic Reports about Christianity and Gnosticism* [Leiden: Brill, 1977]). Yet for the most part this Jewish experimentation with the intermediaries was never perceived as a threat as long as the sovereignty and uniqueness of God remained intact.

151. God is the one sovereign Lord over all creation, and over all nations, even over those who do not acknowledge this God. Even the spiritual powers who oppose God (Satan) in mysterious ways serve God's ultimate purposes which cannot be thwarted. All other beings, however highly exalted, are consistently portrayed as inferior and subservient to the high God of Israel. They could be depicted as highly exalted because they serve the Most High. The uniqueness of God is often described in terms of God's incomparability with any other deity. There is nothing that God can be compared with: "To whom then will you liken God, or what likeness compares with him?" (Isa 40:18). Philo's instruction on the "first and most sacred commandment" serve as a good illustration of Jewish attitudes toward God: "Let us . . . acknowledge and honor one God who is above all, and let the idea that gods are many never even reach the ears of man" (*Decal.* 65). God's uniqueness

world of intermediaries, indeed, provides us with some useful analogies for the early Christian accommodation of the veneration of the risen and exalted Jesus. But the lack of any precedent for such veneration in Judaism makes the Christian practice of worshiping Jesus "genuinely innovative and striking."[152] As Richard Bauckham has argued, the worship of Jesus rather than being a deviation is "a specifically Christian form of Jewish monotheism"[153] which implies "Jesus' inclusion in the unique identity of the one God who alone may be worshiped."[154]

As will be suggested in the coming discussion, the most probable source for belief in the lordship of Jesus lies in the early Christian conviction "that he was the anointed one of God, the Messiah of Israel."[155] As we also are going to argue, it was probably OT texts like Isaiah 45:20-23 which led Paul to the realization that God's salvific purposes would be fulfilled through his faithful Messiah. For as the Messiah essentially accomplishes what God promised to do himself, by bringing salvation to the nations (Isa 45:22), so he is crowned with the "name above any other name" (Phil 2:9). There is an intrinsic link in Paul's thinking between Jesus' messianic role and his function as κύριος.[156] If this is the case there is no way that we can either negate or downplay the political connotations embedded in this language. Within the wide spectrum of messianic expectations the dominant one was that of a mighty warrior-king whose dominion will be "from sea to sea, and from the River to the ends of the earth . . . All kings [will] fall down before him, all nations give him service" (Ps 72:8, 11). That is why the acknowledgment of Jesus as Lord *was* a serious encroachment in another area, the area of Roman imperial politics. Considering the popularity of the κύριος-

---

was characteristically manifested and upheld in religious worship. However widely developed were Jewish speculations about the intermediaries, patriarchs, angels, etc., there is no precedent for any of them being worshiped or prayed to. God alone was the object of prayers and sacrifices.

152. Hurtado, "First-Century Jewish Monotheism," 4.
153. Bauckham, "Worship of Jesus," 129.
154. Bauckham, "Worship of Jesus," 130.
155. Collins, "Worship of Jesus," 238.
156. Cf. Collins: "The veneration and acclamation here [2:9-11] may be read in a political sense (Jesus is Messiah or King in God's stead) or in a religious sense (Jesus is cosmic Lord in God's stead). Both connotations were probably intended and perceived in the first century CE" ("Worship of Jesus," 247, n. 56).

title during the reign of Nero (see coming discussion), for a Graeco-Roman mind the suggestion to "bow down"[157] and acknowledge "X as κύριος" most certainly would have evoked the setting of emperor worship.[158]

6.2.2.3 Κύριος *and* Σωτήρ *Terminology*

The third indication of Paul's critical engagement in Philippians with the imperial cult is the use of the titles κύριος and σωτήρ (2:9-11; 3:20). Paul applied these titles to Jesus. But there was another claimant in the Roman Empire to these same titles, namely, the emperor himself. Paul thus sets up a polemical parallelism, contrasting Christ and Caesar, in order to establish Christ as the one true κύριος and σωτήρ.

The term κύριος as applied to Jesus is a prominent feature in Philippians.[159] In applying the term to Jesus, Paul draws from the tradition which antedates his letters.[160] More significantly, Christological titles in Philippians betray their indebtedness to the OT. Indeed, "Paul serves as both our earliest and most definitive witness [that the confession "Jesus is Lord" comes] not from pagan or imperial influences"[161] but straight from the Septuagint. Two features in Philippians point in this direction. First, Paul uses the phrase ἡμέρα Χριστοῦ Ἰησοῦ three times (1:6, 10; 2:16) in a clear allusion to the

---

157. Rather than being literal, "bowing" in case of Roman emperor should be understood as an unequivocal sign of submission and obedience to his authority (but see Philo, *Leg.* 116).

158. Oakes, *Philippians*, 169.

159. Altogether the title is used fifteen times in the following variations: ὁ κύριος in 4:5; ἐν κυρίῳ in 1:14, 2:24, 29, 3:1; 4:1, 2, 4, 10; ἐν κυρίῳ Ἰησοῦ in 2:19; κύριος Ἰησοῦς Χριστός in 1:2; 2:11; 3:20; 4:23; Χριστοῦ Ἰησοῦ τοῦ κυρίου μου in 3:8. Κύριος in Philippians embraces a whole range of meanings, including Paul's personal relationship to Christ (2:19, 24; 3:8; 4:10), the corporate dimension as the Lord of the church in Philippi (1:2; 3:1; 4:1, 23); and the universal Lord of the whole cosmos (2:10-11; 3:20-21).

160. Cf. 1 Cor 16:22. Most likely the origin of the early Christian confession of Jesus as κύριος stems from the conviction that he was the anointed one of God, the Messiah of Israel; see Collins, "The Worship of Jesus," 238; cf. N.T. Wright: "If Jesus is Messiah, he is of course also Lord, *Kyrios*. The proper contexts for this term, too, are its Jewish roots on the one hand and its pagan challenge on the other. Taking them the other way round for the moment: the main challenge of the term, I suggest, was . . . to the lordship of Caesar, which, though certainly "political" was also profoundly "religious" ("Paul's Gospel and Caesar's Empire," *Reflections* 2 [1998]: 48).

161. Gordon Fee, "Paul and the Trinity: The Experience of Christ and the Spirit for Paul's Understanding of God," in *The Trinity: An Interdisciplinary Symposium on the Trinity* (ed. S. T. Davis et al; Oxford: Oxford University Press, 1999), 60.

well-known OT concept of the "day of the Lord." The concept, which in the OT signified the decisive coming of God, now comes to signify the future coming of Christ. What is of significance is that Paul feels free to drop κύριος leaving just the "day of Christ." One of the remarkable features of Paul's letters is his striking and innovative reapplication of OT citations (which originally contained references to God) to Christ.[162]

Second, as was already stated, Philippians 2:9-11 is written in obvious dependence on Isaiah 45:23. The most remarkable feature of Paul's rendering of the Isaianic passage is the referential shift of the Lord-title from God to Jesus, whereby Jesus becomes "the sharer of the unique lordship of Yahweh and the rightful recipient of such worship and praise as God alone may command."[163] The idea that the whole created universe will pay homage not just through Jesus to God, but to the κύριος Ἰησοῦς Χριστός is indeed an "astonishing"[164] one.

The appropriation of the title κύριος for the emperor had an uneasy start. In traditional Greek and Roman societies the address of a ruling king as κύριος would have been quite inappropriate.[165] Such a usage would have been undoubtedly considered as servile flattery because κύριος never entirely

---

162. Cf. 1 Cor 10:21; 22; 2 Cor 3:16; 1 Thess 3:13; 4:6; 2 Thess 1:7-8; 9; 12 etc.

163. Ralph P. Martin, *Carmen Christi: Philippians ii.5-11 in Recent Interpretation and in the Setting of Early Christian Worship* (Reprint [1967]; New York: Cambridge University Press, 1983), 257.

164. Hawthorne, *Philippians*, 92.

165. See the relevant discussion in Fee, "Paul and the Trinity," 49-72; Werner Foerster, "κύριος κτλ," *TDNT* 3:1081-98; Marco Frenschkowski, "Kyrios in Context Q 6:46, the Emperor as 'Lord', and the Political Implications of Christology in Q," in *Zwischen den Reichen: Neues Testament und Römische Herrschaft. Vorträge auf der Ersten Konferenz der European Association for Biblical Studies* (ed. Michael Labahn and Jürgen Zangenberg; Tübingen: Francke Verlag, 2002): 95-118; Lary W. Hurtado, "Lord," in *DPL* 560-69; Arthur D. Nock, "Early Gentile Christianity," 1:77; Dieter Zeller, "Kyrios," in *DDD* 492-96.

lost its original connotation of slave-ownership.¹⁶⁶ Indeed, Roman emperors, starting with Augustus, quite reluctantly accepted the title κύριος.¹⁶⁷

The situation drastically changes with Nero. Literally hundreds of artifacts (papyri, ostraca) have been discovered which, in place of the usual designation of an emperor as αὐτοκράτωρ, now contain κύριος ἡμῶν. Particularly telling is the extent ("everywhere, down to the remotest village"¹⁶⁸) of the evidence coming from all strata of society. It should be noted, however, that there is a general lack of evidence whether such usage was promoted officially by Rome. What is also important is that the artifacts were found not only in Egypt, but also in Greece. Adolf Deissmann cites a decree of honor found on a marble tablet in Boeotia (67 CE) which contains two references to Nero. The emperor is designated as "lord of the whole world" (ὁ τοῦ παντὸς κόσμου κύριος) and also as "the lord Augustus."¹⁶⁹

It is quite clear that by the time of Paul's missionary endeavor κύριος was used as "a divine predicate intelligible to the whole Eastern world."¹⁷⁰ At the same time κύριος was not yet *an official way* of addressing the emperor. For this reason the designation κύριος is not found on coins, or in official

---

166. As Frenschkowski points out, "*Kyrios* always describes a relationship, it is a part of interrelated word-pair, and this word-pair still mostly is slave-Lord" ("Kyrios in Context," 98). This is probably the main reason why Nock expressed his pessimism with regard to the possible interplay between the usage of the word in Christian and imperial contexts. In one of his extended essays on the Hellenistic background of early Christianity he wrote: "It may be doubted whether there is in the use of *kyrios* any conscious contrast or anything that would be felt as such between Jesus and the Emperor" ("Early Gentile Christianity," 77).

167. In fact, Suetonius tells us that Augustus "always felt horrified and insulted when called 'My Lord' (Suetonius here uses the Latin equivalent of the κύριος – *dominis*), a form of address used by slaves to their owners" (*Aug.* 53.1). Similarly, Tiberius did not allow himself to be addressed as *despotes* (Suetonius, *Tib.* 27; cf. also Tacitus, *Ann.* 2:87). Dio relates Tiberius' rationale for the prohibition: "I am *despotes* only of slaves, but *autokrator* of the army and simply *prokritos* of normal people" (Dio 57.8.2). Overall there is very poor evidence for the emperor's designation as κύριος before Nero.

168. G. Adolf Deissmann, *Light from the Ancient East: The New Testament Illustrated by Recently Discovered Texts of the Graeco-Roman World* (trans. Lionel R.M. Strachan; 1927; repr., Peabody, Ma.: Hendrickson, 1995), 353.

169. For this and other citations on Nero, see Deissmann, *Light,* 353-55. In this regard a small piece of evidence from the book of Acts should not be ignored. It is quite symptomatic that in Acts 25:26 Festus calls Nero simply ὁ κύριος. In light of the overwhelming support from other sources this often questioned and neglected evidence should be considered as "thoroughly credible" (Deissmann, *Light*, 354).

170. Deissmann, *Light,* 350.

correspondence or on state inscriptions. Κύριος in the first century CE is used more like an epithet or a metonym, not an official title bestowed by some senatorial decree. Yet, overwhelming evidence from private letters and documents from the time of Nero on testifies that κύριος becomes a persistently popular designation of the emperor. And it is precisely the case when "popular usage of this kind is more relevant for the NT than is official or literary usage."[171] Popular usage refers to the language that people use in prayer to address their deities. In the Hellenistic culture in which the κύριος-terminology was widely used in evoking gods,[172] it is almost natural to suppose that the same kind of language was used in worshiping the emperor. For these reasons, we concur with Donald Jones that "the least one can say is that *kyrios* as a title in the imperial cult left its imprint on the first century A.D. and the early Christian proclamation of Jesus as Lord would doubtless have confronted it."[173]

In Philippians we encounter one more significant Christological designation of Jesus as the coming σωτήρ (Phil 3:20).[174] Σωτήρ is one of those key terms used in the OT for the identity of God: God is called Savior because he is the one who brings deliverance.[175] Although other human beings may serve as the agents of God's salvation and in this sense can be called saviors,[176] nevertheless, Paul's introduction of the Messiah as the expected Savior (Phil 3:20) is an interesting and innovative thought. The most obvious reason for such innovation is Paul's re-reading of Isaiah 45:20-23. As we already pointed out, in that crucial text, God, who is introduced as a "righteous God and Savior" (v. 21), promises deliverance not only to those who are exiled in Babylon, but indeed to "all the ends of the earth" (v. 22).

---

171. Oakes, *Philippians*, 171.

172. Cf. Deismann: "It is therefore in accordance with Egyptian or Egypto-Semitic custom that in numerous Greek inscriptions, papyri, and ostraca of the earliest Imperial period the title "lord" is attached to the Caesars" (*Light*, 357).

173. Jones, "Roman Imperial Cult," 1031.

174. Surprising as it may be this is the only case of σώτηρ found within the undisputed Pauline letters. If we take into consideration the letter to the Ephesians and the Pastorals we can count another six references (Eph 5:23; 1 Tim 1:1; 2:3; Titus 1:3; 2:10; 3:4).

175. E.g., Deut 32:15; Mic 7:7; Hab 3:18; Pss 24:5; 27:1; 62:2; Isa 12:2; 45:15, 21; 60:16; 63:8).

176. E.g., Judg 2:16; 3:9, 15; 2 Kgs 13:5; Neh 9:27.

Obviously Paul envisions that this prophetic vision is now being fulfilled through the mediation of God's Messiah.

Starting with Julius Caesar, σωτήρ was frequently, although not exclusively,[177] used for emperors. The most basic meaning of the Greek word σωτήρ signified "a person who saves or preserves."[178] Of special importance is the fact that σωτήρ had a prominent place in the imperial cult. As M. Bockmuehl states: "[σωτήρ] was the title commonly used for Caesar in the Roman Emperor cult."[179] One example is found on a famous inscription from Priene (c. 9 BCE) where Augustus is hailed as a "savior (σωτήρ) who brought war to an end and set [all things] in peaceful order."[180] Of Caligula it was said that he "would pour out streams of blessings on Asia and Europe as savior and benefactor" (σωτήρ καὶ εὐεργέτης).[181] The two inscriptions from Eresus (Lesbos) and from Aezani (Phrygia) celebrate Claudius as the "savior of the world" (σωτήρ τᾶ'ς οἰκουμένας)[182] and as "savior god and benefactor" (θεὸς σωτήρ καὶ εὐεργέτης).[183] The same was true with regard to Nero. An inscription from Egypt (60-61 CE) addresses the emperor:[184]

Νέρωνι Κλαυδίωι Καίσαρ[ι] Σεβαστῶι Γερμανικῶ[ι] αὐτοκράτορι, τῶ σωτῆρι καὶ εὐεργέτηι τῆ[ς] οἰκουμένης.

---

177. Cf. Nock "*Soter*, while most often used of Emperors, was at times formally applied to local dignitaries and to Imperial functionaries, in a manner which indicates that it was not felt to be excessive or invidious" ("Soter and Euergetes," in *Essays on Religion and the Ancient World* [ed. Zeph Stewart; Cambridge, Ma.: Harvard University Press, 1972], 727).

178. Jan den Boeft, "Saviour," in *DDD* 733. Originally σώτηρ was applied to gods whose function was protecting and rescuing people. Gradually the term came to be used of people of exceptional bravery or other similar qualities who rescued individuals or communities from their enemies. To these belonged first of all military leaders, politicians, but also philosophers and poets.

179. Bockmuehl, *Philippians*, 235. See also Werner Foester, "σώτηρ κτλ," *TDNT* 7:1010-12; Witherington, *Philippians*, 99-102.

180. Cited in Victor Ehrenberg and A.H.M. Jones, eds., *Documents Illustrating the Reigns of Augustus and Tiberius* (2nd ed.; Oxford: Clarendon Press, 1955; 1976), § 98b.

181. Philo, *Leg.* 22.

182. *IGRR* 4.12.

183. *IGRR* 4.584.

184. *IGRR* 1.1124. A similar ascription of the title of σωτήρ to Nero is found on an inscription from Cyprus (*IGRR* 3.986; 60-61 CE).

> To the emperor Nero Claudius Caesar Augustus Germanicus,
> the savior and benefactor of the world.

It is our contention that this analysis of κύριος and σωτήρ has direct bearing on the correct understanding of Paul's rhetoric in Philippians 3:18-20. Paul's vision of the κύριος who is coming to save his people clashes with the imperial vision, for the coming παρουσία[185] of a military leader or emperor with a rescue mission[186] was a familiar notion. Although the usual Pauline term for the coming of Christ (παρουσία) is missing in Philippians (although see 2:12), the idea is clearly present in the background of the expectation of the Savior, Jesus (Phil 3:20). In Paul's mind the awaited Savior is expected to transform the bodies of humility "by the power that also enables him to make all things subject to himself" (3:21). It is this extraordinary characterization of the κύριος and σωτήρ who is invested with superior power – power that enables him to "subject all things" (3:21)[187] – and to whom universal, indeed, cosmic homage is due, ("every knee should bend, in heaven and on earth and under the earth;" 2:10)[188] that makes the comparison between Christ and Caesar all the more plausible.[189]

---

185. Παρουσία is another of those words which "straddles both Jewish apocalyptic and imperial context" (J.R. Harrison, "Paul and the Imperial Gospel at Thessaloniki," *JSNT* 25 [2002]: 82). The word is often found on the inscriptions announcing the coming of the ruling emperor (for the examples see Deissmann, *Light*, 368-72).

186. Cf. Cicero: "He no doubt is a savior who has provided salvation" (*Ver.* 2.2.154). The salvation was always understood not in abstraction but in some concrete, material way. The savior is the one who provides peace, stability and material goods.

187. As Oakes points out, it is this connection of the savior-figure with the *invested power* which makes the comparison between Christ and the emperor "unequivocal" (*Philippians*, 139, 140-41).

188. Cf. Philo's sincere amazement the universal scope of the homage paid to the emperor: "[A]ll men, all women, all cities, all nations, every country and region of the earth, I had almost said the whole of the inhabited world (πᾶσα ἡ οἰκουμένη), . . . flatter him, dignifying him above measure, and helping to increase his pride and arrogance" (*Legat.* 116). He is especially appalled by the "the barbaric custom . . . of falling down in adoration before him [Gaius]" (*Legat.* 116).

189. Philo, like Paul, seems to be drawing a parallel between the unrighteous Gaius ("the ruler of all the earth and of all the sea," *Legat.* 44) who assumes "the sovereignty of the whole world" (*Legat.* 8), and the righteous Moses to whom God entrusted sovereignty over "all the earth and sea, and of all the rivers." In fact, God "gave him the whole world (πάντα τὸν κόσμον) as a possession" (*Mos.* 1.155).

6.2.3 Paul's Way of Discipleship: Κοινωνία in Christ's Sufferings

The third difference between Paul and his opponents is related to a different path that they choose to follow. While the opponents are the "enemies of the cross" (Phil 3:18) Paul and others are the followers of the crucified Jesus. In our previous discussion we indicated that several features in Philippians 3:18-20 (such as the emotional, reiterated character of the admonition, and the language of enmity read within the context of the Graeco-Roman conventions) strongly suggest that the opponents quite possibly counted themselves among the devotees of Christ. What they seem to oppose was a particular way of discipleship which for Paul implied following the crucified. Why would the "cross" become a stumbling block for at least some Gentile converts to Christianity?

We have already briefly noted the significance of the cross for Paul and his theology.[190] Far from being simply the means of the crucifixion, the cross becomes an important, if not central, theological symbol. "Cross" divides human existence into a "before" and "after"; it becomes "the absolute epistemological watershed."[191] For Paul the crucifixion of Christ is not a commemoration of the event in the past, it is something which continues to create "a new and persisting situation whereby Paul's allegiance is radically changed, his identity revamped."[192] In no small way the cross signifies "the death of one world and the advent of another,"[193] the beginning of the new creation (Gal 6:15; 2 Cor 5:17).

---

190. See on the issue: Alexandra R. Brown, *The Cross and Human Transformation: Paul's Apocalyptic Word in 1 Corinthians* (Minneapolis: Fortress, 1995); idem, "Apocalyptic Transformation in Paul's Discourse on the Cross" *WW* 16 (1996): 427-36. Charles B. Cousar, *A Theology of the Cross: The Death of Jesus in the Pauline letters* (OBT; Minneapolis: Fortress Press, 1990); David E. Fredrickson, "Paul, Hardships, and Suffering," in *Paul in the Greco-Roman World: A Handbook* (ed. J. Paul Sampley; Harrisburg, Pa.: Trinity Press International, 2003), 172-97; Joel B. Green and Mark D. Baker, *Recovering the Scandal of the Cross: Atonement in New Testament and Contemporary Contexts* (Downers Grove, Ill.: InterVarsity, 2000); Martin Hengel, *The Cross of the Son of God* (trans. John Bowden; London: SCM, 1986); J. Louis Martyn, "Epistemology at the Turn of the Ages: 2 Corinthians 5:16," in *Christian History and Interpretation: Studies Presented to John Knox* (ed. W.R. Farmer et al.; Cambridge: Cambridge University Press, 1967), 269-87.
191. Martyn, "Epistemology at the Turn of the Ages," 286.
192. Cousar, *A Theology of the Cross*, 143.
193. J. Louis Martyn, "Apocalyptic Antinomies in Paul's Letter to the Galatians," *NTS* 31

There are several reasons which help us understand the difficulty of the Gentiles' appropriation of the symbolism of the cross. Whereas for Paul the cross constituted a matter of his pride (Gal 6:14), for the majority of the Gentile world it was "a highly offensive and shameful symbol. As a punishment it was largely restricted to the lower classes, provincials and slaves and nearly always was associated with rebellion and treason."[194] Paul's references in Philippians to δοῦλος ("slave," 2:7) and σταυρός ("cross," 2:8), represent, respectively, "the most dishonorable *public status* and the most dishonorable *public humiliation* imaginable in the world of Roman antiquity."[195]

Second, it was not just a matter of pure esthetics but an implicit connection between cross and humility, which was particularly difficult to swallow for potential converts in Philippi. We have indicated in our previous discussion (see ch. 5) that some of the dominant features of Graeco-Roman culture were love for honor, prestige and status. We have also referred to overwhelming epigraphic evidence which testified of the Philippians' particular fondness for honorific titles and descriptions. There are clear indications of similar tendencies within the Philippian Christian community. Paul's criticism of their acting out of "selfish ambition or conceit" (2:3) and their "seeking [their] own interests" (2:21) is an eloquent testimony of at least some people in the community who utilize their membership for personal promotion and self-elevation. For this reason we agree with Cotter's assertion that "in the Philippian context to be an enemy of Christ's cross would mean a person opposed to any sort of humiliation."[196]

Moreover, it was not just the issue of humility and renunciation of status but the prospect of suffering for Christ's sake which could have presented a major obstacle for the Gentile believers.[197] Although suffering in general

---

(1985): 414.

194. DeVos, "Church and Community Conflicts," 285.

195. Joseph H. Hellerman, "The Humiliation of Christ in the Social World of Roman Philippi, Part 2," *BibSac* 160 (2003): 424.

196. Cotter, "Our Politeuma," 97.

197. Cf. Wolfgang Schrage: "Christ and his cross are the ground and cause of the suffering of the Christian." („Leid, Kreuz und Eschaton: Der Perstasenkataloge als Merkmale paulinischer *theologia crucis* und Eschatologie," *EvT* 34 (1974): 162; cited in Cousar, *A Theology of the Cross*, 152). In Philippians there is a close link between humility and suffering: as the humility of Jesus led him to the cross, so the followers of Jesus have to be ready to embrace the same destiny: suffering is a part and parcel of following the crucified

was not a stranger in the 1st century Mediterranean world,[198] there is a pointed difference in how the theme of suffering was treated in the Graeco-Roman and Jewish traditions. As was asserted in ch. 2, Graeco-Roman religion was understood as an effective means for preservation of the well being of an individual and the society as a whole. In other words, worship of a deity should bring peace and harmony, not suffering. No doubt, Jewish understanding of religion was no different. At the same time the reality of living in an almost permanent state of persecution made suffering for the Jews an essential part of their religious experience. The Jews learned how to make sense out of it,[199] learned how to "suffer with joy."[200]

Most probably under the influence of Jewish apocalypticism, the early Christians adopted the thought that "through many persecutions [they] must enter the kingdom of God" (Acts 14:22). For Paul, a faithful student of that tradition, his pointed emphasis on suffering proceeds mostly from his *theological understanding* of a qualitatively different situation which Christ inaugurated by his own sufferings. The time of the messianic woes has begun and thus none of the faithful can escape the privilege of being a part of it. For Paul "the suffering of this present time" (Rom 8:19) had indeed a cosmic significance. The universal "groaning" was a sure sign that the "new creation" is well under way (cf. Rom 8:18-23).

When Paul talks of the prospects of "suffering with Christ" (Phil 1:28-30) he probably means the consequences of the believers' withdrawal from

---

(Phil 1:29).

198. Cf. L. Gregory Bloomquist: "Dread of suffering and death translated into fear of familial suffering and death in the form of dishonor and kinship pollution; political suffering and death translated into the ever-present threat of civil strife; ultimate apocalyptic death was the unthinkable dissolution of the empire itself. The world—from the struggle of daily life to imperial conquest— was a battleground of social suffering and death in which no one could win" ("Subverted by Joy: Suffering and Joy in Paul's letter to the Philippians," *Int* 61 [2007]: 271).

199. For example, the book of Sirach admonishes readers to face difficulties with a Stoic-like attitude: "Whatever happens to you, accept it, and in the uncertainties of your humble state, be patient, since gold is tested in the fire, and the chosen in the furnace of humiliation" (Sir 2:4-5, NJB).

200. Cf. the final prayer of a ninety year old martyr in 2 Macc 6:30: "The Lord in his holy knowledge knows full well that, although I could have escaped death, I am not only enduring terrible pain in my body from this scourging, but also *suffering it with joy* in my soul because of my devotion to him" (2 Macc 6:30, NAB, emphasis added).

worshiping the official gods. Such a behavior could have easily provoked sporadic acts of hatred or violence, social ostracism, and action of the sort. Yet, once again, we should not anachronistically read into the prospect of "suffering" the state sponsored persecution of the Christians with the confiscation of their property, prohibitions against visiting public buildings and markets, indeed with the threat to their own lives which all took place at a much later date.[201]

Our previously suggested scenario for the opponents' identity fits well with the current supposition that they were the proponents of a cross*less* form of Christianity. For as we have seen voluntary associations fulfilled an important social function within Graeco-Roman society. Although religious devotion within such associations was an essential element of their functioning, often an exclusive devotion to a deity was not the primary reason for joining the association. Moreover, we have seen examples of syncretistic practices within associations. If our earlier supposition that early Christianity in Philippi was nurtured through a network of house churches is correct, then it is possible that Paul's opponents in Philippians 3:18-20 is a deviant group of former friends (Paul weeps over their fate) now turned enemies (see previous discussion). Paul has to address the issue of the enemies once again, for their stance has an appealing side for other believers: they suggest a form of Christianity which excludes the prospect of social

---

201. Although there are good reasons to believe that the early Christian proclamation from the start indeed contained a subversive, anti-imperial message (cf. Acts 16:31-32), and thus could not have gone unnoticed by the local authorities, it was still a long way toward any full-scale, state-sponsored persecution of the followers of Jesus. Despite the fact of the swift growth of Christianity in the first thirty to forty years after the death of Jesus Rome for the most part remained ignorant of this new sect. A. Sherwin-White in an article published as early as 1952 convincingly showed that Roman judicial bureaucracy was in effect one of the sure means which precluded the prospect of a wide scale persecution of Christians or other religious minorities (see "The Early Persecutions and Roman Law Again," *JTS* 3 (1952): 199-213). Although Paul himself designates his imprisonment as for the "defense and confirmation of the gospel" (Phil 1:7), it is so far his own mostly rhetorical characterization. There is at this point in Roman law no charge for "preaching Jesus" or being his follower. According to Luke's account in Acts, Paul was not a political prisoner of Rome; on the contrary, Roman authorities play a positive role in securing the life of the apostle (Acts 23:10; 23; 24). Paul's imprisonment at the time of writing the Philippians is the result of his own volition: "You have appealed to the emperor; to the emperor you will go" (Acts 25:12).

ostracism and suffering. Their earthly πολίτευμα serves as a protective umbrella which legitimizes their existence within the society.

Conclusion

Summarizing this part of our discussion I would like to reiterate our line of reasoning. In Philippians 3:18-20 we are introduced to a group of people whom Paul calls "the enemies of the cross of Christ" (3:18). The emphatic structure of Paul's phrase and the use of the word πολίτευμα ("but our πολίτευμα is in heaven," 3:20) led some scholars to the conclusion that Paul in fact borrows the term from his opponents to argue for a different πολίτευμα in heaven. The meaning of πολίτευμα used in the inscriptions of voluntary associations supports our initial supposition that Paul's opponents in Philippians 3:18-20 were members of a voluntary association who at some point accepted Christ as a cultic deity. This supposition was further substantiated by reading Paul's text within the Graeco-Roman conventions of enmity. Voluntary association most naturally could have provided the organizational structure and ideological rationale for their different "walk" (3:18). Furthermore, the supposition was substantiated by the analyses of Paul's polemical description of the opponents in 3:19 which, in our assessment, best fits the socializing practices within voluntary associations. We argued that Paul intentionally chooses an insulting characterization of his opponents to make his point: these are dangerous people! The danger in our view proceeds from the intrinsic link which existed between the socializing practices of associations and religious devotion.

In the second part of this chapter we considered Paul's counter-arguments against his opponents. First of all, Paul capitalizes on the ambiguity of the term πολίτευμα. Whereas for his opponents πολίτευμα is the term used for voluntary associations, Paul uses the term to substantiate his vision for the "Jerusalem above" understood as the heavenly governing body under whose protection and guidance believers live on earth. Second, our analysis of certain terminology in Philippians (equality with God, κύριος and σώτηρ, the worship motif) clearly points to Paul's anti-imperial polemics whereby Jesus is set as an alternative Lord and Savior of the nations.

When the opponents' description in Philippians 3:18-20 is read through this ideological grid, it helps us understand Paul's indignation and harsh characterization of the opponents. Finally, what distinguishes Paul and his opponents is a different understanding of what it means to be a follower of the crucified. For them, Christ is a cultic deity, one among others. For Paul, Christ is the only Lord and Savior who summons his disciples to follow him through renunciation of status and indeed the prospect of coming suffering.

Summary

In the current study, we followed the methodology pioneered by G. Heinrici and E. Hatch, and attempted to read a particular passage from Paul's letter to the Philippians (3:18-20) within the social context of the first century Graeco-Roman city. Overall the method of socio-historical study proved to be a valuable tool for the correct understanding of the formation of the early Christian community. For such formation took place not in isolation but rather in interaction with the concrete realities of the urban life of the Roman Empire.

Hatch's supposition that Christian groups would have been considered "to the eye of the outside observer" as types of voluntary associations drew our attention to the study of this peculiar social institution. Their unofficial status, openness, and egalitarian character stipulated the vast dispersion and popularity of voluntary associations in the ancient world. In our study of the epigraphic evidence we saw examples of voluntary associations where men and women, rich and poor, slaves and highly ranking Roman officials were united under the same bond of religious or occupational devotion. For many, especially underprivileged members of society (slaves, foreigners, women), voluntary associations provided the sense of belonging and opportunities for social mobility. Philippi in this sense was not an exception: the inscriptional evidence confirmed the presence of both professional and religious associations at Philippi.

In many ways the focal point of our discussion, namely, the identity of the "enemies of the cross," is a conspicuous commentary on the uneven and complicated character of the Gentiles' appropriation of the gospel. To bring back Crossan and Reed's metaphor of the two "tectonic plates," Paul's polemic against the "enemies of the cross" in Philippians 3:18-20 is an example of the critical engagement of the Jewish-Christian monotheistic tradition with the pluralistic Graeco-Roman culture. As the Christian gospel intruded further into Gentile territory, its appropriation by the Gentiles could not help but involve certain elements of adaptation and assimilation to the prevailing culture. In terms of organizational structure, for example, Christians did not have to invent a specific "Christian" form. The "small group" setting, like the Graeco-Roman household and/or voluntary associations, was readily available for Christians to use in their formation. The NT evidence points to the fact that it was within such settings that Paul's ministry took place at Philippi.

Moreover being an artisan by trade, his practice of "preaching while working" (1 Thess 2:9) undoubtedly could have created the impression that he was setting up another religious association. It naturally follows that the terminology which was used of voluntary associations (ἐκκλησία, πολίτευμα), or of their officers (ἐπίσκοποι, διάκονοι), became a part of the enriched Christian vocabulary. With the appropriation of certain structural models and terminology, Christian community inherited certain peculiar features and trends, among them the fact that the heads of the households and better off members of the community most naturally assumed special roles within the Christian *ekklēsia*. Like the household and voluntary associations, Christian community, through the practice of patronage, became an effective instrument of social networking. As we indicated in our study, being connected to an influential patron was at times as strong an incentive as the devotion to a deity to join an association. The elevated status of women and their leadership roles in the Philippian church was a reflection of a similar trend within the official and non-official cultic associations in that city. Moreover, the language of friendship, honor, and of internal rivalry used by Paul in the letter to the Philippians points to a similar social dynamic in voluntary associations.

What distinguished Philippi, this relatively small provincial city, was the coveted privileged status of the Roman colony. One of the clear signs of its pro-Roman stance was the prominent display of the imperial cult in Philippi. Some of the inscriptional evidence suggested the involvement of members of voluntary associations in emperor worship. In a city like Philippi, participation in the emperor cult, far from being a meaningless ritualistic exercise, would have been the most natural way to express appreciation for the benefits of the *Pax Romana*. Such participation also conferred legitimacy on those who participated and their sense of belonging to the overall Roman political universe.

We also pursued the task of identifying the "enemies of the cross" in view of the proposed meaning of πολίτευμα. It was Paul's emphatic phrase: "But *our* πολίτευμα is in heaven!" (Phil 3:20) that suggested a polemical juxtaposition of the πολίτευμα of these "enemies" to the one propagated by Paul. The lexical study of the term πολίτευμα confirmed that the word was used of voluntary associations. The structure of Paul's argument in Philippians 1:27-4:3 strongly suggested that the "enemies of the cross" was a deviant group of Christians for whom membership in a voluntary association (πολίτευμα) provided the structure and ideological rationale for their alternative "walk." Paul's emotional tone (3:18) suggests his opponents are professing Christians, at least some of whom Paul knew in person. The reiterated character of the admonition (3:18) also suggests that their different "walk" continued to present a tempting alternative to the rest of the community.

We have also argued that Paul's polemical description of the opponents (3:19) is reminiscent of the socializing practices within voluntary associations. Such practices were at the same time expressions of religious devotion and of political loyalty. It was the opponents' continual devotion to the Roman emperor as to the κύριος and σωτήρ of the nations that Paul finds especially appalling, if not downright blasphemous.[1] The theme of "equality with God" and the motif of worship further corroborated this conclusion. For Paul, the staunch defender of a Jewish monotheistic heritage (cf. 1 Cor 8:6), any claims to be ἴσα θεῷ (as it is implied in the ἰσόθεοι τιμαί terminology) would immediately implicate the false pretender. The seemingly politically innocuous terminology, prompted by Paul's Jewish heritage, attains clear anti-imperial connotations within the context of imperial ideology. For Paul there is only one κύριος, the σωτήρ Jesus, who is worthy

---

1. Cf. D. Cuss, "A Christian of the first century who believed in one God, and who reserved for this God all the divine titles which his pagan countrymen lavished on the emperor and his family, would understand without difficulty the implications of the author of the Apocalypse when he wrote that the heads of the beast 'were marked with blasphemous titles' [Rev 13:1]" (*Imperial Cult*, 51-52).

of veneration; before him "every knee shall bow" including that of the emperor. By their continual devotion to Caesar, the opponents threaten to undermine the essential features of Paul's worldview. This is what made these people especially dangerous; for Paul they are enemies who are doomed for eternal destruction.

In Philippians 3:20 Paul capitalizes on the metaphorical meaning of the word πολίτευμα, which was used for the designation of a governing body within a *polis,* to argue his alternative vision of the heavenly πολίτευμα behind which lurks the notion of the "new Jerusalem" (Gal 4:26). As the genius of the Roman political system introduced the emperor as the central figure of social integration and consolidation, Paul's missionary endeavor brought forth an alternative societal community of the *familia Christi,* members of which were organized around an alternative figure of societal integration, namely, κύριος Jesus. A particularly scandalous element of Christian proclamation was the fact that this Jesus himself fell victim to Roman imperial policy and was executed as an insurrectionist, but now was held to be entitled to universal authority and acclaim. Yet, as Jesus, on the way to glory, humbled himself to the point of death, so his followers were to organize their lives accordingly, not excluding the call to "participate in his sufferings" (Phil 3:10). These initially unknown and unnoticed followers of the Nazarene became in time a mortal threat to the imperial system because in their proclamation the very center of Roman political and social integration was challenged.

APPENDIX 1

Cults Attested at and Near Philippi

(Adapted from Valerie Abrahamsen, *Women and Worship*, 16-18)

Table 1

Cult/Deity	Archeological or other evidence	Era	Remarks
Hera-Juno	-one inscription from forum -possibly eight rock reliefs, all questionable	Imperial	-designated "Regina" by Thracians -Hadrian's wife identified with her on inscription
Athena-Minerva	-marble sculpture from forum temple (placed between two Victories) -possibly three rock reliefs	Imperial	-identified with Diana in one inscription from Koumbalitsa
Aphrodite-Venus	-chapel and statue at Dikili-Tash – possibly six rock reliefs (these could, however, be "female figures")	Imperial	-shown with objects from women's daily life -goddess of marriage

Cult/ Deity	Archeological or other evidence	Era	Remarks
Men-Luna	-one rock relief, with attributes of Luna and Bendis -possibly one acropolis inscription to Luna	Imperial (and earlier?)	in relief, wears Phrygian cap with star, leans on a spear; is feminine here through sexually ambiguous elsewhere -Mên cult on Thasos (syncretized with Dionysos)
Sabazios	-Strabo references (for Thrace) -Macrobius references (for Thrace) -possible rock reliefs (as syncretized with Dionysos)	Imperial and earlier	-throughout Thrace, member of a trinity also consisting of two goddesses: Demeter-Juno-Kybele and Artemis-Bendis-Mên
Isis (with Serapis and Telesphorus/ Horus)	-sanctuary on acropolis hill -inscriptions -altar at city gate (moved there in antiquity) -possibly several rock reliefs (most of these could be "female figures") -votive ear among reliefs	-Imperial and earlier -early Byzan-tine	-Isis as "Regina" in two inscriptions (one from Drama) -has priests in cult -healing deity -Imperial coins minted at Thessaloniki portrays Serapis -important site at Amphipolis -Isis most common of the three deities (Isis, Serapis, Horus) at Philippi

Cults Attested at and Near Philippi

Cult/ Deity	Archeological or other evidence	Era	Remarks
Kybele-Mother of the Gods-Cotys	-inscriptions from near Philippi – colossal statue from forum – marble head from baths -possibly three rock reliefs -sanctuary near Sylvanus inscription -Strabo references (for region)	Imperial (and earlier on Thasos)	-may be related to Imperial cult at Philippi -in connection with Attis, may have healing qualities -highly attested on Thasos and elsewhere in Thrace, including coinage
Mars-Jupiter-Ares	-two reliefs, including one at theater -rock relief associated with Dionysos -Herodotus references (for region)	Imperial and earlier	god of gladiators and soldiers in arena
Liber Pater and Libera (sometimes with Hercules)	-three inscriptions from baths – inscriptions from Drama, Raktcha and Kalambaki (one each) -funerary stelai in region	-Imperial -Early Byzantine (especially on Thasos)	Agricultural deities syncreticized to Dionysos, especially vis-à-vis funerary rites
Nemesis and Nike-Victoria	-reliefs and inscriptions at theater -one rock relief -coins -statues associated with forum temples -forum inscriptions	Imperial	protector of arena participants

Cult/ Deity	Archeological or other evidence	Era	Remarks
Dionysos-Bacchus	-Herodotus references (for region) -sanctuary near Sylvanus inscription? -two phalluses and a Centaur among rock reliefs -pre-Roman coins -several rock reliefs -Hellenistic temple	Imperial and earlier	-closely allied with Liber Pater, Horseman and Sabazios -associated with frenzied rites, mysteries and orgies -heavy female participation in above -concern for veneration of the dead and the afterlife
Emperor and Empress	-two temples in forum -numerous inscriptions in forum	Imperial	worship patterns seem generally to follow those of rest of empire

APPENDIX 2

Membership List of the Silvanus Association at Philippi

(*CIL* 3.633.2; Pilhofer, *Phillipi*, II: 170-72)

Col. 1
L(ucius) Volattius Urbanus sac(erdos)
L(ucius) Nutrius Valens iun(ior)
Hermeros Metrodori
C(aius) Paccius Mercurialis
P(ublius) Vettius Victor
C(aius) Abellius Anteros
Orinus coloniae
M(arcus) Publicius Valens
Crescens Abelli
C(aius) Flavius Pudens
M(arcus) Varinius Chresimus
M(arcus) Minucius Ianvarius
P(ublius) Hostilius Philadelphus
P(ublius) Herennius Venustus
L(ucius) Domitius Ikarus
M(arcus) Publicius Laetus
C(aius) Abellius Agathopus
C(aius) Curtius Secundus
P(ublius) Ofillius Rufus
C(aius) Horatius Sabinus
Ti(berius) Claudius Magnus

T(itus) Flav[iu]s Clymenus
L(ucius) Domitius Callistus
C(aius) Decimus Germanus
M(arcus) Publicius Primigenius
C(aius) Paccius Trophimus
L(ucius) Atiarius Firmus
P(ublius) Vettius Aristobulus
Chrysio Pacci

Col. 3
Hostilius Natales
C(aius) Paccius Mercuriales l(ibertus)
M(arcus) Alfenus Aspasius sacerdos
C(aius) Valerius Firmus
Velleius Palbes
A(ulus) Velleius Onesimus
Phoibus colon(iae)
C(aius) Flavius Pudens
L(ucius) Volattius Firmus
M(arcus) Publicius Cassius
C(aius) Abellius Secundus
Atilius Fuscus
L(ucius) Domitius Venerianus

L(ucius) Domitius Primigenius
L(ucius) Atiarius Thamyrus
Col. 2
M(arcus) Herennius Helenus
C(aius) Atilius Fuscus
C(aius) Atilius Niger
Tharsa coloniae
Phoebus coloniae
L(ucius) Laelius Felix
M(arcus) Plotius Gelos
P(ublius) Trosius Geminus
M(arcus) Plotius Valens
M(arcus) Plotius Plotianus f(ilius)
M(arcus) Plotius Valens f(ilius)
L(ucius) Atiarius Successus
C(aius) Licinius Valens
C(aius) Velleius Rixa

L(ucius) Volattius Urbanus
C(aius) Iulius Philippus
L(ucius) Domitius Icario
Canuleius Crescens
L(ucius) Atiarius Moschas
Fontius Capito
M(arcus) Glitius Carus
L(ucius) Atiarius Suavis
Domitius Peregrinus
Col. 4
Iulius Candidus
Valerius Clemens

APPENDIX 3

Graeco-Roman and Jewish Literary Sources on Πολιτευμα

Aeschines (4th century BCE):

Against Timarchus 1.86: "Demophilus had previously brought in a measure (πολίτευμα) of the following sort..."

Against Timarchus 1.86: "... the revision of the lists and the measures (πολιτευμάτων)..."

On the Embassy 2.8: "...and the peace and the politics of Eubulus (Εὐβούλου πολιτευμάτων)..."

On the Embassy 2.172: "...we preserved our democratic form of government (τὸ τῆς δημοκρατίας πολίτευμα)."

Against Ctesiphon 3.79: "... what is the reason that policies (τῶν αὐτῶν πολιτευμάτων) identical with those of Demosthenes..."

Against Ctesiphon 3.105: "...no slight exposure of Demosthenes' policies (Δημοσθένους πολιτευμάτων)."

Against Ctesiphon 3.230: "...today in consequence of the policies of Demosthenes (τῶν Δεμοσθένους πολιτευμάτων)..."

Against Ctesiphon 3.254: "...in consequence of the policies of Demosthenes (τῶν Δεμοσθένους πολιτευμάτων)".

Appian, *Civil Wars* (1st century CE):

1.3.21: "...he got the leadership of the people quickly by one measure of policy (ἑνὶ πολιτεύματι)."

2.2.13: "... Caesar's support through one political act (δι' ἑνὸς πολιτεύματος)."

3.1.2.: "...by one capital stroke of the policy (ἑνι τοιῷδε πολιτεύματι)."

Aristotle, *Politics* (384-322 BCE):

3.1278b: "For the government (τὸ πολίτευμα) is... supreme over the state (τῆς πόλεως)..."

3.1278b: "...and the constitution is the government (πολίτευμα δ' ἐστὶν ἡ πολιτεία)."

3.1279a: "... 'constitution' (πολιτεία) means the same as 'government' (πολίτευμα)."

3.1279a: "...and the government (πολίτευμα) is the supreme power in the state."

3.1283a: "...who claim to be sovereign over the government (τοῦ πολιτεύματος)."

3.1283b: "...to be sovereign (κύριους εἶναι) over the government (τοῦ πολιτεύματος)."

3.1283b: "...the other virtuous men in the state (ἐν τῷ πολιτεύματι)..."

3.1293a: "...the poor becomes sovereign over the government (τοῦ πολιτεύματος)."

3.1293a: "...the rest of the citizens who go into the government (εἰς τὸ πολίτευμα)..."

4.1297: "In some states the citizen-body (τοῦ πολιτεύματος) consists not only..."

5.1301b: "...for the magistrates alone of the class that has political power (τῷ πολιτεύμασι)..."

5.1302b: "...the power of the government (τὴν δύναμιν τοῦ πολιτεύματος)..."

5.1303b: "...struggle among all people in the state (ἐν τῷ πολιτεύματι)."

5.1305b: "...the jury-courts are not made up from the government (ἐκ τοῦ πολιτεύματος)."

5.1306a: "...for the government (τοῦ παντὸς πολιτεύματος) being in the hands of a few..."

5.1308a: "...outside the constitution and those in the government (ἐν τῷ πολιτύματι)."

5.1308a: "...there are a greater number in the governing class (ἐν τῷ πολιτεύματι)..."

6.1321a: "...a share in the government (τοῦ πολιτεύματος) upon the multitude..."

6.1321a: "...among the members of the governing classes (ἐν τῷ πολιτεύματι)."

7.1332b: "...that those in the government (ἐν τῷ πολιτύματι) should be sufficiently numerous..."

Epictetus (mid. 1st to 2nd century CE):

3.1: "...will you introduce them also into the state (εἰς τὸ πολίτευμα) with the habit?.."

Demosthenes (384-322 BCE):

On the Chersones 8.70: "...made havoc of the chief resources of the state (πολιτευμάτων)."

On the Chersonese 8.72: "...devise political measures (πολιτεύμαθ')..."

On the Chersonese 8.72: "... must always go with the measures (πολιτεύμασι)..."

On the Accession of Alexander 17.7: "... on the ground that their rule (ἀδικήματος ὄντος τοῦ πολιτεύματος) is an outrage."

On the Crown 18.108: "...that no measure of mine (πολίτυμ' ἐμόν) was invidious."

On the Crown 18.109: "...both in domestic and in Hellenic policy (πολιτεύμασι)."

On the Crown 18.110: "... the rest of my policy (λοιπῶν πολιτευμάτων)..."

On the Crown 18.108: "... for the very fact that all the measures (πολιτεύματα)..."

On the Crown 18.122: "...talk, not deeds and policy (τοῖς πολιτεύμασιν) were the criterion of patriotism."

On the Crown 18.136: "...refusing to surrender the just claims of the commonwealth (πολίτευμα) ..."

On the Crown 18.257: "... I decided to take part in public affairs (πολιτεύμαθ)..."

On the Crown 18.297: "... guilty in the eyes of the world (πολιτευμάτων)."

On the Crown 18.302: "All the purposes were accomplished by my decrees (ἐμοῖς πολιτεύμασιν)."

Agaisnt Androtion 22.47: "...I desire also to subject the politics (τὰ πολιτεύματα)..."

Against Aristogon 2 26.16: "... anyone can see from his public measures (πολίτευμα) was an enactment..."

Diodorus Siculus, *Library* (1st century BCE):

12.11.3: "Establishing a democratic form of government (πολίτευμα δημοκρατικόν)..."

12.12.2: "...and the government (τὸ πολίτευμα) enjoyed a blessed life of freedom..."

15.40.1: "For having been used to oligarchic institutions (ὀλιγαρχιλοῖς γὰρ πολιτεύμασι)."

15.45.2: "...who had held control over the government (τοῦ πολιτεύματος)."

Isocrates (436-338 BCE):
7.78: "...for from the same political institutions (ἐκ τῶν αὐτῶν πολιτευμάτων) there must always spring like or similar ways of life."

Josephus (1st century CE):
C. Ap. 2.145: "...our whole constitution of the government (τοῦ πολιτεύματος)..."

C. Ap. 2.164: "Some legislators have permitted their governments (τῶν πολιτευμάτων) to be under monarchies, others put them under oligarchies, and others under a republican form..."

C. Ap. 2.165: "...but he ordained our government (τὸ πολίτευμα) to be... a Theocracy (θεοκρατίαν)."

C. Ap. 2.184: "... the entire settlement of our government (τοῦ πολιτεύματος) altered."

C. Ap. 2.251: "...to procure political decrees (τοῦ πολιτεύματος) from the people."

C. Ap. 2.257: "...provided that the commonwealth (τὸ πολίτευμα) should keep itself pure."

Ant. 1.5: "...and the constitution of our government (τοῦ πολιτεύματος), as interpreted out of the Hebrew Scriptures."

Ant. 1.13: "...and changes of the form of our government (πολιτευμάτων)..."

Ant. 11.157: "...corruptions were introduced into their state (τὸ πολίτευμα)."

Ant. 12.108: "... and the principal men of their commonwealth (τοῦ πολιτεύματος)."

Philo (1st century CE):
Agr. 81: "... women... enrolled in the lists of the republic of virtue (τῷ τῆς ἀηετῆς ἐγγεγραμμέναι πολιτεύματι)."

Jos. 69: "...entitled to be enrolled as a free citizen in the greatest and most admirable state in the whole world (πολιτεύματι τοῦδε τοῦ κόσμου)."

Op. mundi 143: "... having been enrolled in the largest and most perfect commonwealth (πολιτεύματι)."

Plato, *Laws* (429-347 BCE):
12.945d: "...then the whole of the state (τὰ πάντα πολιτεύματα) and country flourishes."

Plutarch, *Lives* (1st century CE):

Alc. 16.1: "But all this statecraft (πολιτεύμασι) and eloquence and lofty purpose..."
Per. 12.1: "... more than all the public measures (τῶν πολιτευμάτων) of Pericles..."
Sol. 9.2: "...these should be supreme in the government (τοῦ πολιτεύματος)."
Sol. 15.3: "For the first of his public measures (πολίτευμα) was an enactment..."
Thed. 4.4: "... the integrity and purity of public life (τοῦ πολιτεύματος)."
Them. 35.2: "...he desired to rule again as before, and to direct the state (πολιτεύματος)."

Polybius (203-120 BCE):

[nation]:
1.58.7: "The two nations (τὰ δὲ πολιτεύματ') engaged were like the well-bred game-cocks..."
1.64.5: "...the two nations (μὲν τῶν πολιτευμάτων) were closely matched."

[country]:
5.9.8: "Antigonus... did not return to his own country (τὸ πάτριον πολίτευμα)."

[commonwealth]:
3.3.7: "... the growth of the commonwealth of Rhodes (τοῦ Ῥοδίων πολιτεύματος)."
6.46.7: "...two things on which the safety of a commonwealth (πολίτευμα) depends, – courage in the face of the enemy and concord at home."
6.56.6: "...which keeps the Roman commonwealth (τὸ Ῥωμαίων πολίτευμα) together."

[republic]:
3.90.14: "... the awe and respect which the Republic (τοῦ Ῥωμαίων πολιτεύματος) has inspired in its allies."
6.3.1: "Of the Greek republics (Ἑλληνικῶν Ῥωμαίων) ..."
24.13.1: "Republic of Rome (πολιτεύματος τῶν Ῥωμαίων)..."
30.5.6: "For the fact that the republic of Rhodes (τὸ πολίτευμα τῶν Ῥωδίων)..."
38.12.11: "... some of the kings and republics (τῶν πολιτευμάτων)."

[league]:
2.10.5: "... who had all his life served the Achaean league (τῶν Ἀχαιῶν πολιτεύματι)."
2.46.1: "...cities (πόλεις) not only in alliance (συμπολιτευμένας) with them..."
2.46.1: "... and other officers of the league (πολιτεύματος)."
4.1.3: "...for the league (τὸ πολίτευμα) of the latter has made extraordinary progress."
24.10.3: "... the very bonds of our league (πολιτεύμασιν)."

[city]:
4.1.3: "...and restored the confidence of the whole city (πολίτευμα)."
30.7.9: "... the Macedonians in their own cities (ἐν τοῖς ἰδίοις πολιτεύμασι)."
30.14.2: "... tended towards Rome, in every city (πᾶσι τοῖς πολιτεύμασιν)."

[government]:
2.41.6: "...maintain intact in their league a democratic form of government (πολίτευμα)."
4.25.7: "...restoring to their ancestral form of government (πάτρια πολιτεύματα)..."
6.3.11: "Again there have been many instances of oligarchical governments (ὀλιγαρχικὰ πολιτεύματα)..."

[statesmen]:
3.8.3: "But the leading statesmen (πρώτους ἄνδρας ἐπὶ τοῦ πολιτεύματος)..."
3.85.7: "...the chief men of the state (οἱ προεστῶτες τοῦ πολιτεύματος)..."
28.9.4: "...or individually to kings and statesmen (τοῖς βασιλεῦσι καὶ τοῖς πολιτευομένοις)."

[state]:
1.3.7: "Now, had the states (τὰ πολιτεύματα) that were rivals..."
1.12.8: "...treating of the most important states (πολιτευμάτων)."
1.13.12: "Moreover, the two states (τὰ πολιτεύματα) themselves were..."
1.13.13: "...national characteristics and resources of the two states (τοῦ πολιτεύματος)."
1.26.9: "...and the vast resources of the contending states (πολιτευμάτων)."

Graeco-Roman and Jewish Literary Sources on Πολίτευμα   199

4.23.9: "...management of the state (τὸ πολίτευμα) and the chief offices ..."
4.47.4: "...was at once voted against Byzantium (τῶν Βυζαντίων πολιτεύματος) on these grounds..."
5.86.8: "...without difficulty all the states (πάντων τῶν πολιτευμάτων)..."
6.18.5: "...the strength which is developed by the state (τοῦ πολιτεύματος)."
6.18.5: "...the peculiar constitution of the state (τοῦ πολιτεύματος)..."
6.52.11: "...taken by the Roman state (τοῦ πολιτεύματος) to turn out men..."
6.56.10: "If it were possible to form a state (πολίτευμα συναγαγεῖν) wholly of philosophers..."
8.2.7: "The strength of the state (τοῦ πολιτεύματος δύναμιν)..."
21.17.10: "...and nearly all the nations and states (ἐθνῶν καὶ πολιτευμάτων)..."
23.12.8: "...active career in a state (πολιτεύματι)..."
23.14.1: "...in the course of the active career in an aristocratic state (ἐν ἀριστοκρατικῷ πολιτεύματι)."
30.6.8: "...succeeded in inducing their several states (τὰ πολιτεύματα)."
30.32.8: "In the other states (ἐν δὲ τοῖς ἄλλοις πολιτεύμασι)..."

[constitution]:
1.3.7: "...majority of the Greeks have no knowledge of the previous constitution (πολιτεύματος)."
2.47.1: "...Cleomenes had revolutionized the constitution (τό τε πάτριον πολίτευμα) of his country."
2.70.1: "...and after reestablishing their ancient constitution (πολίτευμα τὸ πάτριον)..."
3.2.6: "I shall show that its [constitution's] (τοῦ πολιτεύματος) peculiar character..."
3.4.1: "And if our judgment of individuals and constitutions (πολιτευμάτων)..."
3.8.2: "...destroying the constitution (τὸ πολίτευμα) and reducing Carthage to a despotism."
3.118.8: "...by the peculiar excellence of their political constitution (τῇ τοῦ πολιτεύματος)."
3.118.12: "...establishing other constitutions (τῶν πολιτευμάτων)..."
4.81.14: "...which followed the entire destruction of the ancient constitution (πάτριον πολίτευμα)."
4.84.3: "...and in enjoyment of their several constitutions (τοῖς ἰδίοις πολιτεύμασι)."
6.1.4: "...remarks about to be made on this constitution (τῶν πολιτευμάτων)."

6.3.8: "Lycurgus, who was the first to construct a constitution (πολίτευμα)..."

6.10.6: "...which had also assigned to it an adequate share in the constitution (τὸ πολίτευμα)."

6.11.11: "...whether the constitution (τὸ πολίτευμα) as a whole were an aristocracy or democracy or despotism."

6.12.9: "...describing the constitution as despotic (βασιλικόν ἐστι τὸ πολίτευμα)."

6.14.1: "...what part is left for the people in the constitution (ἐν τῷ πολιτεύματι)?"

6.14.12: "...that the chief power of the state was the people's, and the constitution was democracy (δημοκρατικόν ἐστι τὸ πολίτευμα)."

6.18.5: "...that the constitution (τὸ πολίτευμα) is seen to posses within itself the power..."

6.43.1: "...historians have recorded as constitutions (τῶν πολιτευμάτων) of eminent excellence."

6.46.9: "...to speak of the two constitutions (τῶν πολιτευμάτων)..."

6.50.3: "...we must acknowledge that the Spartan constitution (πολίτευμα) is deficient..."

6.51.1: "Now the Carthaginian constitution (Καρχηδονίων πολίτευμα)..."

6.51.4: "...the difference between the two constitutions (τὰ πολιτεύματα)..."

9.36.4: "...and restored your laws (τοὺς νόμους) and ancestral constitution (πολίτευμα)."

10.2.9: "...in the establishment of the Lacedaemonian constitution (τὸ Λακεδαιμονίων πολίτευμα)."

Strabo, *Geography* (64 BCE-21CE):

6.3.4: "One evidence of their bad policies (πολιτευμάτων)..."

7.7.11: "...this term being applied to decrees, or statutes (τὰ πολιτεύματα) and rules."

12.3.37: "...on portion of these two governments (τῶν δυεῖν πολιτευμάτων)..."

Bibliography

1. Primary Sources

1.1 Ancient Texts and Translations

Aeschines. Aeschines with an English translation by Charles Darwin Adams. Cambridge, Ma., Harvard University Press; London, William Heinemann Ltd. 1919.

Appian. *The Civil Wars*. Translated by Horace White. London. MacMillian and Co., Ltd. 1899.

Aristotle. Aristotle in 23 Volumes, Vol. 21, translated by H. Rackham. Cambridge, Ma, Harvard University Press; London, William Heinemann Ltd. 1944.

Aristotle. Aristotle in 23 Volumes, Vol. 22. Translated by J. H. Freese. Cambridge and London. Harvard University Press; William Heinemann Ltd. 1926.

Aristides in four volumes. Text and translation by C. A. Behr. Cambridge: Harvard University Press, 1973.

Asconius. *Asconius Pedianud, Quintus: Commentaries of Five Speeches of Cicero*. Translated by Simon Squires. Bristol: Bristol Classical Press, 1990.

Babylonian Talmud. 17 vols. Ed. I. Epstein. London: Soncino, 1935-42.

Biblica Hebraica Stuttgartensia. Eds. W. Rudolph, K. Elliger. New ed. Stuttgart: Deutsche Bibelgesellschaft, 1977.

The Dead Sea Scrolls Study Edition (Translations).Edited by Florentino García Martínez and Eibert J. C. Tigchelaar. Leiden; New York : Brill, 1998.

The Mishnah : A New Translation. Edited by Jacob Neusner. New Haven, Ct. : Yale University Press, 1988.

Midrash Rabbah. 10 vols. Reprint (1 ed. 1939). Edited by H. Freedman and M. Simon. London: Soncino Press, 1961.

The Nicene and Post-Nicene Fathers. Vol. II: St. Augustine: The City of God. Christian Doctrine. Edited by Philip Schaff. Grand Rapids: Eerdmans, 1983.

Novum Testamentum Graece. Ed. E. Nestle et al. 27th ed. Stuttgart: Deutsche Bibelgesellschaft, 1993.

Cicero, M. Tullius. The Orations of Marcus Tullius Cicero, literally translated by C. D. Yonge. London. George Bell & Sons. 1903.

Charles, Robert Henry (ed.): *Commentary on the Pseudepigrapha of the Old Testament*. 2vols.Bellingham, Wa. : Logos Research Systems, Inc., 2004.

Demosthenes. LCL. Translated by J. H. Vince. Cambridge, Harvard University Press, 1939-40.

The Digest of Justinian, Edited by C. H. Monro. Cambridge, Mass.: Cambridge University Press, 1904).

Dio, Cassius. *Dio's Rome. An Historical Narrative Originally Composed in Greek during the Reigns of Septimius Severus, Geta and Caracalla, Macrinus, Elagabalus and Alexander Severus: and Now Presented in English Form*. Edited by Herbert Baldwin Foster. Volumes 1-6. Troy New York: Pafraets Book Company, 1905. Online: http://www.gutenberg.org/etext/18047.

Diodorus Siculus. 12 vols. LCL. Translated by C.H. Oldfather et al. Cambridge, Mass.: Harvard University Press, 1933-67.

Epictetus. *The Discourses of Epictetus*, with the Encheridion and Fragments. Translated by George Long. London: George Bell and Sons. 1890.

Euripides. 8 vols. Translated by A.S. Way, D. Koracs. Cambridge: Harvard University Press, 1912-99.

Herodotus. LCL. Translated by A.D. Godley. Cambridge: Harvard University Press, 1920-25.

Horace. *The Odes and Epodes*. LCL. Translated by J.C. Rolfe. Cambridge: Harvard University Press, 1914.

Isocrates. Isocrates with an English Translation in three volumes, by George Norlin. Cambridge, Harvard University Press; London, William Heinemann Ltd. 1980.

Josephus, Flavius. *The Works of Josephus : Complete and Unabridged*. Translated by William Whiston. Peabody, Ma.: Hendrickson, 1996, c1987.

Livy. 14 vols. LCL. Translated by B.O. Foster et al. Cambridge: Harvard University Press, 1919-59.

Minor Attic Orators, Volume I: Antiphon, Andocides. LCL. Translated by K. J. Maidment and J. O. Burtt. Cambridge : Harvard University Press, 1941-1954.

Philo, of Alexandria ; Yonge, Charles Duke: *The Works of Philo : Complete and Unabridged*. Peabody, Ma.: Hendrickson, 1996, c1993.

Plato. Plato in Twelve Volumes, Vols. 10 & 11 translated by R.G. Bury. Cambridge, MA, Harvard University Press; London, William Heinemann Ltd. 1967 & 1968.

Pliny the Elder. *The Natural History*. 10 vols. LCL. Translated by H. Rackham, W.H.S. Jones. Cambridge, Ma.: Harvard University Press, 1939-62.

Plutarch. *Lives*. 11 vols. LCL. Translated by B. Perrin. Cambridge, Ma.: Harvard University Press, 1914-26.

Polybius. *The Histories*. 6 vols. LCL. Translated by W.R. Paton. Cambridge: Harvard University Press, 1922-27.

Septuaginta: With morphology. Edited by A. Ralphs. Stuttgart : Deutsche Bibelgesellschaft, 1935. Repr.1979.

Strabo. *The Geography of Strabo*. 8 vols. LCL.Translated by H. L. Jones, Cambridge: Harvard University Press, 1917-32.

Suetonius. 2 vols. LCL. Translated by J.C. Rolfe (rev. 1998). Camridge: Harvard University Press, 1913-14.

Tacitus.*The Histories and the Annals*. 5 vols. LCL. Translated by J. Jackson. Cambridge: Harvard University Press, 1925-37.

Virgil. *Ecologues, Georgics, Aenid;* 2 vols. LCL. Translated by H.R. Gairclough, G.P. Goold (rev. 1999). Cambridge: Harvard University Press, 1916-18.

1.2 Inscriptions

Epigraphes Ano Makedonias (Elimeia, Eordaia, Notia Lynkestis, Orestis). Tomos A', Katalogos epigraphon. Edited by Thanasis Rizakes and Giannis Touratsoglou. Athens 1985.

Catalogue of the Greek Papyri in the John Rylands Library, Manchester. Vol. 1. Edited by A. S. Hunt; Vol. 2. Edited by J. de M. Johnson, V. Martin, and A. S. Hunt. Manchester, 1911–15.

Collection of Greek Inscriptions in the British Museum. 5 vols. Edited by Charles Thomas Newton. London 1874-1916.

Corpus cultus equitis Thracii. Vol. 1. *Monumenta orae Ponti Euxini Bulgariae*. Edited by Zlatozara Gočeva und Manfred Oppermann. Leiden 1979.

Corpus der griechisch christlichen inschriften von Hellas. Vol. 1. Edited by Nikos A. Bees. Chicago: Ares Publishers, 1978.

Corpus inscriptionum graecarum. 4 vols. Berlin 1828-1877.

Corpus Inscriptionum Latinarum. Berlin, 1862–1909.

Corpus Papyrorum Judaicarum. 3 vols. Edited by Avigdor Tcherikover and Alexander Fuks. Cambridge: Harvard University Press, 1957.

Die Inschriften von Ephesos. Vol. 2. Edited by Christoph Börker and Reinhold Merkelbach. Vol. 6. Edited by Reinhold Merkelbach and Johannes Nollé. Bonn, 1980.

Die Inschriften von Smyrna. 2 vols. Edited by Georg Petzl. IGSK 23. Bonn: Habelt, 1982-90.

Inscriptions de Délos. Vol. 4, nos. 1497-2219. Edited by Pierre Roussel and Marcel Launey. Paris 1937.

Inscriptiones Graecae. 14 vols. Edited by G. Dittenberger et al. Berlin, 1873-1939.

Inscriptiones graeae ad res romanas pertinentes. Vol. 4. Edited by René Cagnat with Georges Lafaye. Paris 1908-1927. Reprint: Chicago, Ares 1975.

Inscriptiones graecae in Bulgaria repertae. Vol. 4. *Inscriptiones in territorio Serdicensi et in vallibus Strymonis Nestique repertae* Edited by Georgi Mihailov. Sofia, 1966.

Inscriptiones Graecae Insularum Maris Aegaei. Edited by H. von Gaertringen and W. R. Paton. Berlin, 1895.

Inscriptions grecques et latines de la Syrie, XXI. Inscriptions de la Jordanie, 4: Pétra et la Nabatène Méridionale, du Wadi al-Hasa au Golfe de ʿAqaba, ed. Maurice Sartre. Paris 1993.

Inscriptions grecques et latines reueillies en Asie Mineure. Edited by Philippe Le Bas and William Henry Waddington. Hildesheim: Olms, 1870. Repr. 1972.

Mouseion kai Bibliotheke tes Euangelikes Scholes (Smyrna). Edited by Athos Duchesne, Louis, and Charles Bayet. Paris 1876.

Orientis Graeci Inscriptiones Selectae. 2 vols. Edited by W. Dittenberger. Leipzig, 1903–5.

Sardis, VII. Greek and Latin Inscriptions, Part I. Edited by Buckler, William Hepburn, and David Moore Robinson. Leiden 1932.

Supplementum Epigraphicum Graecum. Vols. 26-41. Edited by Henry W. Pleket and Ronald S. Stroud. Amsterdam 1979-1994.

Sylloge Inscriptionem Gracarum. 4 vols. Edited by G. Dittenberger. Leipzig: Apud S. Hirzlium, 1917-24.

Tituli Asiae Minoris, IV. Tituli Bithyniae linguis Graeca et Latina conscripti, 1. Paeninsula Bithynica praeter Chalcedonem. Nicomedia et ager Nicomedensis cum septentrionali meridianoque litore sinus Astaceni et cum lacu Sumonensi. Edited by Friedrich Karl Dörner, with the assistance of Maria-Barbara von Stritzky. Vienna 1978.

The Oxyrhynchus Papyri. Vols. I.–VI. Edited by B. P. Grenfell and A. S. Hunt. London, 1898–1927.

Barton, S.G. and G. H. R. Horsley. "A Hellenistic Cult Group and the New Testament Churches." *Jahrbuch Für Antike Und Christentum* 24 (1981): 7-41.

Buckler, W.H. and J. Keil. „Two Resolutions of the Dionysiac Artists from Angora." *Journal of Roman Studies* 16 (1926): 245-52.

Collart, Paul. "Le théâtre de Philippes." *Bulletin de correspondance hellénique* 52 (1928): 74-124.

_____. "Le sanctuaire des dieux égyptiens à Philippes," *Bulletin de correspondance hellénique* 53 (1929): 70-100.

_____. "Inscriptions de Philippes."*Bulletin de correspondance hellénique* 57 (1933): 313-79.

_____. "Inscriptions de Philippes."*Bulletin de correspondance hellénique* 62 (1938): 409-32.

Collart, Paul. *Philippes, ville de Macedoine depuis ses origins jusqua'a la fin de l'époque romaine.* 2 vols. Paris: Boccard, 1937.

Cousin, Georges. "Insriptions du sanctuaire de Zeus Panamaros." *Bulletin de correspondance hellénique* 28 (1904): 20-53.

Cumont, Franz. "Notices épigraphizues. V. Inscriptions de Macédoine," *Revue de l'Instruction publique en Belgique,*" 41 (1898): 338-53.

Deschamps, Gaston and Georges Cousin. "Inscriptions du temple de Zeus Panamaros." *Bulletin de correspondance hellénique* 15 (1891): 169-209.

Horsley, G.H.R., ed. *New documents illustrating early Christianity: a review of the Greek inscriptions and papyri published in 1976.* Vol.1. Ancient History Documentary Research Centre. Macquarie University, 1981.

_____. *New documents illustrating early Christianity: a review of the Greek inscriptions and papyri published in 1977.* Vol. 2. Ancient History Documentary Research Centre. Macquarie University, 1982.

_____. *New documents illustrating early Christianity: a review of the Greek inscriptions and papyri published in 1979.* Vol. 4. Ancient History Documentary Research Centre. Macquarie University, 1987.

_____. *New Documents Illustrating Early Christianity: Linguistic Essays, with Cumulative Indexes to Vols. 1–5.* Vol. 5. Ancient History Documentary Research Centre. Macquarie University, 1989.

Lemerle, Paul. "Inscriptions latines et greques de Philippes. I. Inscriptions latines." *Bulletin de correspondance hellénique* 58 (1934): 448-83.

———. "Inscriptions latines et greques de Philippes (suite)." *Bulletin de correspondance hellénique* 59 (1935): 126-64.

———. "Le testament d'un Thrace a Philippes." *Bulletin de correspondance hellénique* 60 (1936): 336-43.

———. *Philippes et la Macédoine orientale à l'epoque chrétienne et byzantine*. BEFAR 158. Paris: Boccard, 1945).

Llewelyn S.R and R.A. Kearsley, eds. *New documents illustrating early Christianity: a review of the Greek inscriptions and papyri published in 1980-81*. Vol. 6. Ancient History Documentary Research Centre 6. Macquarie University, 1992.

Mertzides, Stauros. Οἱ Φίλιπποι. Constantinople, 1897.

Perdrizet, Paul. "Inscriptions de Philippes: Les Rosalies," *Bulletin de correspondance hellénique* 24 (1900): 299-323.

Pilhofer, Peter. *Philippi, Band II: Katalog der Inschriften von Philippi*. Wissenschaftliche Untersuchungen Zum Neuen Testament 119. Tübingen: Mohr Siebeck, 2000.

Robert, Louis. "Hellenica V, Inscriptions de Philippes publiées par Mertzidès." *Revue de Philologie* 13 (1939): 136-50.

Roberts, Colin H., Theodore C. Skeat, and Arthur D. Nock. "The Gild of Zeus Hypsistos." *Harvard Theological Review* 29 (1936): 39-88.

Tod, Marcus N. "Macedonia. Inscriptions." *Annual of the British School at Athens* 23 (1918-19): 67-97.

Weber, Patrick and Michel Sève. "Un monument honorifique au forum de Philippes. *Bulletin de Correspondance Hellénique* 112 (1988): 467-79.

2.3 Sourcebooks

Beard, Mary, John A. North, and S. R. F. Price. *Religions of Rome*. Vol.2: *A Sourcebook*. Cambridge: Cambridge University Press, 1998.

Braund, David. *Augustus to Nero: A sourcebook on Roman History, 31BC–AD 68*. Totowa: Barnes and Noble Books, 1985.

Deissmann, Gustav Adolf. *Light from the Ancient East. The New Testament Illustrated by Recently Discovered Texts of the Graeco-Roman World*. Translated by Lionel R.M. Strachan. 1927. Repr., Peabody, Ma.: Hendrickson Publishers, 1995.

Ehrenberg, Victor and A.H.M. Jones, eds. *Documents Illustrating the Reigns of Augustus and Tiberius*. 2nd edition. Oxford: Clarendon Press, 1976.

Lewis, Naphtali, and Meyer Reinhold, eds. *Roman Civilization: Selected Readings. Vol. 2: The Empire.* Records of Civilization, Sources and Studies. New York: Columbia University Press, 1951.

Shelton, Jo-Ann. *As the Romans Did: A Sourcebook in Roman Social History.* 2nd ed. ed. New York: Oxford University Press, 1998.

Sherk, R.K., ed. *Roman Documents from the Greek East: Senatus Consulta and Epistulae to the Age of Agustus.* Baltimore: John Hopkins, 1969.

Smallwood, E. Mary. *Documents illustrating the principates of Gaius, Claudius and Nero.* London: Cambridge University Press, 1967.

3. Reference Works

Alexander, Patrick H., and Society of Biblical Literature. *The SBL Handbook of Style: For Ancient near Eastern, Biblical, and Early Christian Studies.* Peabody, Ma.: Hendrickson, 1999.

Arndt, William, Frederick W. Danker, Walter Bauer (eds.). *A Greek-English Lexicon of the New Testament and Other Early Christian Literature.* Revised and edited by Frederick William Danker.—3rd. ed. Chicago: University of Chicago Press, 2000.

Blass, Friedrich, Albert Debrunner, Robert Walter Funk. *A Greek Grammar of the New Testament and Other Early Christian Literature.* Chicago: University of Chicago Press, 1961.

Francis Brown, Samuel Rolles Driver, Charles Augustus Briggs (eds.). *Enhanced Brown-Driver-Briggs Hebrew and English Lexicon.* electronic ed. Oak Harbor, Wa.: Logos Research Systems, 2000.

Freedman, Daniel N. (ed.). *The Anchor Bible Dictionary.* 6 vols. New York: Doubleday, 1992.

Gould, J. and W.L. Kolb (eds.). *A Dictionary of Social Sciences.* New York: The Free Press, 1964.

Hammond, N. G. L. and H. H. Scullard (eds.). *The Oxford Classical Dictionary.* Oxford: Clarendon Press, 1970.

Hatch, E. and H.A. Redpath. A Concordance to the Septuagint and the Other Greek Versions of the Old Testament (Including the Apocryphal Books. 3 vols. Reprint (1st ed. 1897-1906). Graz: Akademiesche Druck-U. Verlagsanstalt, 1954.

Hawthorne, Gerald F., Ralph P. Martin, Daniel G. Reid (eds.). *Dictionary of Paul and His Letters.* Downers Grove, Ill.: InterVarsity Press, 1993.

Hornblower, S. and A. Spawforth, eds. *Oxford Classical Dictionary.* 3d ed. Oxford: Clarendon Press, 1996.

Kittel, G. (ed). *Theological Dictionary of the New Testament.* 10 vols. Translated and edited by Geoffrey W. Bromiley. Grand Rapids: Eerdmans, 1964-76.

Klauck, Hans-Josef. *The Religious Context of Early Christianity: A Guide to Graeco-Roman Religions Studies of the New Testament and Its World.* Edinburgh: T & T Clark, 2000.

Liddell, Henry George and Robert Scott. *A Greek-English Lexicon.* Edited by Henry Stuart Jones and Roderick McKenzie. Oxford: Oxford University Press, 1996.

Moulton, James Hope and George Milligan. *The Vocabulary of the Greek Testament.* London: Hodder and Stoughton, 1930.

Porter, Stanley E. and Craig A Evans (eds.). *Dictionary of New Testament Background : A Compendium of Contemporary Biblical Scholarship.* Downers Grove, Ill.: InterVarsity Press, 2000.

Stillwell, Richard , William Lloyd MacDonald and Marian Holland McAllister. *The Princeton Encyclopedia of Classical Sites.* Princeton, N.J.: Princeton University Press, 1976.

Hildegard Temporini and Wolfgang Haase (eds.). *Austieg und Niedergang der römischen Welt: Geschichte und Kultur Roms im Spiegel der neuren Forschung.* Berlin; New York: W. de Gruyter, 1972-80.

Van der Toorn, K., Bob Becking, Pieter Willem van der Horst (eds.). *Dictionary of Deities and Demons in the Bible.* 2nd extensively rev. ed. Leiden: Brill; Grand Rapids: Eerdmans, 1999.

4. Secondary Literature

Abrahamsen, Valerie. "Women at Philippi: The Pagan and Christian Evidence." *Journal of Feminist Studies in Religion* 3 (1987): 17-30.

_____. "Christianity and the Rock Reliefs at Philippi." *Biblical Archaeologist* 51 (1988): 46-56.

_____.*Women and Worship at Philippi: Diana/Artemis and Other Cults in the Early Christian Era.* Portland: Astarte Shell Press, 1995.

Agouridis, S. "The Role of Women in the Church at Philippi," *Bulletin of Biblical Studies* 1 (1980): 77-85.

Alcock, Susan E. *Graecia Capta: The Landscapes of Roman Greece.* Cambridge: Cambridge University Press 1996.

Bibliography

Alföldy, Geza. *The Social History of Rome*. Translated by D. Braund and F. Pollock. London: Croom Helm; Totowa: Barnes and Noble Books, 1985.

Ascough, Richard S. "*Translocal Relationships among Voluntary Associations and Early Christianity.*" *Journal of Early Christian Studies* 5 (1997): 223-41.

_____. *What Are They Saying About the Formation of Pauline Churches?* New York: Paulist, 1998.

_____. "The Thessalonian Christian Community as a Professional Voluntary Association." *Journal of Biblical Literature* 119 (2000): 311-328.

_____."Greco-Roman Philosophic, Religious, and Voluntary Associations." Pages 3-19 in *Community Formation in the Early Church and in the Church Today*. Edited by Richard N. Longenecker. Peabody, Ma.: Hendrickson Publishers, 2002.

_____. *Paul's Macedonian Associations: The Social Context of Philippians and 1 Thessalonians*. Wissenschaftliche Untersuchungen Zum Neuen Testament 2. Reihe 161. Tübingen: Mohr Siebeck, 2003.

_____. "Voluntary Associations and the Formation of Pauline Christian Communities: Overcoming the Objections." Pages 149-183 in *Vereine, Synagogen und Gemeinden im Kaiserzeitlichen Kleinasien* . Edited by Andreas Gutsfeld and Dietrich-Alex Koch. Tübingen: Mohr Siebeck, 2006.

Bakirtzis, Charalambos & Helmut Koester, ed. *Philippi at the Time of Paul and after His Death*. Harrisburg, Pa.: Trinity Press International, 1998.

Balch, David L. "The Genre of Luke-Acts," *Southwestern Journal of Theology* 33 (1990): 5-19.

_____."Paul, Families, and Households." Pages 258-92 in *Paul in the Greco-Roman World: A Handbook*. Edited by J. Paul Sampley. Harrisburg, Pa.: Trinity Press International, 2003.

Banks, Robert J. *Paul's Idea of Community: The Early House Churches in Their Historical Setting*. Grand Rapids: Eerdmans, 1988.

Barclay, John M.G. "Deviance and Apostasy. Some Applications of Deviance Theory to the First-Century Judaism and Christianity." Pages 114-27 in *Modelling Early Christianity: Social-Scientific Studies of the New Testament in Its Context*. Edited by Philip Francis Esler. London: Routledge, 1995.

Barker, Margaret. *The Great Angel. A Study of Israel's Second God*. Louisville, Ky.: Westminster John Knox Press, 1992.

Bauckham, Richard J. "The Worship of Jesus in Philippians 2: 9-11." Pages 128-39 in *Where Christology Began : Essays on Philippians 2*. Edited by Ralph P. Martin and Brian J. Dodd. Louisville, Ky.: Westminster John Knox Press, 1998.

_____. *Jesus and the God of Israel: God Crucified and Other Studies on the New Testament's Christology of Divine Identity.* Grand Rapids: Eerdmans, 2008.

Baumgarten, Albert. "Graeco-Roman Voluntary Associations and Ancient Jewish Sects." Pages 93-112 in *Jews in a Graeco-Roman World*. Edited by Martin Goodman. Oxford: Clarendon Press, 2004.

Beard, Mary, John A. North, and S. R. F. Price. *Religions of Rome*. Volume I: *A History*. Cambridge: Cambridge University Press, 1998.

Beare, Francis Wright. *Philippians*. London: A. & C. Black, 1973.

Becker, Jürgen. "Paul and His Churches." Pages 132-210 in *Christian Beginnings: Word and Community from Jesus to Post-Apostolic Times*. Edited by Jürgen Becker. Translated by Annemarie S. Kiddler and Reinhard Krauss. Louisville, Ky.: Westminster/John Knox Press, 1993.

Benko, S. "Pagan Criticism of Christianity during the Fires Two Centuries AD," Pages 1055-1118 in *ANRW.* Principat II. 23.2. Edited by Hildegard Temporini and Wolfgang Haase. Berlin: de Gruyter, 1980.

Berry, Ken L. "The Function of Friendship Language in Philippians 4:10-20." Pages 107-124 in *Friendship, Flattery, and Frankness of Speech: Studies on Friendship in the New Testament World*. Edited by John T. Fitzegerald. Leiden: Brill, 1996.

Black, David. "The Discourse Structure of Philippians: A Study in Textlinguistics." *Novum Testamentum* 37 (1995):16-49.

Bloomquist, L. Gregory. *The Function of Suffering in Philippians*. Journal for the Study of the New Testament. Supplement Series 78. Sheffield: JSOT Press, 1993.

_____. "Subverted by Joy: Suffering and Joy in Paul's letter to the Philippians," *Interpretation* 61/3 (2007): 270-82.

Blumenfeld, Bruno. *The Political Paul: Justice, Democracy and Kingship in a Hellenistic Framework*. Journal for the Study of the New Testament. Supplement Series 210. London: Sheffield Academic Press, 2001.

Bockmuehl, Markus N. A. "The Form of God" (Phil.2:6). Variations on a Theme of Jewish Mysticism," *Journal of Theological Studies* 48 (1997): 1-23.

_____. *The Epistle to the Philippians*. Black's New Testament Commentaries 11. Peabody, Ma.: Hendrickson, 1998.

Booij, Thijs. "Some Observations on Psalm 87." *Vetus Testamentum* 37 (1987): 16–25.

Bormann, Lukas. *Philippi: Stadt Und Christengemeinde Zur Zeit Des Paulus.* Supplements to Novum Testamentum 78. Leiden: Brill, 1995.

Bos, Johanna W.H. "Psalm 87." *Interpretation* 47 (1993): 281–85.

Böttger, Paul Christoph. „Die Eschatologische Existenz der Christen: Erwägungen zu Philipper 3 20." *Zeitschrift Für die Neutestamentliche Wissenschaft* 60 (1969): 244-63.
Bowersock, Glen Warren. "The Imperial Cult: Perceptions and Persistence." Pages 171-82 in *Jewish and Christian Self-Definition*. Vol. 3. Edited by Ben F. Meyer and E.P. Sanders. Philadelphia: Fortress Press, 1980–83.
Branick, Vincent P. *The House Church in the Writings of Paul*. Zacchaeus Studies New Testament. Wilmington: Michael Glazier, 1989.
Brent, Allen. *The Imperial Cult and the Development of Church Order: Concepts and Images of Authority in Paganism and Early Christianity before the Age of Cyprian*. Supplements to Vigiliae Christianae, 45. Boston: Brill, 1999.
Brosend, William F. "The Means of Absent Ends." Pages 348-62 in *History, Literature and Society in the Book of Acts*. Edited by Ben Witherington; Cambridge: Cambridge University Press, 1996.
Brown, Alexandra R. *The Cross and Human Transformation: Paul's Apocalyptic Word in 1 Corinthians*. Minneapolis: Fortress Press, 1995.
———. "Apocalyptic Transformation in Paul's Discourse on the Cross." *Word & World* 16 (1996): 427-36.
Bruce, Frederick F. *The Epistle to the Galatians: A Commentary on the Greek Text*. New International Greek Testament Commentary. Grand Rapids: Eerdmans, 1982.
Brunt, Peter A. *Italian Manpower 225 B.C.–A.D. 14*. Oxford: Oxford University Press, 1987.
Campbell, John B. "Veterans." Page 1592 in *The Oxford Classical Dictionary*. Edited by N. G. L. Hammond and H. H. Scullard. Oxford: Clarendon Press, 1970.
Carter, Warren. *The Roman Empire and the New Testament: An Essential Guide*. Nashville: Abingdon Press, 2006.
Charlesworth, M. "Some Observations on Ruler-Cult Especially in Rome." *Harvard Theological Review* 28 (1935): 5-44.
Chester, Andrew. "Jewish Messianic Expectations and Mediatorial Figures and Pauline Christianity." Pages 17–89 in *Paulus und das Antike Judentum*. Edited by Martin Hengel and Ulrich Heckel. Tübingen: Mohr Siebeck, 1991.
Clark, M. "*Spes* in the Early Imperial Cult: 'The Hope of Augustus'." *Numen* 30 (1983): 80-105.

Clarke, Andrew D. *Serve the Community of the Church: Christians as Leaders and Ministers* First-Century Christians in the Graeco-Roman World. Grand Rapids: Eerdmans, 2000.

Collange, J.F. *The Epistle of Saint Paul to the Philippians.* London: Epworth Press, 1979.

Collins, Adela Yarbro. "The Worship of Jesus and the Imperial Cult." Pages 234-57 in *The Jewish Roots of Christological Monotheism: Papers from the St. Andrews Conference on the Historical Origins of the Worship of Jesus.* Edited by Carey C. Newman, James R. Davila and Gladys S. Lewis. Leiden: Brill, 1999.

Collins, John N. *Diakonia: Re-interpreting the Ancient Sources.* New York: Oxford University Press, 1990.

Cormack, J.M.R. "High Priests and the Macedoniarchs from Beroa." *Journal of Roman Studies* 33 (1943): 39-44.

Cosgrove, Charles H. "The Law Has Given Sarah No Children," *Novum Testamentum* 29 (1987): 219-35.

Cotter, Wendy. "Our Politeuma is in Heaven: The Meaning of Philippians 3.17-21." Pages 92-104 in *Origins and Method: Towards a New Understanding of Judaism and Christianity: Essays in Honour of John C. Hurd.* Journal for the Study of the New Testament. Supplement Series 86. Edited by Bradley H. McLean. Sheffield: JSOT Press, 1993.

_____. "The Collegia and Roman Law: State Restrictions on Voluntary Associations, 64 BCE – 200AD." Pages 74-89 in *Voluntary Associations in the Graeco-Roman World.* Edited by John S. Kloppenborg and Stephen G. Wilson. London: Routledge, 1996.

Cousar, Charles B. *A Theology of the Cross: the Death of Jesus in the Pauline letters.* Overtures to Biblical Theology. Minneapolis: Fortress Press, 1990.

Crossan, John Dominic, and Jonathan L. Reed. *In Search of Paul: How Jesus's Apostle Opposed Rome's Empire with God's Kingdom.* New York: HarperSanFrancisco, 2004.

Cuss, Dominique. *Imperial Cult and Honorary Terms in the New Testament.* Paradosis; Contributions to the History of Early Christian Literature and Theology. Switzerland: Fribourg University Press, 1974.

Dahl, Nils A. "Euodia and Syntyche and Paul's Letter to the Philippians." Pages 3-15 in *The Social World of the First Christians: Essays in Honor of Wayne A. Meeks.* Edited by L. Michael White and O. Larry Yarbrough. Minneapolis: Fortress Press, 1995.

Dalton, William J. "The Integrity of Philippians." *Biblica* 60 (1979): 97-102.

Danker, Frederick W. "Associations, Clubs, Thiasoi " Pages 501-3 in vol. 1 of *The Anchor Bible Dictionary*. Edited by David Noel Freedman. New York: Doubleday, 1992.

Davies, Paul E. "The Macedonian Scene of Paul's Journeys." *Biblical Archaeologist* 26 (1963): 91-106.

Den Boeft, Jan. "Saviour." Pages 733-36 in *Dictionary of Deities and Demons in the Bible Dictionary*. Edited by K. van der Toorn, Bob Becking, Pieter Willem van der Horst. 2nd extensively rev. ed. Leiden: Brill; Grand Rapids: Eerdmans, 1999.

De Vos, Craig Steven. *Church and Community Conflicts: The Relationships of the Thessalonian, Corinthian, and Philippian Churches with Their Wider Civic Communities*. SBL Dissertation Series 168. Atlanta, Ga.: Scholars Press, 1999.

Dix, Dom Gregory. *The Shape of the Liturgy*. New Edition with an Introduction by Dr. Simon Jones. Norfolk: Biddles Ltd., King's Lynn, 1945; repr. New York: Continuum, 2007.

Dunn, James D.G. "Was Christianity a Monotheistic Faith from the Beginning?" *Scottish Journal of Theology* 35 (1982): 303–36.

Edson, Charles. "Cults of Thessalonica (Macedonica III)." *Harvard Theological Review* 41 (1948): 153-204.

Ellis, Earle. "Paul and his coworkers." Page 183 in *Dictionary of Paul and His Letters*. Edited by Gerald F. Hawthorne et al. Downers Grove, Ill.: InterVarsity Press, 1993.

Emerton, John A. "The Problem of Psalm 87." *Vetus Testamentum* 50 (2000): 183–99.

Esler, Philip F. *Community and Gospel in Luke-Acts: The Social and Political Motivations of Lukan Theology*. Society for the New Testament Monograph Series 57. Cambridge: Cambridge University Press, 1987.

Fears, J.R. "The Cult of Jupiter and Roman Imperial Ideology." Pages 3-141and 827-9 in *ANRW*. Principat II. 17.1 &2. Edited by Hildegard Temporini and Wolfgang Haase. Berlin: de Gruyter, 1981.

Fee, Gordon D. *Paul's Letter to the Philippians*. New International Commentary on the New Testament 50. Grand Rapids: Eerdmans, 1995.

———. "Paul and the Trinity: The Experience of Christ and the Spirit for Paul's Understanding of God," Pages 49-72 in *The Trinity. An Interdisciplinary Symposium on the Trinity*. Edited by Stephen T. Davies, Daniel Kendall, and Gerald O'Collins. Oxford: Oxford University Press, 1999.

Ferguson, John. "Classical Religions," and "Ruler-Worship," Pages 749-60 and 766-79 in *The Roman World*. Edited by John Wacher. Vol. 2. London: Routledge, 2002.

Filson, Floyd V. "The Significance of the Early House Churches," *Journal of Biblical Literature* 58 (1939): 105-12.

Fisher, Nicholas R.E. "Roman Associations, Dinner Parties, and Clubs." Pages 1199-1225 in *Civilization of the Ancient Mediterranean : Greece and Rome*. Edited by Michael Grant and Rachel Kitzinger. Vol.2. New York: Scribner's, 1988.

Fishwick, Duncan. "The Development of Provincial Ruler Worship in the Western Roman Empire." Pages 1201-1253 in *ANRW*. Principat II.16.2. Edited by Hildegard Temporini and Wolfgang Haase. Berlin; New York: de Gruyter, 1978.

_____. *The Imperial Cult in the Latin West: Studies in the Ruler Cult of the Western Provinces of the Roman Empire*. Etudes Préliminaires Aux Religions Orientales Dans L'empire Romain108. Leiden: Brill, 1987.

Fitzgerald, Aloysius. "The Mythological Background for the presentation of Jerusalem as Queen and False Worship as Adultery in the OT." *Catholic Biblical Quarterly* 34 (1972): 403-16.

Fitzgerald, John T., ed. *Friendship, Flattery, and Frankness of Speech: Studies on Friendship in the New Testament World*. Leiden: Brill, 1996.

_____. "Philippians in the Light of Some Ancient Discussions of Friendship." Pages 141-60 in *Friendship, Flattery, and Frankness of Speech: Studies on Friendship in the New Testament World*. Edited by John T. Fitzegerald. Leiden: Brill, 1996.

_____. "Christian Friendship: John, Paul, and the Philippians." *Interpretation* 61 (2007): 284-96.

Foerster, Werner. "κύριος κτλ." Pages 1081-98 in vol. 3 of *Theological Dictionary of the New Testament*. Edited by Gerhard Kittel, Geoffrey William Bromiley and Gerhard Friedrich. Grand Rapids: Eerdmans, 1964.

_____. "σώτηρ κτλ." Pages 1010-12 in vol. 7 of *Theological Dictionary of the New Testament*. Edited by Gerhard Kittel, Geoffrey William Bromiley and Gerhard Friedrich. Grand Rapids: Eerdmans, 1964.

Fowl, Stephen E. *Philippians*. Two Horizons New Testament Commentary 11. Grand Rapids: Eerdmans, 2005.

Fowler, W. Warde. *Roman Ideas of Deity in the Last Century before the Christian Era: Lectures Delivered in Oxford for the Common University Fund.* Freeport: Books for Libraries Press, 1969.

Frame, James Everett. *A Critical and Exegetical Commentary on the Epistles of St. Paul to the Thessalonians.* International Critical Commentary. Vols.52-53. Edinburgh: T. & T. Clark, 1912.

Fredrickson, David E. "Paul, Hardships, and Suffering." Pages 172-97 in *Paul in the Greco-Roman World: A Handbook.* Edited by J. Paul Sampley. Harrisburg, Pa.: Trinity Press International, 2003.

_____."Envious Enemies of the Cross of Christ (Philippians 3:18)." *Word & World* 28, no. 1 (2008): 22-28.

Friesen, Steven J. "Networks of Religion and Society at Ephesus: Men and Women in Provincial Highpriesthood." Paper presented at the annual meeting of the Archeology of the NT World Group of the SBL. San Francisco, 1992.

_____. *Imperial Cults and the Apocalypse of John: Reading Revelation in the Ruins.* Oxford: Oxford University Press, 2001.

Frenschkowski, Marco. "Kyrios in Context Q 6:46, the Emperor as "Lord", and the Political Implications of Christology in Q." Pages 95-118 in *Zwischen den Reichen: Neues Testament und Römische Herrschaft. Vorträge auf der Ersten Konferenz der European Association for Biblical Studies.* Edited by Michael Labahn and Jürgen Zangenberg. Tübingen: Francke Verlag, 2002.

Garland, David E. "The Composition and Unity of Philippians. Some Neglected Literary Factors." *Novum Testamentum* 27 (1985): 141-73.

Garnsey, Peter and Richard P. Saller. *The Roman Empire: Economy, Society, and Culture.* Berkeley: University of California Press, 1987.

Gasque, W. Ward. "The Historical Value of Acts." *Tyndale Bulletin* 40 (1989): 136-57.

Geertz, Clifford. *The Interpretation of Cultures: Selected Essays.* New York: Basic Books, 1973.

George, Timothy. *Galatians.* New American Commentary 30. Nashville: Broadman & Holman Publishers, 2001, c.1994.

Gilbert, George H. "Women in Public Worship in the Pauline Churches." *Biblical World* 2 (1893): 38-47.

Ginsburg, Michael. "Roman Military Clubs and Their Social Functions." *Transactions and Proceedings of the American Philological Association* 71 (1940): 149-56.

Gnilka, Joachim. *The Epistle to the Philippians.* New Testament for Spiritual Reading 17. New York: Herder and Herder, 1971.

Graham, Ronald William. "Women in the Pauline Churches: A Review Article." *Lexington Theological Quarterly* 11 (1976): 25-33.

Green, Joel B. "Internal Repetition in Luke-Acts: Contemporary Narratology and Lukan Historiography." Pages 283-99 in *History, Literature and Society in the Book of Acts.* Cambridge: Cambridge University Press, 1996.

Green, Joel B and Mark D. Baker. *Recovering the Scandal of the Cross: Atonement in New Testament & Contemporary Contexts.* Downers Grove, Ill.: InterVarsity Press, 2000.

Hayman, Peter. "Monotheism – a Misused Word in Jewish Studies," *Journal of Jewish Studies* 42 (1991): 1–15.

Harland, Philip A. "Honouring the Emperor or Assailing the Beast: Participation in Civic Life among Associations (Jewish, Christian and Other) in Asia Minor and the Apocalypse of John." *Journal for the Study of the New Testament* 77 (2000): 99-121.

⎯⎯⎯⎯. *Associations, Synagogues, and Congregations: Claiming a Place in Ancient Mediterranean Society.* Minneapolis: Fortress Press, 2003.

⎯⎯⎯⎯. "Spheres of Contention, Claims of Pre-eminence: Rivalries among Associations in Sardis and Smyrna." Pages 53-63, 259-62 in *Religious Rivalries and the Struggle for Success in Sardis and Smyrna.* Studies in Christianity and Judaism 14. Waterloo: Wilfrid Laurier University Press, 2005.

Harrison, J.R. "Paul and the Imperial Gospel at Thessaloniki." *Journal for the Study of the New Testament* 25 (2002): 71-96.

Hatch, Edwin. *The Organization of the Early Christian Churches: Eight Lectures Delivered before the University of Oxford, in the Year 1880, on the Foundation of the Late Rev. John Bampton.* London: Longmans Green, 1901.

Hawthorne, Gerald F. *Philippians.* Word Biblical Commentary 43. Waco: Word Books, 1983.

Heen, Erik M. "Phil 2:6–11 and Resistance to Local Timocratic Rule: *Isa Theō* and the Cult of the Emperor in the East." Pages 125-54 in *Paul and the Roman Imperial Order.* Edited by Richard A. Horsley. Harrisburg, Pa.: Trinity Press International, 2004.

Heinrici, Georg. "Die Christengemeinden Korinths und die religiösen Genossenschaften der Griechen," *Zeitschrift für die Neutestamentliche Wissenschaft* 19 (1876): 465-526.

Hellerman, Joseph. "The Humiliation of Christ in the Social World of Roman Philippi, Part 2," *Bibliotheca Sacra* 160 (2003): 421-33.

_____. "Brothers and Friends in Philippi: Family Honor in the Roman World and in Paul's Letter to Philippians." *Biblical Theology Bulletin* 39 (2009): 15-25.

Hendrix, Holland L. "Philippi (Place)." Pages 313-17 in *Anchor Bible Dictionary*. Edited by David Noel Freedman. Vol. 5. New York: Doubleday, 1992.

Hengel, Martin. *Acts and the History of Earliest Christianity*. SCM Press, 1979.

_____. *The Cross of the Son of God*. Translated by John Bowden. SCM Press, 1986.

Hock, Ronald F. "The Workshop as a Social Setting for Paul's Missionary Preaching." *Catholic Biblical Quarterly* 41 (1979): 438-50.

_____. *The Social Context of Paul's Ministry: Tentmaking and Apostleship*. Philadelphia: Fortress, 1980.

Holloway, Paul A. *Consolation in Philippians: Philosophical Sources and Rhetorical Strategy*. Cambridge: Cambridge University Press, 2001.

Hoover, Roy W. "The Harpagmos Enigma: A Philological Solution," *Harvard Theological Review* 64 (1971): 95-119.

Horbury, W. "The Messianic Associations of the 'Son of Man'" *Journal of Theological Studies* 36 (1985): 34-55.

Hurtado, Larry W. *One God, One Lord: Early Christian Devotion and Ancient Jewish Monotheism*. Philadelphia: Fortress Press, 1988.

_____. "What Do we Mean by 'First-Century Jewish Monotheism?'," Pages 348–68 in *Society of Biblical Literature 1993 Seminary Papers*. Edited by E.H. Lovering. Atlanta, Ga.: Scholars Press, 1993

_____."Lord." Pages 560-69 in *Dictionary of Paul and His Letters*. Edited by Gerald F. Hawthorne, Ralph P. Martin, Daniel G. Reid. Downers Grove, Ill.: InterVarsity Press, 1993.

_____."First-Century Jewish Monotheism." *Journal for the Study of the New Testament* 71 (1998): 3–26.

_____. *Lord Jesus Christ: Devotion to Jesus in earliest Christianity*. Grand Rapids: Eerdmans, 2003.

Jeffers, James S. "Jewish and Christian Families in First-Century Rome." Pages 128-50 in *Judaism and Christianity in First-Century Rome*. Edited by Karl P. Donfried and Peter Richardson. Grand Rapids: Eerdmans, 1998.

Jewett, Robert. "The Epistolary Thanksgiving and the Integrity of Philippians." *Novum Testamentum* 12 (1970): 40-53.

———. "Conflicting Movements in the Early Church as Reflected in Philippians." *Novum Testamentum* 12 (1970): 362–90.

Jobes, Karen H. "Jerusalem, our Mother: Metapepsis and Intertextuality in Galatians 4:21-31." *Westminster Theological Journal* 55 (1993): 299-320.

Jones, Donald L. "Christianity and the Roman Imperial Cult." Pages 1023-1054 in *ANRW*. Principat II. 23.2. Edited by Hildegard Temporini and Wolfgang Haase. Berlin; New York: de Gruyter, 1980.

Judge, Edwin Arthur. *The Social Pattern of the Christian Groups in the First Century: Some Prolegomena to the Study of New Testament Ideas of Social Obligation*. London: Tyndale Press, 1960.

Kajanto, Iiro. *The Latin Cognomina*. Helsinki: Societas Scientiarum Fennica, 1965.

Kee Alistair. "The Imperial Cult: the Unmasking of an Ideology." *Scottish Journal of Religious Studies* 6 (1985): 115.

Kennedy, H.A.A."Apostolic Preaching and Emperor Worship." *Expositor* 7 (1909): 289-307.

———. *The Epistle to the Philippians*. Expositor's Greek Testament. Vol. 3. Grand Rapids: Eerdmans, 1983.

Keppie, Lawrence. *Colonization and Veteran Settlement in Italy 47-14 BC*. British School at Rome Suppl. Publ. London: British School at Rome, 1983.

Kim, Seyoon. *Christ and Caesar: The Gospel and the Roman Empire in the Writings of Paul and Luke*. Grand Rapids: Eerdmans, 2008.

Klauck, Hans-Joseph. *The Religious Context of Early Christianity: A Guide to Graeco-Roman Religions*. Minneapolis: Fortress Press, 2003.

Klijn, A.F.J. "Paul's Opponents in Philippians iii." *Novum Testamentum* 7 (1964): 278–84.

Kloppenborg, John S. "Edwin Hatch, Churches and Collegia." Pages 212-38 in *Origins and Method: Towards a New Understanding of Judaism and Christianity. Essays in Honour of John C. Hurd*. Edited by Bradley H. McLean. Journal for the Study of the New Testament. Supplement Series 86. Sheffield: JSOT Press, 1993.

———."Collegia and *Thiasoi*: Issues in Function, Taxonomy and Membership." Pages 16-30 in *Voluntary Associations in the Graeco-Roman World*. Edited by John S. Kloppenborg and Stephen G. Wilson. London: Routledge, 1996.

Klöpper, Albert. *Der Brief des Apostel Paulus an die Philipper*. Berlin: G. Reimer, 1893.

Koester, Helmut. "The Purpose of the Polemic of a Pauline Fragment (Philippians iii)." *New Testament Studies* 8 (1961–62): 318).

Koukouli-Chrysantaki, Chaido. "Colonia Iulia Augusta Philippensis." Pages 5-35 in *Philippi at the Time of Paul and after His Death*. Edited by Charalambos Bakirtzis and Helmut Koester. Harrisburg, Pa.: Trinity Press International, 1998.

Krentz, Edgar. "Military Language and Metaphors in Philippians." Pages 105-27 in *Origins and Method : Towards a New Understanding of Judaism and Christianity : Essays in Honour of John C. Hurd*. Edited by Bradley H. McLean. Sheffield: JSOT Press, 1993.

Lampe, Peter and Ulrich Luz, "Post-Pauline Christianity." Pages 242-80 in *Christian Beginnings: Word and Community from Jesus to Post-Apostolic Times*. Edited by Jürgen Becker and S. Kidder. Translated by A.S. Kidder and R. Krauss. Louisville, Ky.: Westminster John Knox Press, 1993.

Lane Fox, Robin. *Pagans and Christians*. SanFrancisco: Harper and Row, 1986.

Lane, William L. "Social Perspectives on Roman Christianity During the Formative Years from Nero to Nerva: Romans, Hebrews, 1 Clement." Pages 196-244 in *Judaism and Christianity in First-Century Rome*. Edited by Karl P. Donfried and Peter Richardson. Grand Rapids: Eerdmans, 1998.

Lazarides, D. "Philippi (Krenides)." Pages 704-5 in *The Princeton Encyclopedia of Classical Sites*. Edited by Richard Stillwell, William Lloyd MacDonald and Marian Holland McAllister. Princeton: Princeton University Press, 1976.

Levick, Barbara. *Roman Colonies in Southern Asia Minor*. Oxford: Clarendon, 1967.

Limberis, Vasiliki. "The Eyes Infected by Evil: Basil of Caesarea's Homily, on Envy." *Harvard Theological Review* 84, no. 2 (1991): 163-84.

Lincoln, Andrew T. *Paradise Now and Not Yet. Studies in the Role of the Heavenly Dimension in Paul's Thought with Special Reference to His Eschatology*. Cambridge: Cambridge University Press, 1981.

Longenecker, Richard N. *Galatians*. Word Biblical Commentary 41. Dallas: Word Books, 1990.

Lüdemann, Gerd. *Early Christianity According to the Traditions in Acts: A Commentary*. Translated by John Bowden. Minneapolis: Fortress Press, 1989.

Lüderitz, Gert. "What Is Politeuma?" Pages 183-225 in *Studies in Early Jewish Epigraphy*. Edited by J. W. van Henten and Pieter Willem van der Horst. Leiden: Brill, 1994.

Luter, A. Boyd. "Partnership in the Gospel: The Role of Women in the Church at Philippi." *Journal of the Evangelical Theological Society* 39 (1996): 411-420.

MacMullen, Ramsay. *Roman Social Relations, 50 B.C. to A.D. 284.* New Haven: Yale University Press, 1974.

_____. "Conversion: A Historian's View." *Second Century* 5 (1985): 67-81.

Maier, Christl M. "Psalm 87 as a Reappraisal of the Zion Tradition and Its Reception in Galatians 4:26," *Catholic Biblical Quarterly* 69 (2007): 473-486.

Malherbe, Abraham J., *Social Aspects of Early Christianity.* Fortress Press, 1983.

_____."Paul's Self-Sufficiency (Philippians 4:11)." Pages 125-140 in *Friendship, Flattery, and Frankness of Speech: Studies on Friendship in the New Testament World.* Edited by John T. Fitzegerald. Leiden, New York, Köln: E.J. Brill, 1996.

_____. *The Letters to the Thessalonians: A New Translation with Introduction and Commentary.* Anchor Yale Bible. New York: Doubleday, 2000.

Malina, Bruce J. *The New Testament World: Insights from Cultural Anthropology.* Rev. ed. Louisville, Ky.: Westminster John Knox Press, 1993.

_____. "Early Christian Groups: Using small group formation theory to explain Christian organizations." Pages 92-109 in *Modelling Early Christianity: Social-Scientific Studies of the New Testament.* Edited by Philip F. Esler. London: Routledge, 1995.

Malinowski, Francis X. "The Brave Women of Philippi." *Biblical Theology Bulletin* 15 (1985): 60-64.

Mann, John C. *Legionary Recruitment and Veteran Settlement During the Principate.* Institute of Archeology Occasional Publication 7. Edited by M.M. Roxan. London: Institute of Archeology, 1983.

Marchal Joseph A. "With Friends like these. . . : A Feminist Rhetorical Reconsideration of Scholarship and the Letter to the Philippians." *Journal for the Study of the New Testament* 29 (2006) 77-106.

Marshall, I. Howard. *The Epistle to the Philippians.* Epworth Commentaries. London: Epworth Press, 1992.

Martin, Ralph P. *Philippians.* Grand Rapids: Eerdmans, 1980, c. 1976.

_____. *Carmen Christi; Philippians ii. 5-11 in Recent Interpretation and in the Setting of Early Christian Worship.* London: Cambridge , 1967. Reprint. New York: Cambridge University Press, 1983.

Martyn, J. Louis. "Epistemology at the Turn of the Ages: 2 Corinthians 5:16," Pages 269-87 in *Christian History and Interpretation: Studies Presented to John Knox.* Edited by W.R. Farmer, C.F.D. Moule, R.R. Niebuhr. Cambridge: Cambridge University Press, 1967.

―――――. "Apocalyptic Antinomies in Paul's Letter to the Galatians," *New Testament Studies* 31 (1985): 410-24.

McLean, Bradley H. "The Agrippinilla Inscription: Religious Associations and Early Church Formation." Pages 239-70 in *Origins and Method: Towards a New Understanding of Judaism and Christianity. Essays in Honour of John C. Hurd.* Edited by Bradley H. McLean. Journal for the Study of the New Testament. Supplement Series 86. Sheffield: JSOT Press, 1993.

Mearns, Chris. "The Identity of the Opponents at Philippi." *New Testament Studies* 33 (1987): 194–204.

Meeks, Wayne A. "The Social Context of Pauline Theology." *Interpretation* (1982): 266-77.

―――――. *The First Urban Christians: The Social World of the Apostle Paul.* New Haven: Yale University Press, 1983.

Melick, Richard R. *Philippians, Colossians, Philemon.* New American Commentary 32. Nashville: Broadman Press, 1991.

Moberly, Walter L. "How Appropriate is 'Monotheism' as a Category for Biblical Interpretation?" Pages 216–34 in *Early Jewish and Christian Monotheism.* Edited by Loren T. and Wendy E.S. North Stuckenbruck. London: T & T Clark International, A Continium Imprint, 2004.

Nock, Arthur Darby. "On the Historical Importance of Cult Associations." *Classical Review* 38 (1924): 105-9.

―――――."Early Gentile Christianity and Its Hellenistic Background." Pages 49-133 in *Essays on Religion and the Ancient World.* Edited by Zeph Stewart. Cambridge, Ma.: Harvard University Press, 1972.

―――――. "Soter and Euergetes." Pages 720-35 in *Essays on Religion and the Ancient World.* Edited by Zeph Stewart; Cambridge: Harvard University Press, 1972.

Oakes, Peter. "Philippians: From People to Letter." Ph.D. diss,. University of Oxford, 1995.

―――――. *Philippians: From People to Letter.* Cambridge: Cambridge University Press, 2001.

O'Brien, Peter Thomas. *The Epistle to the Philippians: A Commentary on the Greek Text.* New International Greek Testament Commentary. Grand Rapids: Eerdmans, 1991.

Ogilvie, R. M. *The Romans and Their Gods in the Age of Augustus* Ancient Culture and Society. London: Chatto & Windus, 1969.

Osiek, Carolyn. *Philippians, Philemon.* Abingdon New Testament Commentaries. Nashville: Abingdon Press, 2000.

———. "*Diakonos* and *Prostatis*: Women's Patronage in Early Christianity." *Hervormde teologiese studies* 61 (2005): 347-370.

Osiek, Carolyn, Margaret Y. MacDonald, and Janet H. Tulloch. *A Woman's Place: House Churches in Earliest Christianity*. Minneapolis: Fortress Press, 2006.

Papazoglou, Fanoula. "Macedonia under the Romans." Pages 192-207 in *Macedonia: 4000 Years of Greek History and Civilization*. Edited by M.B. Sakellariou. Ekdotike Athenon, 1983.

Perkins, Pheme. "Christology, Friendship and Status: The Rhetoric of Philippians." Pages 509-20 in *Society of Biblical Literature 1987 Seminar Papers*. Edited by Kent H. Richards. Society of Biblical Literature, 1987.

Pervo, Richard I. *Profit with Delight: The Literary Genre of the Acts of the Apostles*. Minneapolis: Fortress Press, 1987.

Peterlin, Davorin. *Paul's Letter to the Philippians in the Light of Disunity in the Church*. Supplements to Novum Testamentum 79. Leiden: Brill, 1995.

Pilhofer, Peter. *Philippi. Band I: Die Erste Christliche Gemeinde Europas*. Wissenschaftliche Untersuchungen Zum Neuen Testament 87. Tübingen: Mohr Siebeck, 1995; 2000.

Pleket, H. W. "An Aspect of the Emperor Cult: Imperial Mysteries." *Harvard Theological Review* 58 (1965): 331-347.

Polard, T.E. "The Integrity of Philippians." *New Testament Studies* 13 (1966-67): 57-66.

Poland, Franz. *Geschichte des griecheschen Vereinswesens*. Leipzig: Teubner, 1909.

Portefaix, Lilian. *Sisters Rejoice: Paul's Letter to the Philippians and Luke-Acts as Seen by First-Century Philippian Women*. Coniectanea Biblica New Testament Series 20. Stockholm: Almqvist & Wiksell International, 1988.

Porter, Stanley E. *Paul in Acts*. Library of Pauline Studies. Peabody, Ma.: Hendrickson, 2001.

Price, S. R. F. *Rituals and Power: The Roman Imperial Cult in Asia Minor*. Cambridge: Cambridge University Press, 1984.

———. "Gods and Emperors: The Greek Language of the Roman Imperial Cult." *Journal of Hellenic Studies* 104 (1984): 79-85.

Reed, Jeffrey T. "Philippians 3:1 and the Epistolary Hesitation Formulas: The Literary Integrity of Philippians, Again." *Journal of Biblical Literature* 115 (1996): 63-90.

———. *A Discourse Analysis of Philippians: Method and Rhetoric in the Debate over Literary Integrity*. Journal for the Study of the New Testament. Supplement Series 136. Sheffield: Sheffield Academic Press, 1997.

Reimer, Ivoni Richter. *Women in the Acts of the Apostles: A Feminist Liberation Perspective*. Translated by Linda M. Maloney. Minneapolis: Fortress Press, 1995.

Reilly, Linda Collins. *Slaves in Ancient Greece: Slaves from Greek Manumission Inscriptions*. Chicago: Ares Publication, 1978.

Reumann, John H. P. "Church Office in Paul, especially in Philippians." Pages 82-91 in *Origins and Method: Towards a New Understanding of Judaism and Christianity: Essays in Honour of John C. Hurd*. Journal for the Study of the New Testament. Supplement Series 86. Edited by Bradley H. McLean. Sheffield: JSOT Press, 1993.

_____. "Contributions of the Philippian Community to Paul and to Earliest Christianity." *New Testament Studies* 39 (1993): 438-57.

_____. "Philippians, Especially Chapter 4, as a "Letter of Friendship": Observations on a Checked History of Scholarship." Pages 83-106 in *Friendship, Flattery, and Frankness of Speech: Studies on Friendship in the New Testament World*. Edited by John T. Fitzegerald. Leiden: Brill, 1996.

_____. "Philippians and the Culture of Friendship." *Trinity Seminary Review* 19 (1997): 69-83.

_____. *Philippians: A New Translation with Introduction and Commentary*. Anchor Yale Bible. New Haven: Yale University Press, 2008.

Rostovzeff, Michael Ivanovitch. *The Social & Economic History of the Hellenistic World*. Oxford: Clarendon Press, 1941.

_____. The Social and Economic History of the Roman Empire. 2d ed. ed. Oxford: Clarendon Press, 1957.

Saller, Richard P. *Personal Patronage under the Early Empire*. Cambridge: Cambridge University Press, 1982.

Salmon, Edward Togo. *Roman Colonization under the Republic Aspects of Greek and Roman Life*. Ithaca, N.Y.: Cornell University Press 1970.

Sandnes, Karl Olav. "Equality within Patriarchal Structures: Some New Testament perspectives on the Christian fellowship as a brother- or sisterhood and a family." Pages 150-82 in *Constructing Early Christian Families: Family as social reality and metaphor*. Edited by Halvor Moxnes. London: Routledge, 1997.

_____. "The Role of the Congregation as a Family within the Context of Recruitment and Conflict in the Early Church." Pages 333-46 in *Recruitment, Conquest, and Conflict : Strategies in Judaism, Early Christianity, and the Greco-Roman World*. Edited by Peder Borgen, Vernon K. Robbins and David B. Gowler. Atlanta, Ga.: Scholars Press, 1998.

_____. *Belly and the Body in the Pauline Epistles*. Monograph Series. Society for New Testament Studies 120. Cambridge: Cambridge University Press, 2002.

Schaper, Joachim. *Eschatology in the Greek Psalter*. Wissenschaftliche Untersuchungen Zum Neuen Testament. 2. Reihe 76. Tübingen: Mohr Siebeck, 1995.

Schaps, D. "The Woman Least Mentioned: Etiquette and Women's Names." *Classical Quarterly* 27 (1977): 323–30.

Schmithals, William. „Die Irrlehrer des Philipperbriefes." *Zeitscrift für Theologie und Kirche* 54 (1957): 297-341.

_____. "The False Teachers of the Epistle to the Philippians." Pages 65-122 in *Paul and the Gnostics*. Translated by J.E. Steely. Nashville: Abingdon, 1972.

Schrage, Wolfgang. „Leid, Kreuz und Eschaton: Der Perstasenkataloge als Merkmale paulinischer *theologia crucis* und Eschatologie," *Evangelische Theologie* 34 (1974): 160-175.

Schwemer, Anna Maria. "Himmlische Stadt und Himlisches Bürgerrecht bei Paulus (Gal 4,26 und Phil 3,20)," Pages 230-35 in *La Cité de Dieu = Die Stadt Gotte : 3. Symposium Strasbourg, Tübingen, Uppsala, 19.-23. September 1998 in Tübingen*. Edited by M. Hengel, S. Mittmann, and A. M. Schwemer. WUNT 129. Tübingen: Mohr Siebeck, 2000.

Segal, Alan F. *Two Powers in Heaven: Early Rabbinic Reports about Christianity and Gnosticism*. Leiden: Brill, 1977.

_____. "'Two Powers in Heaven' and Early Christian Trinitarian Thinking." Pages 73–95 in *The Trinity: An Interdisciplinary Symposium on the Trinity*. Edited by Stephen T. Davies, Daniel Kendall, and Gerald O'Collins. Oxford: Oxford University Press, 1999.

Sherwin-White, Adrian N. "The Early Persecutions and Roman Law Again." *Journal of Theological Studies* 3 (1952): 199-213.

_____. "The Roman Citizenship. A Survey of Its Development into a World of Franchise." Pages 23-58 in *ANRW*. Principat I.2. Edited by Hildegard Temporini. Berlin: de Gruyter, 1972.

Silva, Moisés. *Philippians*. Baker Exegetical Commentary on the New Testament 11. Grand Rapids: Baker Book House, 1992.

Smallwood, E. Mary. *The Jews under Roman Rule: From Pompey to Diocletian*. Studies in Judaism in Late Antiquity 20. Leiden: Brill, 1976.

Smith, Dennis E. "Meals and Morality in Paul and His World." Pages 319-39 in *Society of Biblical Literature 1981 Seminar Papers*. Edited by Kent Harold Richards. San Francisco: Scholars Press, 1981.

Smith, Mark S. "The Structure of Psalm 87." *Vetus Testamentum* 37 (1987): 16–25.

Stevenson, George H. and Andrew W. Lintott. "Clubs, Roman." Pages 352-3 in *The Oxford Classical Dictionary*. Edited by N. G. L. Hammond and H. H. Scullard. Oxford: Clarendon Press, 1970.

Stowers, Stanley K. "Social Status, Public Speaking and Private Teaching: The Circumstances of Paul's Preaching Activity." *Novum Testamentum* 26 (1984): 59-82.

_____. "Friends and Enemies in the Politics of Heaven: Reading Theology in Philippians." Pages 89-104 in *Pauline Theology. Vol.1: Thessalonians, Philippians, Galatians, Philemon*. Edited by Jouette M. Bassler. Minneapolis: Fortress Press, 1991.

Sumney, Jerry L. *Philippians: A Greek Student's Intermediate Reader*. Peabody, Ma.: Hendrickson, 2007.

Tannehill, Robert C. *The Narrative Unity of Luke-Acts: A Literary Interpretation*. 2 vols. Minneapolis: Fortress Press, 1986.

Tarn, W.W. and G.W. Griffith. Hellenistic Civilization. 3d ed. London: E. Arnold, 1952.

Taylor, Nicholas H. "The Social Nature of Conversion in the Early Christian World." Pages 128-36 in *Modelling Early Christianity : Social-Scientific Studies of the New Testament in Its Context*. Edited by Philip Francis Esler. London: Routledge, 1995.

Tellbe, Mikael. "The Sociological Factors behind Philippians 3:1-11 and the Conflict at Philippi." *Journal for the Study of the New Testament* 55 (1994): 97-121.

_____. *Paul between Synagogue and State: Christians, Jews, and Civic Authorities in 1 Thessalonians, Romans, and Philippians*. Coniectanea Biblica. New Testament Series 34. Stockholm: Almqvist & Wiksell, 2001.

Theissen, Gerd. *Social Reality and the Early Christians: Theology, Ethics, and the World of the New Testament*. Translated by Margaret Kohl. Minneapolis: Fortress Press, 1992.

_____. "The Social Structure of Pauline Communities: Some Critical Remarks on J.J. Meggitt, Paul, Poverty and Survival." *Journal for the Study of the New Testament* 84 (2001): 65-84.

Thomas, W. Derek. "Place of Women in the Church at Philippi." *Expository Times* 83 (1972): 117-120.

Thurston, Bonnie Bowman, Judith Ryan, and Daniel J. Harrington. *Philippians and Philemon*. Collegeville: Liturgical Press, 2004.

Tod, Marcus N. *Sidelights on Greek History.* Oxford: Blackwell, 1932.

Van Bremen, Riet. "Women and Wealth." Pages 223-42 in *Images of women in antiquity* Edited by Averil Cameron and Amélie Kuhrt. Croom Helm, 1983.

Vermes, Geza. *Scripture and Tradition in Judaism. Haggadic studies.* Leiden: Brill, 1961.

Vincent, Marvin Richardson. *A Critical and Exegetical Commentary on the Epistles to the Philippians and to Philemon.* International Critical Commentary 50. Edinburgh: T & T Clark, 1897.

Vollenweider, Samuel. „Der „Raub" Der Gottgleichheit: Ein Religionsgeschichtlicher Vorschlag zu Phil 2.6 (-11)." *New Testament Studies* 45 (1999): 413-33.

Wallace Daniel B. *Greek Grammar beyond the Basics – Exegetical Syntax of the New Testament.* Zondervan, 1999.

Wanamaker, Charles A. *The Epistles to the Thessalonians: A Commentary on the Greek Text.* The New International Greek Testament Commentary. Grand Rapids: Eerdmans, 1990.

Watson, Duane F. "A Rhetorical Analysis of Philippians and Its Implications for the Unity Question." *Novum testamentum* 30 (1988): 57-88.

_____. "New Jerusalem." Page 1095 in vol. 4 of *The Anchor Bible Dictionary*. Edited by Daniel N. Freedman. 6 vols. New York: Doubleday, 1992.

Watson, George Ronald. *The Roman Soldier: Aspects of Greek and Roman Life.* Ithaca: Cornell University Press, 1969.

White, L. Michael. "Morality Between Two Worlds: A Paradigm of Friendship in Philippians." Pages 210-15 in *Greeks, Romans, and Christians. Essays in Honor of Abraham J. Malherbe.* Edited by David L. Balch, Everett Ferguson, and Wayne A. Meeks. Minneapolis: Fortress Press, 1990.

_____. "Visualizing The "Real" World of Acts 16: Toward Construction of a Social Index." Pages 234-61 in *The Social World of the First Christians: Essays in Honor of Wayne A. Meeks.* Edited by L. Michael White and O. Larry Yarbrough. Minneapolis: Fortress Press, 1995.

Williams, Demetrius K. *Enemies of the Cross of Christ: The Terminology of the Cross and Conflict in Philippians.* Journal for the Study of the New Testament. Supplement Series 223. London: Sheffield Academic Press, 2002.

Wilson, Bryan. *Magic and the Millennium.* London: Heinemann, 1973.

Wilson, Stephen G. "Voluntary Associations: An Overview." Pages 1-15 in *Voluntary Associations in the Graeco-Roman World.* Edited by John S. Kloppenborg and S. G. Wilson. London: Routledge, 1996.

Witherington, Ben. "Lydia." Page 422 in vol. 4 of *The Anchor Bible Dictionary*. Edited by Daniel N. Freedman. 6 vols. New York: Doubleday, 1992.

———. *Friendship and Finances in Philippi: The Letter of Paul to the Philippians*. The New Testament in Context. Valley Forge, Pa.: Trinity Press International, 1994.

———. *The Acts of the Apostles: A Socio-Rhetorical Commentary*. Grand Rapids: Eerdmans, 1998.

Wright, N. T. "Paul's Gospel and Caesar's Empire." *Reflections* (*Center for Theological Inquiry*) 2 (1998): 42-65.

Zanker, Paul. *The Power of Images in the Age of Augustus*. 1st paperback ed. ed. Jerome Lectures ; 16th Ser. Ann Arbor: University of Michigan Press, 1988.

Zeller, Dieter. "Kyrios," Pages 492-96 in *Dictionary of Deities and Demons in the Bible Dictionary*. Edited by K. van der Toorn, Bob Becking, Pieter Willem van der Horst. 2nd extensively rev. ed. Leiden: Brill; Grand Rapids: Eerdmans, 1999.

Zetterholm, Magnus. *The Formation of Christianity in Antioch: A Social-Scientific Approach to the Separation between Judaism and Christianity*. London: Routledge, 2003.